Urban Rhythms

Pop Music and Popular Culture

Urban Rhythms

Pop Music and Popular Culture

Iain Chambers

St. Martin's Press, Inc., 175 Fifth Avenue, New York, NY 10010
Printed in Hong Kong
Published in the United Kingdom by Macmillan Publishers Ltd.
First published in the United States of America in 1985

Library of Congress Cataloging in Publication Data

Chambers, Iain.
　Urban rhythms.
　Includes index.
　Bibliography: p. 253
　Discography: p. 213
　1. Music, Popular (Songs, etc.)–Great Britain–
History and criticism. 2. Music and society.
3. Great Britain–Popular culture. I. Title.
ML3492.C52　1985　780'.42'0941　84-22848
ISBN　0-312-83469-1
ISBN 0-312-83468-3 (pbk.)

Contents

List of Illustrations

Acknowledgements

Not all of the work and influences drawn upon in putting this book together carry readily identifiable names, but those that do I would like to thank sincerely.

To Simon Frith I owe a very special debt for his painstaking attention to my many tentative expressions and drafts. Stuart Hall provided invaluable criticism and frequently suggested a more effective shape for my looser musings. Lidia Curti, Dick Hebdige and Larry Grossberg forced me to clarify my thinking on many points that I might well have preferred to have left in lazy ambiguities. Their comments, conversation, and their own work, have provided me with arguments, encouragement and inspiration.

Gino Coppola generously gave up time to prepare several of the illustrations.

I would also like to thank *New Musical Express*, *Melody Maker*, *Sounds* and *Black Music & Jazz Review* for letting me look through back numbers in their offices, Jean Kennedy for her help in obtaining permission to use some of the illustrations, and Anthea Brodrick, Steven Kennedy, Janet Clayton and Keith Povey for preparing the manuscript for publication.

Finally, it is to those whose anonymous labours have daily shaped the imaginative possibilities of pop music into a rich, contemporary reality that this book is intended as a modest tribute.

I would also like to thank Intersong Music Ltd for permission to quote from James Brown's 'Superbad'; Warner Bros Music Ltd for permission to quote from Van Morrison's 'Astral

Weeks'; Virgin Music (Publishers) Ltd for permission to quote from Big Youth's 'Marcus Garvey Dread'; and Bogle-L'Ouverture Publications Ltd for permission to quote from Linton Kwesi Johnson's poem 'Yout Scene'.

Introduction: Chasing the Traces

The unspecified menace of hooded eyes beneath a greased quiff while in the background a futuristic looking juke-box blares out American rock 'n' roll; the bedsitter, a late night cup of coffee and Joni Mitchell on the turntable; the physical thud of a bass co-ordinating the shuffle of dancers in the bluish grey smoke of a crowded inner-city reggae club – these are just three of the many images that can be collected from the story of pop. In this book I will attempt to examine the sense of this diversity, tracing out some of the different uses to which pop music in Britain has been bent in its almost thirty years of existence.

In attempts to pin down pop's 'meaning', song lyrics have often seemed tempting, occasionally fashionable, anchors to employ. Yet the semantic ambiguities of the music continually slip this attempted arrest. Under Afro-American musical influences, pop has even been involved in attempts to subvert language altogether. From Elvis Presley's hiccuping enunciation on 'Heartbreak Hotel' to the choked incoherence of James Brown mouthing the elusive timbres of soul, words have largely served to relay a metalanguage of acoustic immediacies. These sounds communicate to the body of the dancer or listener long before the explicit has had time to fall into place: 'words are sounds we feel before they are statements to understand' (Greil Marcus).

Pop music is a field of continual novelties. In some cases, these merely involve the latest twist in marketing strategy, the quick business eye for a possible trend. More frequently, fresh proposals represent a real intrusion upon an earlier organisation of the music and its surrounding culture. Whenever a

sound powerful enough to threaten existing arrangements
emerges, previous interpretations, choices and tastes are put
in question. In the successive cultural struggle, the powers of
the record companies, radio and television, and the music
press to shape the situation briefly surface from their daily and
subconsciously administered obscurity. Aesthetic criteria and
judgements that were once taken for granted have suddenly to
be justified and defended.

In the following histories I have chosen to concentrate on
such moments. The unforseen accents of new musicl languages not only force a transformation of pop's previous
boundaries, but, in the process, throw a light across the whole
field of pop. It is these irruptions, often drawing upon the
more 'hidden' sounds of Afro-America and the Afro-
Caribbean (R & B, soul, reggae), that most strikingly illumin-
ate the perpetual remaking of pop's sonorial and cultural
prospects.

From a disco or the purchase of a Walkman to turning on
the radio and reading the *New Musical Express* each week, it is
the *reproducibility* of sound that dominates the surfaces of pop.
Recorded music also links together a massive record industry,
and its subsidiaries, to various musical choices and cultural
uses. For, after the commercial power of the record companies
has been recognised, after the persuasive sirens of the radio
acknowledged, after the recommendations of the musical press
noted, it is finally those who buy the records, dance to the
rhythms and live to the beat who demonstrate, despite the
determined conditions of its production, the wider potential of
pop.

As a consequence of this last perspective, records and songs
can no longer be considered as isolated critical objects.
Rescued from a traditional aesthetic vacuum, particular
sounds become specific indications or symptoms of cultural
tendencies weaving across the musical field. We will discover
that these tendencies are muliple; that they sometimes clash
and elsewhere overlap; that they rest on sexual divisions as
well as on precise subcultural styles, on race as well as
commerce.

Records will be regularly mentioned. They are collected into a Discography at the end of the book. Indicated as potential witnesses for the histories presented, they are the 'sonorial forms of knowledge' (Jacques Attali) that have acted as points of departure for the writing. They represent an absent but integral dimension: a sonorial infrastructure across which my own observations have been hung. Where possible, they should be listened to.

Chapter 1

Living in a Modern World

'Those who sneer at Elvis Presley should... redirect their antagonism. Presley just had to happen. He is a symptom of the times. What we should examine and try to understand is the plaguey circumstances that produced him.'

(Tony Brown, *Melody Maker*, 1956)

In a brief article on the English pop singer Tommy Steele written in 1957, Colin MacInnes referred to the 'strange ambivalence' of Steele and other British singers like him who achieved recording success 'at the cost of splitting their personalities and becoming bi-lingual: speaking American at the recording studio, and English in the pub round the corner afterwards' (MacInnes, 1961, p. 14). This was usually dismissed at the time as a superficial affectation, an empty commercial pose. Still, the apparently effortless transition between the different worlds of Britain and 'America' had by the late 1950s become a distinctive feature of much of the former's youth culture.

Grudgingly acknowledged as a symptom of wider change, 'Americanisation' had also often become the bitter synonym for the unwelcomed rush of the industrial world. Sixteen years earlier, in 1941, George Orwell had noted a new, 'rather restless' spirit in British popular culture, 'centring on tinned food, *Picture Post* and the internal combustion engine' (Orwell, 1970, p. 98). Rapid transport, rapid communication and fast food: these were all important signs of a culture coming to be based on the indiscriminate circulation of goods and messages – ones not necessarily tied to any particular social or cultural place. The facile movement of bodies, sounds, images and

1

information threatened to break up a particular reality 'by overcoming the uniqueness of every reality' (Walter Benjamin).

The triumphant immediacy that the reproductive capacities of contemporary industrial society has released – an Elvis Presley record selling a million copies, a film viewed by many millions, a painting reproduced thousands of times – annihilates the ritual space between the previously separate spheres of 'art' and everyday life. The objects of culture are loosened from the tyranny of 'tradition' (Benjamin, 1973). The shiny surfaces of contemporary urban culture mock earlier aesthetic securities and bounce previous criteria back in the shocked faces of its critics, effectively locking them out. On the other side, just beneath the sheen of the plastics and chrome, on the inside of the fashion screen, and well beyond the limited access imposed by traditional art, a complex minutiae of choices, pleasures, desires and possibilities are being continually imprinted. The seemingly banal concerns that once filled the cinemas, stuffed the juke-boxes with coins, crowded the dance halls and coffee bars – those 'events without prestige' (Henri Lefebvre) – have all along explored a profounder vein.

In 'free time' or 'leisure', in that temporary release that industrial society permits from the world of work, obligation and the narrow tracks of a bludgeoning routine, the perpetual chronicle of daily existence comes to be interrogated by the disruptive emergence of the repressed. Banal assumptions about the nature and scope of leisure are confronted by charged symptoms of unsuspected complexity: no 'pleasures' are finally innocent, no pastimes ultimately purposeless. Edgar Morin caught this rich, though rarely appreciated side of modern popular culture most effectively when he proposed that it was a culture 'in solution', immersed in contemporary society and history, and one that poses problems neither previously formulated nor considered (Morin, 1962).

Popular culture

'A region where goods confront needs more or less transformed into desires.'

(Henri Lefebvre)

Figure 1. Jitterbugging in the 1940s

The principal criticism launched against 'mass' or popular culture with increasing vigour after 1945 was that it was 'plastic' and 'inauthentic'. An 'ersatz' culture of ephemeral emotions, ruled by Hollywood 'stars' and sultry youths in the 'Hit Parade', seemed to be orchestrating a spectacle of consumerism. Writers and commentators, who elsewhere displayed marked disagreement in social and political outlook, came together in a revealing bloc when confronted by this phenomenon. Commercial popular culture and the 'soma' of Americana that was apparently drugging the nation in the late 1940s and 1950s was roundly condemned.[1]

The Second World War, the stationing of US troops in Britain after 1942 in preparation for the invasion of continental Europe, 'swing' music and the comedy shows of the American

Forces Network, and the effects of both on the British public and the BBC, clearly left influential traces.[2] But the USA was by no means a novelty to British popular culture by this time. American influences can be followed back through advertising, cinema, popular music, dance and entertainment to the late nineteenth century and the London music hall.[3] Various aspects of American popular culture were already extremely prominent in Britain by the end of the First World War. This was particularly due to the success of its two most widely reproduced forms: cinema and dance music. In the Lancashire of the 1920s, 'Label's, Turner's, Rafferty's and Bailey's were the pioneers and were later joined by another eight schools in the task of teaching the Charleston, black bottom, foxtrot, tango and waltz to the youths of Rochdale' (Wild, 1979, p. 148).

An American domination of such popular entertainment media as dance, light music and cinema, together with a small but keen interest in jazz was clearly well established before 1939. In the post-1945 world, where it was 'the rebuilding of the world economy around the United States' that 'formed the framework in which Britain's experiments in social democracy went ahead' (Gamble, 1981, p. 104), the American shaping of popular British culture was destined to grow in importance.

But for all the resentment that surrounded the transglobal spread of Coca-Cola, chewing gum and Hollywood, British reactions were often steeped in a far older bile than simply anti-Americanism. It was the novel and unsolicited ingression of new tastes coming from 'below', and their evident powers to challenge and redraw some of the traditional maps of cultural habits, that generated many an acid but apprehensive rebuttal.

> It is a life without point or quality, a vulgar world whose inhabitants have more money than is good for them, barbarism with electric light... a cockney tellytopia, a low grade nirvana of subsidised houses, hire purchase extravagance, undisciplined children, gaudy domestic squalor, and chips with everything.[4]

The indiscriminate technological reproduction of cultural artefacts, the uncontrolled racket of unashamed commerce, and the rude transatlantic styles of tail-fin cars, electric guitars and rainbow-checked jackets, was the stuff of cultural nightmares for old world patricians. A frightful liberty ruled only by the dollar sign or its sterling equivalent.

For there we have it. The howls of protest and outrage that accompanied the flamboyant signs of a post-war recovery and, by the second half of the 1950s, a newly discovered consumerism were not only directed westwards across the Atlantic. The fundamental target was industrial society itself. It was industry and technology as a whole that was on trial, accused of destroying 'culture' and 'values' in the modern world. Official sentiments and taste continued to maintain a steady orbit around the attractively simple idea that deep down 'culture' and industry are diametrically opposed forces. 'Educated' comment and opinion leaders, generally far removed from the daily workings and experience of post-war popular urban culture, claimed that it contained the alarming ability to 'level down' culture and sweep it away.[5] 'Culture' was replaced by commerce, reduced to the level of hair shampoo and oven-ready chickens.

By the 1950s, popular culture was clearly flourishing without the parochial blessing and participation of *that* culture. It was increasingly indifferent to the accusations launched against it from 'above'. Existing beyond the narrow range of school syllabuses, 'serious' comment and 'good taste', popular concerns broke 'culture' down into the immediate, the transitory, the experienced, and the lived. It revealed a constructed, contradictory and *contested* history of producing viable daily experiences: ones that make 'sense', that contain pleasures, that are livable.

The mutual involvement of industry and culture, of commercial production and popular taste, and the necessary generation of a new aesthetics also points to a division of labour that unties the once presumed authorial voice of the culture product. Where the individual presence of a writer or painter suggested a singular moment of production, the collective technological processes involved in radio, cinema, television and recorded music fragment the figure of the 'artist' and disperse the idea of any simple point of 'origin'.

With pop music, for example, the singer's voice, the songwriter's intentions, the group's sound – passing through an arranger, record producer, studio engineer, record company distribution and radio airplay – becomes completely redimensionalised. There is no longer an easily identifiable 'source', no obvious 'author', but a plurality of 'authors': 'So, when everyone's gone home you then take what you recorded and completely change it' – Glyn Johns, record producer (Wale, 1972, p. 67).

The market for such products is not, of course, 'free'. You select, and your selection is determined by what is on offer and your means for obtaining it. But mass reproduction does not simply represent the grey monolith of an implacable industrial production. Revealing a 'market-orientated originality' (Walter Benjamin), a culture is produced via distinctive patterns of consumption; through choice, taste and use a meaningful pattern, or 'bricolage', is put together. The purchase is worked over, accrues a use, a 'sense'; you envelope the commodity with desire. It comes to be set in the geography of a *particular* and individual reality. In the process, new moments of cultural power, decision, choice and intervention are diffused, learnt and applied. The history of contemporary British popular culture is also a history of these developments.

Commercial in organisation and distinctly urban in tone: these are the two principal features of popular culture today. Its amorphous sweep, which through cinema, radio, records and television seeps into every corner of our daily lives, has frequently been understood to constitute a major threat to what was assumed to have once been a more 'healthy' and 'genuine' culture of 'the people'. Yet, looking with care into an earlier epoch, before 'Americanisation' provided a tidy explanation, we find that popular urban culture, at least in Britain, has borne all the signs of a modern entertainment industry for quite some time. By the 1860s, the music hall had already 'made a commodity of "having a good time"' (Waites, 1981). And at the end of the nineteenth century, popular sports such as cricket and football were fully professional and being supported out of spectators' pockets. A distinct popular culture could be discerned, organised around the pub, the music hall, the sporting paper, football and the race track (Stedman-Jones, 1974). As has recently been observed, nearly all the tendencies evident in the contemporary situation, in particular those that go under the rubric of 'commercialisation', were already present in urban British popular culture by 1880 (Cunningham, 1980).[6]

When, in *The Uses of Literacy* (first published in 1957), Richard Hoggart protested against a 'new' (sic) commercial mass culture 'unbending the springs of action' of an older, more solid, urban working class culture, he was unwittingly indicating something else. Urban popular culture was not, as he believed, being 'devalued' by commerce, by glossily advertised 'invitations to a candy floss world', as unmistakably shifting gear and shape. To the remaking of the relation between the worlds of production and leisure and the rise of a commercial popular culture that took place in the late nineteenth century, the post-1945 world contributed a massive expansion in consumerism. The recognition of internal markets, now that the British Empire was rapidly becoming a fading memory, was accompanied by a major growth in the production of consumer goods – cars, fridges, washing machines, televisions – and attendant service industries. It was in this sharply altered economic and social climate that the 'shiny barbarism' of consumerism and imitations of American postures by those 'fond of jive and boogie-woogie' (Hoggart, 1958), took place. However exaggerated were the reported noises of this change, an earlier working-class insularity and its defensive 'culture of consolation' (Stedman-Jones, 1974) was being prised open. A less precise, more amorphous popular urban culture was relentlessly taking root. Or, as the teenage male hero of Colin MacInne's *Absolute Beginners* put it: it was uncool to be 'anti-American'.

Popular music

Leaving the wider tendencies in British popular culture for the moment, let us turn to the particular world of popular music and the emergence of 'pop'. It is tempting to see in the change of terminology from 'popular' to 'pop' that occurred in the mid-1950s a simple historical divide between the field of commercial popular music in general and a more precise area

associated with a 'teenage' public. But the abbreviation of the
term involved more than a purely generational division in
taste. It also suggested a precise musical and cultural shift.
The voices of Little Richard and Elvis Presley came out of a
musical tradition quite different from that of Frank Sinatra,
Rosemary Clooney and the other doyens of post-war American popular music. This sonorial clash lies behind much of
the subsequent history of popular music and the arrival of
'pop' as a distinctive sound.

In November 1956, the American singer Johnny Ray
topped the British Hit Parade for several weeks with the song
'Just Walking in the Rain' (see Discography). It typifies the
then archetypal format employed in commercial popular
music: the thirty-two bar structure. This means that the
song's musical 'core' consists of two cells, each of eight
measures or bars. These alternate with one another, either
A/A/B/A or A/B/A/B. London's Denmark Street, the heart of
the British popular music industry, or 'Tin Pan Alley', had
been pouring out hundreds of songs employing this structure
since the beginning of the century. In New York, initially
around Union Square, an even larger and more influential
musical industry produced thousands of such song types for
eager American ears.

Critics of twentieth-century popular music have consistently castigated the use of such a musical formula: surely the
clearest sign of standardised, if not automated, commercial
production they argued.[7] They conveniently forget that the
vast body of known musics, both European and non, have
persistently worked with generally agreed musical structures
whose skeletal frames have remained relatively fixed. The
major exception here, not the rule, has been nineteenth-
century European classical music.

The unintended irony, and partial explanation for subsequent critical acrimony, is that it is the European classical
tradition that stands as an authoritative shadow over the
compositional techniques of Tin Pan Alley. Distilled through
the popularising approaches of the operetta, Viennese dance,
the musical and the show, it has been the 'classical' tradition
that has largely legitimised and guided the aesthetic criteria
and musical canons that are employed in white commercial

music. Harmonic architecture and linear development – the apex of classical music concerns – may well have been simply translated into the idea of an attractive melody or memorable tune, but the logic was cut from the same cloth.

Further, to explain the musical form of 'Just Walking In The Rain' as simply embodying the reflex of the market in its composition is frankly to miss the overall texture of the musical event. Johnny Ray's own 'open' singing style, markedly different from the popular 'crooning' styles of Frank Sinatra and Bing Crosby, is also important. Together with the whistling that opens and accompanies much of the song, it gives the piece its individual character. No doubt the three songwriters would have cheerfully agreed with the gloomy verdict of the popular culture critics that the whistling was the necessary 'hook', the calculated ornament or sonorial novelty, required to put this tried song formula up among the hits. But such criticism also inadvertently suggests a quite different dimension: where a concern for melody and linear harmonic structures – the 'tune' – radically falls away to be replaced by intense variations on the 'ornamental'.

The exploration of this second possibility had been taking place elsewhere, in another musical continent. The chart appearances by the mid-1950s of black performers like Fats Domino, Little Richard and Chuck Berry had occasionally provided direct evidence of this alternative. But, despite the exceptional shock at the time of Elvis Presley and his other wild stablemates on the Memphis Sun label (Jerry Lee Lewis, Carl Perkins, Bill Riley) integrating their music with 'Negro' sounds, it tended to continue as an obscured and subterranean conection. The white American singer Pat Boone built his early career on producing 'acceptable' versions of black rhythm and blues material. In his version, Little Richard's 'Long Tall Sally' acquires 'clarity and an engaging relaxation' (*Melody Maker*, 7 July 1956). He was merely the latest example in a long history of the popular music industry applying bland camouflaging to Afro-American sounds.

Black American music has been crucial to developments in white popular music and dance since the beginning of the century, from ragtime through dance bands to 'swing' and rock 'n' roll. But until the 1960s, with the rare exception of

Louis Armstrong or Duke Ellington, its direct presence remained in the barely acknowledged undergrowth of the
popular music industry. The complex interchange betwen the
subordinated traces of black Africa and the institutions of
white America (its work discipline, the Church, organised
entertainment) and, via these, European musics, created the
volatile matrix of Afro-American sonorities. Throughout this
encounter a persistent tension has been maintained, first by
slavery and then racism and social marginalisation, preserving much of the autonomous sense of black American music:
'soul is survival', as James Brown rightly reminds us. It was
out of this history, out of the blues and gospel, and their
subsequent meshings in jazz, R & B and soul music, that a
diverse musical syntax, quite distinct from European-derived
'popular song', developed.

While the thirty-two bar format is the musical cornerstone
of Tin Pan Alley, in the Afro-American tradition it is the
twelve bar blues: three chords alternating in a fixed patten.[8]
From the perspective of European classical harmony, this
offers an even more rigid and correspondingly 'poorer' musical frame than that used by the white popular music industry.
The 'blues scale' is also sparse: consisting of five rather than
the seven notes of the official European scale.[9] This produces
a telling disorientation for our ears as the blues singer
stretches and slides over those intervals ('blue notes') we are
accustomed to expect. Such a sensation of 'foreignness' is the
most recognisable aural trait of the blues and Afro-American
music in pop – the slides, slurs, bent, 'dirty' and uncertain
notes in the voice, guitar, saxophone and bass.[10] It remains
the irreducible testimony of the clash between a legitimised,
white European-derived tradition and a barely recognised
Afro-American one.

Seeking a set of spaces quite distinct from those occupied by
the sequential structures of European harmony, Afro-
American music appears to extract its shape from 'within'. A
horizontal simplicity – in the case of the blues only three
chords acting as a guideline – is exchanged for an unsuspected
complexity. Notes are chopped up, jammed together, halved,
augmented, twisted, stretched and dropped. This insistence
on exploring the vertical interiors of the music finds Jackie

Figure 2. **Blues and soul, music and survival: Rev. Gary Davis**

Wilson squeezing thirty-two notes into the monosyllable 'for' in the Dominoes's recording of 'Danny Boy' (Miller, 1971).

In this diverse musical logic, far more important than differences in harmony, or the 'lack' of it, is rhythm. It is here that the sharpest distinction between European and Afro-American musics lies. Both European classical and white popular music is highly underdeveloped in this area, tending merely to emphasise a regular pulse. Afro-American music, on the contrary, harks back through the New World overlay of Baptist hymns, French dances, Celtic tunes and Latin rhythms, to the percussive traditions of West Africa. It sets to bend, tease and subvert the regularity of the beat. It is polyrhythmic.

The combination of different rhythmic layers, overlapping and intersecting, and the vertical clusters of notes they carry, direct our attention to the interior, the 'inside', of the musical experience. Whether it is the blues, soul music, reggae or disco, we are drawn into an insistent 'now'. It is no accident that Afro-American music consistently resorts to tactile adjectives to describe its effects: 'hot', 'funky', 'feeling'. The music does not obey the narrow sequential logic, so akin to writing, of a beginning, middle and end, but the visceral intensity of speech. Only weakly tied to linear harmonic structures, often freed from a pre-existing notational anchorage, and encouraged by continual shifts around 'blue notes', chordal and rhythmic variations, the immediate intensity of improvisation becomes a privileged mode in Afro-American music.[11]

The effects of the interplay between the above musical languages – those of Afro-America and white commercial popular music – did not take place in isolation, but inside a series of long-term shifts that characterise popular music in the inter-war and post-war period. In both the United States and Britain, a previous style of popular music production, tied to composed scores (often written by salaried composers) and sheet music sales, gave way in the 1920s and 1930s to the growing impact of radio and records. On both sides of the Atlantic, the radio permitted dance bands and singers to enter millions of homes simultaneously, establish a national following, and become successful recording stars. The rise of Benny Goodman and 'swing' music in the USA during the mid-1930s was the most clamorous example. But it was not unique.

In the same period, the BBC was broadcasting live music five nights a week from London's West End hotels. Between 10.30 and midnight, Ambrose and his Orchestra, and the bands of Henry Hall, Roy Fox, Jack Payne and others, transmitted their foxtrots, tangos, quicksteps and waltzes from the Mayfair, the Savoy and the Dorchester. Despite the BBC's vigorous campaign against US influences – the 'Trans-atlantic octopus' of the entertainment world – the 'crooning' singing style, complete with transatlantic accent, also became extremely popular.[12] Al Bowlly was its major glory. The fag-end of the music hall, now known as 'variety', was swamped by these wireless celebrities. Once they had established a reputation through radio broadcasts most London dance bands were guaranteed a public success wherever they played.

Inevitably, it was in the United States that the potential of

electrical reproduction to undo the older, more rigid, organisation of popular music was most vigorously illustrated. At
the close of the 1930s, a commercial war broke out between
the music publishers' copyright association and American
radio stations when the former raised their fees. The radio
stations replied by setting up their own copyright organisation. But in doing this they were forced to seek their music
outside the existing control of Tin Pan Alley. Then between
August 1942 and October 1943, the American Federation of
Musicians went on strike for higher payment for recording
services. The record companies, now tapping the lucrative
outlet of the juke-box, and finding themselves starved of new
recorded material owing to the strike, were forced to concede
to the musicians' demands. These two events marked the
practical demise of Tin Pan Alley's previous stranglehold over
commercial popular music.

Among the immediate consequences of the second event
was that 'swing' music, tied to the older music copyright
association (that controlled by Tin Pan Alley) and consequently banned by the radio, was then struck by the musicians' recording boycott. Forced out of public hearing it went
into a dramatic decline. The bands of Benny Goodman, Harry
James and Tommy Dorsey disbanded within weeks of each
other in 1946. The space in public popularity was taken over
by individual singers (who had not been involved in the
musicians' strike): Bing Crosby and, above all, Frank Sinatra.
But it was the first event that turned out to be more
important. Setting up an alternative copyright organisation,
US broadcasting opened itself to previously excluded sounds,
in particular country and western music and, more discreetly,
to black music.

By the early 1950s, if you lived in a large US city, whether
Memphis or Chicago, you could flip your radio dial and there
would be a good chance of finding the blues and R & B
coming from some station. A disc jockey in this period was
Riley B. King – later better known as B. B. King. He had a R
& B show on the Memphis station WDIA. Among his avid
listeners was a young Elvis Presley. No longer so easily
ghettoised in the separate market of 'race records', or restricted to the secluded world of jazz 'cognoscenti', black

American music began bypassing some of the bleaching processes of the popular music industry and finding new ears.

The disappearance of older cultural patterns and their replacement by new possibilities in the flush of the post-war period was also accompanied by some important changes in the music's technological reproduction. The introduction of the mobile hand microphone and the replacement of the fragile, shellac, 78 rpm by the more durable, smaller, plastic, 45 rpm, were significant novelties. But the most important notice for the future was issed towards the end of 1948. It was then that recording tape was introduced for the first time.

Tape promised a new flexibility in recording procedures. Previously, recordings had attempted to produce a carbon copy of the 'interpretation' that the singer had brought with him or her to the recording studio. This was as true of the studied expression of a Caruso as of the 'spontaneity' of a blues sung by Bessie Smith. The widespread adoption of recording tape by the early 1950s replaced the earlier system of recording directly on to a lacquer coated aluminium disc: 'cutting a disc'. With the earlier system a musical error or poor performance led to the throwing away of the costly disc. There was no incentive to explore the peculiar potential of electrical recording, simply to use the studio as quickly and as economically as possible. Tape, on the other hand, allowed the possibility of re-recording the same piece many times over until a satisfactory 'take' was achieved. Even more significantly, it permitted cutting, splicing and editing: the final sound, the record that was released, could be completely put together in the recording studio. Little Richard's 'Keep-A-Knockin' began as a fifty-seven second demo-tape which was then skilfully edited into a two minute ten second record. Splicing bits of tape together, adding additional effects like echo, mixing and editing in a second moment, were not merely technical, they were also musical, possibilities.

Recording tape transposed the record from the status of a frozen snapshot to that of a musical montage. Recorded music was brought to the point where the geographical and temporal co-ordinates of an 'original' interpretation were weakened and finally lost in the particular 'performance' constructed in the recording process. The claims of written composition and

musical intentions prior to recording were continually interrupted and undercut by the electronic speech of studio
production.[13] The request for 'authenticity' was rendered
meaningless by mechanical reproduction (Benjamin, 1973).

The new possibilities offered by the recording studio and
the mass distribution of the subsequent sound by radio and
record also eased the passage towards a further possibility:
that of an important overlap between some of the previously
ignored edges of white popular music (country, 'hillbilly',
southern gospel) and the officially shunned musical immediacies of black America. This was a connection, by no
means inevitable, that was only welded into historical shape –
and its profoundest symptom at the time was rock 'n' roll – by
the appearance of another protagonist: the gathering together
of major changes in youth culture into the more precise figure
of the 'teenager'.

Youth, leisure and pleasure

> 'The young are an alien species.'
>
> (William Burroughs)

> 'It's our culture, our entertainment, our form of art. Most
> people won't listen to anything else but pop music. You get
> the beat, get the urge to dance: you know, chat a bird up
> and start dancing. Your feet are tapping and then your
> hands start. It just builds up inside of you.'
>
> (BBC radio programme)

Faced with youth as a social protagonist, most commentators
have instinctively looked to changes in the nature of leisure for
their explanation. This brings us back to the major upheavals
in post-war popular culture and the manner in which these
often dramatically registered in Britain from the early 1950s
onwards. The startling outline of the 'teddy boy', with his
heavily greased hair styled just so, wearing a drape jacket and
sporting an 'American slouch', or, more simply, the loudness
of both the 'teenager's' wardrobe and music, were blatant
signs of what was uneasily felt to constitute the sheer exag-

geration of a vulgar mass culture. It was in particular the loosely defined 'teenager' – a product, yet also a major consumer, of commercial popular culture – who was considered the messenger of this change.

The public centrality of youth in the festival of consumerism, well under way by the late 1950s, was by no means accidental. At first this was unavoidably accentuated when certain groups of young people in the 1950s came into contact with the expanded consumer market with some money in their pockets. The availability on a vast scale, often for the first time, of cheap and fashionable clothing, plastic pop records, chain store cosmetics and transistor radios, seemed to drive a further wedge into the 'generation gap'. Of course, this was also a suitably inflated metropolitan image of the teenage life: a powerful myth with its own peculiar strength to hang in the imagination and subsequent memory. The lives of the majority of Britain's teenagers invariably turned out to be a lot flatter and meagre in their daily realities.

But 'youth' also referred to wider circumstances, to the modernising drive that – if it only touched parts of British commerce – was the guiding idea behind developments in the increasingly proximate fields of advertising and the visual arts. The industrial reorganisation for consumer production meant that there was a perpetual announcement of the birth of the new and the necessary passing away of yesterday's model, style and fashion. It was 'youth', which subsequent experience has shown to be more a floating symbol denoting 'modernity' – today's people, tomorrow's world – rather than a particular stage of physical life, that promised the requisite succession of present 'moments', that perpetual 'NOW'.[14]

Such change drew on a greater economic and psychic investment in leisure. Leisure was no longer simply a moment of rest and recuperation from work, the particular zone of family concerns and private edification. It was widened into a potential life-style made possible by consumerism. To buy a particular record, to choose a jacket or skirt cut to a particular fashion, to meditate carefully on the colour of your shoes is to open a door onto an actively constructed style of living. The importance of such actualities, the attraction of their presence in the present can become crucial, permitting a sense of 'escape from self-awareness as a history of bad investments, of time wasted' (Brooks, 1982). In contrast to the anonymous drudgery of the working week, selected consumer objects provide the possibility of moving beyond the colourless walls of routine into the bright environs of an imaginary state. For, it is not changes in popular culture that threaten to reduce us to an undifferentiated 'mass', but the structure and organisation of work. At this point, modern leisure is transformed into the very fabric of personal life, the most significant context in which we have the chance to affirm our 'selves'.

It is above all the body, enveloped in sound, in dance, that stands at the cross-roads of pop music and leisure time. Dancing, where the explicit and implicit zones of socialised pleasures and individual desires entwine in the momentary rediscovery of the 'reason of the body' (Nietzsche), is undoubtedly one of the main avenues along which pop's 'sense' travels. Suspended over the predictable rhythms of the everyday, to dance often involves loaded steps, a pattern of obliquely registered tensions. These represent not only the contradictory pulls between work and pleasure, but also between a commonsensical view of pleasure ('letting off steam', 'a well-earned break', 'enjoying yourself') and a deeper, internalised moment where a serious self-realisation – sexual and social, private and public – is being pursued.

Such an investment is not only peculiar to dance, however. It is central to the varied universe of pop, binding romance, popular tastes and pleasures to its multiple surfaces. Pop music's widely assumed banality now acquires a different face. Recognising this, we are encouraged, as Walter Benjamin put it,' to brush history against the grain'.

Chapter 2

A Formative Moment, 1956–63

'Rhythm-crazed teenagers terrorised a city last night.'
(*Daily Sketch*, 1956)

1956 is the year when it begins. There were naturally earlier precedents. Without scurrying through the often obscured American cross-currents of the blues and white country music, we could still step back into the early 1950s or even late 1940s. But it was 1956 when in Britain the scattered signs came together in the recognisable shape of rock 'n' roll. From that moment on it becomes possible to refer to a new and distinctive 'pop music'.

In the opening week of April, preceded by Winifred Atwell's piano on 'Poor People Of Paris', and the Dream Weavers with 'It's Almost Tomorrow', Kay Starr occupied third position in the British Hit Parade with the ambiguously titled 'Rock And Roll Waltz'. The song's title (notice the genteel conjunctive rather than the rushed slang of 'n') suggests an anticipatory compromise that strains to hold together two incompatible worlds. Through the course of the year, the fracture between the musical heritage associated with waltzes ('light' or 'popular' music) and that of rock 'n' roll (unmistakably 'pop') acquires growing importance.

Before 1956, British popular music was dominated by US sounds: a musical cocktail that ran from show business to light jazz. Its recurrent image was that of the 'crooner'. British recording artists – Dickie Valentine, Joan Regan, Denis Lotus, Anne Shelton – supplemented American successes with their own 'cover' versions. Rock 'n' roll's noisy arrival was, as we have already seen, by no means the harbinger of a US cultural invasion. The deep novelty of rock 'n' roll lay elsewhere: it was a potent message from an 'other America', an 'America' which until then had largely remained beyond British earshot.

Glancing through the pages of Britain's two leading music papers in 1955, *Melody Maker* and *New Musical Express*, we find show business trumpeter Eddie Calvert and the 'cool' jazz saxophonist Gerry Mulligan, singers Kay Starr and Dickie Valentine, jazz vocalist Sarah Vaughan and Billy Eckstine, guitarists Barney Kessel and Bert Weedon. It exudes a stable sense of impresarios, musical 'standards' and show business: the soporific odour of a world in which 'tuneful melodies', 'popular standards' and 'entertainment' could be confidently discussed and clarified. The combination was frilly at the edges yet apparently solid. Photographs of female film stars with only the slightest connection to the music scene (Jayne Mansfield, Sabrina), and the *de rigueur* pin-up shots of women singers in low-cut dresses or bathing suits, appeared alongside weighty jazz record reviews and eulogies to Sinatra.

Continuing to turn the pages of *Melody Maker*, and moving into 1956, there are brasher sounds to be noticed creeping into print. In the early summer we read:

> Comes the day of judgement, there are a number of things for which the American music industry, followed (as always) panting and starry-eyed by our own, will find itself answerable to St. Peter. It wouldn't surprise me if near the top of the list is 'Rock-and-Roll'... Viewed as a social phenomenon, the current craze for Rock-and-Roll material is one of the most terrifying things to have had happened to popular music... The Rock-and-Roll technique, instrumentally and vocally, is the antithesis of all that jazz has been striving for over the years – in other words, good taste and musical integrity.[1]

The flag of 'good taste', together with the regularly employed image of its negation: 'Americanisation', indicates a growing polemic around the idea of what exactly should constitute 'popular music'.

Yet, while writers in *Melody Maker* began a campaign to

Figure 3. An 'authentic' sound: Big Bill Broonzy

silence rock 'n' roll, not only American jazz and crooners but
also the blues continued to receive regular coverage. The
potential link between this latter music and rock 'n' roll was
studiously avoided. In part this was facilitated because only a
certain form of blues was seriously considered. The contemporary urban electric style was largely ignored; the interest
in the music was more academic. The concern was with the
prehistory and makings of jazz, now a 'respectable' music,
with the 'authentic' sounds – hence acoustic not electric,
'human' not mechanical – of a 'folk music'. Big Bill Broonzy –
lionised in British jazz circles in the 1950s – was encouraged to
abandon his electric Chicago style and go back to the rural
music he had been playing in Mississippi in the 1930s. A
stubborn insistence on 'authenticity' produced the paradox of
highly artificial results.

In fact, under the threat of the rock 'n' roll 'craze', the most arbitrary distinctions were rapidly drawn up into fiercely patrolled aesthetic boundaries. Yet how was it that in Britain in 1956 there could be such a deep rift between the upholding of some forms of commercially successful popular music and the adamant denial of a novelty that by the end of the year was admitted to have been the most significant event in the musical calendar? What exactly was this distinction whereby Elvis's singing was 'ersatz' and 'mannered' (*Melody Maker* review of 'Heartbreak Hotel') while that of Norman Wisdom or David Whitfield was not? To understand this a bit better it is necessary to gaze further afield. Then perhaps it will become possible to grasp the wider sense of what were then understood to be such obvious distinctions between 'good' and 'bad' popular music.

'Bopping the blues'

The musical language of rock 'n' roll was foreign compared to what had previously dominated British tastes. The majority of objections raised by the popular music establishment insisted that rock 'n' roll was loud and brash, that, quite simply, it was not music but a noise, and worse still, a vulgar commercial noise. But the real strangeness of the music when it fell on fresh ears was the exciting disturbance of an explicit, almost bacchanal emphasis of the body in the singing voice.

When we put the records on and hear Elvis sing 'Heartbreak Hotel', 'All Shook Up', or Gene Vincent 'Be Bop A Lula', our attention is drawn away from the subliminal persistence of the 4/4 pulse towards the jerky triplet rhythms sewn into the vocal. The voice and such other 'lead' instruments as the guitar and the piano push against the beat. The twitching drive in the music emphasises the 'sound' itself as the object of the song. It is the seemingly physical presence of the 'performance' that captures our interest. The instrumental styles, with the recurrent piano *glissandi* of Jerry Lee Lewis, the crashing chords on Little Richard's records, the thumped bass (listen to the opening of 'Heartbreak Hotel'), 'honking' saxophones, and shrill, cutting, guitar breaks, lend further emphasis. We enter into the sensation of the immediate, the *particular* musical performance that, once committed to vinyl, is repeatable a million times over.

Richard Middleton has suggested that such musical 'heat' and the physical exertions demanded of live rock 'n' roll shows were frantic symptoms of the explosive exchange between black music and the white popular tradition (Middleton, 1972). Certainly, black music, building its effects on a vertical axis, emphasised the particularity of the individual perform-ance; which, unlike an 'interpretation', remains accountable only to itself. This, together with the wider evidence of energies released from the encounters of subordinated black and white popular musics in post-war America, suggests that we need to look at rock 'n' roll with a diverse eye from that widely adopted by official comment in the 1950s. For, in the context of traditional musical concerns, what rock 'n' roll had to show was largely unrecognisable.[2]

Along with its charged vocal and instrumental 'attack', this new music also brought in a distinct percussive approach. Intitially this could be heard in the 'pumping' piano sound borrowed from the 'honky tonks' and white 'country-boogie', but it was soon transferred to the rapidly learnt rhythmic possibilities of the more portable and cheaper guitar. In the United States this was hardly surprising. The guitar was the central instrument in many forms of popular music-making, both black and white. The entrance of the electric guitar in the late 1940s, first in jazz and then in urban blues and country and western music extended its sound. The electric guitar went on to supplant the acoustic guitar everywhere: in the sophisticated Texas blues style of T-Bone Walker or the brooding sounds of Muddy Waters and John Lee Hooker, and became an integral part of country music with Merle Travis, Chet Atkins, Ernest Tubb and others in Nashville. American rock 'n' roll, with its debt to both country music and the blues, was dominated by it, as were subsequent developments in the later 1950s. (Listen to the varied sounds of Bo Diddley, Chuck Berry, Buddy Holly and the Everly Brothers, all indicated in the Discography.)

In Britain, the adoption of the guitar was more striking. Lacking the American precedents, the guitar was considered a rather exotic instrument, largely confined to the rhythm sections of dance bands. It was rock 'n' roll and the subsequent popularity of skiffle that established it in British pop. The Shadows, who were also Cliff Richard's backing group, were particularly influential. The 'Shads', with the lead guitar of Hank Marvin, and what would later become the classic group line-up of lead and rhythm guitars, bass and drums, probably inspired more British pop beginnings than any other single musical event.

This new instrumental style was often inserted in other contexts as the needle later swung away from the raw sounds of rockabilly and rock 'n' roll. Elvis was regularly accompanied by the country–gospel quartet the Jordanaires, but then white gospel music was as important in Elvis's musical make-up as the blues.[3] Elsewhere, the modifications were more gratuitous. Many records used a backcloth of uninspired strings that rarely even had the saving grace of 'kitsch'. With some black R & B material, on the other hand, the sugary romanticism implied by adding orchestral touches sometimes changed from being a perfunctory background to becoming a dramatic musical extension. Such is the case with the Drifters' 'There Goes My Baby' (1959), where the gospel overtones of Ben E. King's voice hang over the stark violin figures in a counterpoint of desperate hopelessness.

All these American accents, transported to a fresh context, represented musical possibilities open to novel cultural investment. Britain, more than any other country in the 'Old World', was in a position to comprehend and explore these. A partly shared cultural, and a common linguistic, matrix was part of the 'special relationship' which permitted a deep ingression of US popular culture in Britain. But it also gave British culture the possibility of an increased access to the diversities and deeper strata of US musics upon which rock 'n' roll had been constructed. US musical forms were taken up and eventually translated into British cultural concerns, later becoming an integral part of British pop. In this two-way traffic, the 'America' displayed in the teddy boy style, the Elvis fan, or the later rhythm and blues and soul fanatic, had a lot to say about British popular culture.

'One of the embarrassments of democracy'[4]

The 1950s: a landscape of teddy boys, rock 'n' roll, the literature of the 'angry young men', CND, 'Trad' jazz, the abolition of National Service, the growth in television and car ownership – all apparently explained and wrapped up in Harold Macmillan's phrase, 'You've never had it so good'. Initial responses to these varied manifestations were plainly diverse, but nearly all were couched in defensive terms. The reaction to rock 'n' roll quickly became part of the wider aspersions cast on the social and cultural upheavals that Britain was experiencing at the time.

Much of the criticism was directed at the assumed powers of persuasion of the mass media, the effects of 'affluence', and the growing tendency to see in youth the 'most advanced point of social change' (Hall and Jefferson, 1976). So, the stunning outline of the teddy boy, or the more widespread presence of pop music and teenage styles, offered an opportunity for a sweeping diagnosis of Britain's social and cultural ills. Pop music as the teenage territory of popular music, and rock 'n' roll as its most candid form, were part of a new problem-ridden reality. In the prevailing pragmatic and rationalising temper of the times, rock 'n' roll and teenage pop music seemed a rather unsavoury din, a sort of potential refusal of the cultural consensus.

Nowhere was this considered to be more obvious than in the case of the teddy boy. The hysteria surrounding teddy boys after the Clapham Common murder in 1953, where a boy was dragged from a bus and stabbed to death, developed the theme of physical and sartorial violence already rehearsed in the Ealing film *The Blue Lamp* (1949), featuring Dirk Bogarde as the youth menace, and *Cosh Boy* three years later. However, contrary to popular belief, the style of the teds was not simply the aggressive physical counterpart of rock 'n' roll music. Teds began to appear in south London in 1954, and by the time rock 'n' roll had fully emerged in 1956 this florid male subculture was on the wane in the metropolis. What is undoubtedly true is that in capturing a wider imagination, diffusing drape jackets, 'brothel creepers' (extremely thick crepe soled shoes), narrow 'drain pipe' trousers and hair styles

Figure 4. Teddy boys... dressed up for each other

sculptured in Brylcreem in the provinces, a strong convergence between rock 'n' roll and the subcultural style was
retrospectively forged.

The precise details of a history are frequently subsumed
under the ardent views that command allegiance in popular
beliefs. For many, both then and since, the teds simply
represented the first crucial moment in the post-war period in
which an identifiable way of dressing, a particular music, a
certain hair style, along with coffee bars, dance halls, certain
street corners and particular parts of town merged into a
murky and slightly alien haze. Out of that fog stepped the
'teenager'. The term 'teenager' was then rapidly transformed
into a catchword for an assumed nether world existing
between controlled childhood and adult responsibility. It was
seen as a brief flight into hedonism and conspicuous consumption (hence publicly deplored although sometimes secretly
envied) until the 'real' world of work and the family once
again reasserted itself.

In practice, this youthful 'fling' was quite a bit greyer than
some of its images might suggest. For those that made the
teenage culture of the 1950s theirs was not a classroom
adolescence (the prevailing context of white US youth culture), but one firmly tied to the weekly rhythms of Saturday
night and Monday morning. It was predominantly a culture
of young working-class youth, the expression of those who had
left school at fifteen and gone out to work. What this 'teenage
culture' promised was the increased possibility for a generational style previously excluded not only by economic means
but also cultural ones. This was particularly attractive for
working-class youth faced with older cultural forms that were
either disappearing or being dispersed.

By the mid and late 1950s new elements helped to broaden
out and deflect the previously rapid transit from the school
yard to the works yard and the pub. It becomes a softer focus
re-run of the Boy's world in Graham Greene's *Brighton Rock*:
the enlarged possibilities of post-war recovery smoothing out
and blunting the sharper and more brutal silhouettes of the
1930s. While jobs may well have continued to be as dead-end
as before the war, wages had risen five times and the spending
power of working adolescents doubled. At the end of the

decade, Mark Abrams noted 'that not far short of 90% of all teenage spending is conditioned by working class taste and value' (Abrams, 1959). This also reflected a structural change in the family economy. In a moment when teenage income was no longer fully essential for the home youth spending moved out, sharply differentiating itself from an increased adult attention on home consumption (the television, the fridge, perhaps a car).

It is here, in working-class youth's public consumption, that we begin to find some of the material scaffolding across which the sense of pop music was stretched. In the land of eleven-pluses, grammar school and BBC accents, rock 'n' roll and pop music in general proposed an imaginative and alternative idea of 'culture' to that officially on offer. It was a novel terrain that lacked the solid landmarks of Richard Hoggart's nostalgic vision of urban working-class life (1958), but in its 'contradictory mixture of the authentic and the manufactured' (Hall and Whannel, 1964) was an important notification of a changed reality.

While the teds served momentarily to fix a set of spectacular stylistic options, their self-conscious selection of sartorial devices (the 'winkle-picker' shoes, the velvet-collared jackets and quiffs that advertised *their* presence) became, usually at a less dramatic level of definition, part of a wider set of youth styles. In Colin MacInnes's hero of *Absolute Beginners* (1959) we are presented with a later urban male elegance whose attention to detail is decidely 'alternative' to that of the 'straight' adult world, to the absent style of the 'squares'.

The narcissistic attention that emerges among urban male working-class youth in the post-war period, anticipated by the unrespectable and widely despised 'spivs', but more openly celebrated by the teds, is an important precedent for successive generations. It looks forward to the very different style of the later 'Modernists' or mods, and re-works a traditional working-class concern for looking 'smart' or 'flash' in a more mobile, increasingly media-conscious consumer context.

Such fixings of style – the carefully assembled collage of clothes, hair, music, argot and body – had an importance that is frequently overshadowed in the immediate subcultural glare. For beyond the particular subcultural genesis – the teds

as South London, unskilled, working-class males taking over
Savile Row's attempt to relaunch an Edwardian style for
young aristocratic men about town in the early 1950s and
crossing it with a cinematic 'hard-boiled' American idiom –
these spectacular displays acted as important generators.
They offered stylistic suggestions to young males who did not
directly participate in a particular subculture. To the
'weekend' ted, as to those with even more tentative associations with an active subculture, these new horizons promised
an alternative sense of youth culture from that suggested by
official agencies (' ...where good boys played ping-pong',
Melly, 1972).

Often admired from afar, and directly embraced by only a
select few, subcultural 'solutions' had the important effect of
mediating and diffusing the two major expressive forms
invoked by British youth cultures over the following decades:
pop music and clothes. Between these two poles a profound
urban romanticism was conducted. Moving rapidly outside
London and into the provinces it gave a fresh and richer sense
to the leisure institutions of Saturday night, whether it was in
the dance halls and youth clubs or merely out on the streets
hanging about.

Pop music was eventually to become increasingly difficult
to identify with any one social group. This is not to suggest (as
some commentators prophesied) that class distinctions were
abolished. But the mass media, in particular television, were
forced to seek out the 'popular' in ways that decidedly affected
and changed the manner in which they had previously
handled and responded to ideas of 'class' and 'popular
culture'.[5] The reality of the situation was again often quite
diverse from the public imagery. But there did begin to
register a general weakening of more traditional forms of
cultural consensus and an expanding passage through the
increased 'heterogeneity of social experience' (Howell, 1976)
towards the construction of new possibilities. This emergence
of a 'popular' audience supporting the new media of television, rock 'n' roll, pop music, and 'mass culture' in general,
still continued to run up against persistent social and cultural
barriers. While a wide access to records made pop music far
more 'open' to diverse social groups than earlier musics (both

of 'high' and 'low' origins), in its initial period pop's 'vulgar' sonorities were generally considered only fit for cultural consumption by working-class youth and wayward elements in the grammar schools.

So, despite more accessible conditions, despite the social indifference of a recorded music, 'designed for reproducibility' (Walter Benjamin), early pop was largely to be found within working-class youth culture. This was not simply the effect of an economic cut-off point that divided teenage workers from those still at school. It clearly also involved ideological reasoning. Rare was the grammar school boy, and even rarer the girl, who could surmount the cultural barriers of their school, family and social situation and turn to the despised sounds of pop. A grammar school girl in a northern industrial town:

> The coffee bars and snack bars etc., are the main congregating grounds for other teenagers, but I personally do not patronise these establishments, preferring to drink hot Nescafé at home rather than cool insipid liquid to the blaring of a juke box at eight pence a time in a howling hole of humanity.
>
> (Jackson, 1968, p. 143)

Behind the depressing prison hollowness of such sentiments a furtive exit was available and increasingly explored as the 1950s wore on and the new decade opened. While few grammar school boys looked to rock 'n' roll and pop as a cultural option, several did turn to the Trad jazz revival, the folk song movement (in which some girls also actively participated), and to contemporary US urban blues. But for the moment it remained an underground movement. Its growing presence throughout the late 1950s, especially in the Trad jazz following, occasionally received an indirect fillip, as with the skiffle boom (1956–8), but its real importance in British pop was not to emerge fully until the early 1960s.

Quite clearly, it was not only working-class teenagers who bought records after 1956 and turned them into hits. Many previously established performers successfully continued their lives in the Hit Parade, and when they dropped out were

replaced by up-dated, younger versions. Russ Conway, Shirley Bassey, Matt Monroe and Frank Ifield owed their popularity to a wide audience who unashamedly liked show
business and television variety, and were keen on 'catchy
tunes' performed by glamorous 'stars'. But, all the same,
something had changed. But the late 1950s, it was no longer
possible to fit the diverse sounds of Buddy Holly, the many
US black male and female groups, or such native voices as
Cliff Richard and Billy Fury, into a pre-rock 'n' roll sense of
popular music.

Pop's striking beginnings in rock 'n' roll initially set
British popular music back on its defensive heels. It also
accelerated a series of internal contradictions. Popular music
journalists found themselves caught between bemoaning the
'tastelessness' of rock 'n' roll while being forced to swallow its
popularity. In the brief but bitter critical barrage laid down
against this new American music, it was clear that discussions
about 'taste' and 'musicianship' were only the thin edge of a
far wider cultural wedge.

When 'Hound Dog' was released – and believe me 'released' is the word – I sat up and took rather special notice.
Lo these many times have I heard bad records, for sheer
repulsiveness coupled with the monotony of incoherence,
'Hound Dog' hit a new low in my experience... There must
be some criteria left, even in popular music. If someone is
singing words, one surely has the right to demand that the
words are intelligible? ...How much further can the public
be encouraged to stray from the artistry of Ella Fitzgerald,
or the smooth swinging musicianship of Frank Sinatra?
(*Melody Maker*, 10 October 1956)

The writer, Steve Race, goes on to rehearse the familiar
catechism that linked commercial popularity ('which allows
itself to cater for one demented age group to the exclusion of
the masses who still want to hear a tuneful song, tunefully
sung') to the feared future of 'Americanisation': 'And I fear for
this country which ought to have had the good taste and the
good sense to reject music so decadent' (ibid).

But 'good taste' was clearly powerless against the forces

that had spawned an 'ersatz' Elvis Presley, the 'commercial' pop record and such mutants as the electric guitar. While rock 'n' roll was being decimated in print, *Melody Maker* succumbed to other pressures and on 7 April 1956 introduced the American practice of carrying a weekly Top Twenty chart of the best selling records.[6] But what was really challenging critical criteria in popular music was not only the disruption of taste categories encouraged by rock 'n' roll, or the 'misuse' of the 'Queen's English' by Elvis, an ex-truck driver from Tupelo, Mississippi, but the discovery of a previously unknown musical and cultural experience.

Musical practices on tours and in the dance halls, as well as British record company policy, changed to meet this growing reality far more rapidly than the critics. By the end of 1956, several popular dance bands had spawned 'rock 'n' roll combos'. Such were the beginnings of Tony Crombie's Rockers, The Rockin' Horses, Kenny Flame and his Rockets, The Rockin' Sinners. Their typical line-up consisted of saxophone, piano, guitar, bass, drums and a vocalist. These tentative gestures by British musicians, cut off from the musical practices that had gone into the making of rock 'n' roll, were weak and imitative. But in their own way they were the bearers of the news. In 1956, the news was American rock 'n' roll.

An 'American model'

'He lives in Birmingham, not Hollywood – a dead empire in a sunset world, yet still hopes that somehow an Eden will pull off the trick, Super Mac will open up those golden gates and here along the M1 the orange trees of California will begin to blossom. There must be a lucky card, a permutation no one has found, a new body movement more appealing than the last.'

(Ray Gosling)

'The Americans have colonised our subconscious.'

(Wim Wenders)

That state of mind which was 'America' for many British youngsters in the 1950s bore two unmistakable imprints: Hollywood film and popular music. These, along with the effects they induced in their British equivalents, were among the most immediate experiences that went into the formation of a popular culture repertoire in those years. For many young men, the formalised gangster film types of the late 1940s and then the problematic male youth hero (Montgomery Clift, Marlon Brando, James Dean), fixed and condensed in a masculine style life as an imaginative gesture. As the American critic Robert Warshow wrote of the gangster: 'for the gangster there is only the city; he must inhabit it in order to personify it: not the real city, but that dangerous and sad city of the imagination which is so much more important, which is the modern world' (McArthur, 1972, p. 28). Such is the New York or the Los Angeles of the imagination. In the British context the personification of urban surroundings might seem less dramatically motivated, but an imaginative relationship to them is decidely unsuppressed.

> The Royal was a large luxuriously decorated ballroom. It was full of atmosphere: dimmed lighting, a licenced bar and small tables around the dancing area. This was the luxury we had seen on film. Now we had the setting, so we became the actors. One boy might fancy himself as Errol Flynn, and chat up one bird after another. One might be a second Bob Hope, cracking jokes all night. Then there were the more aggressive ones: Humphrey Bogarts, George Rafts and all the gangster types.
>
> (Barnes 1976, p. 174)

In this active relationship of the 'imaginary' to the 'real' (Morin, 1962), a teenage style, necessarily diverse from surrounding circumstances, and increasingly American in inspiration, flourished. Dick Hebdige has suggestively referred to this as an 'existential option' (Hebdige, 1979). The borrowings by British male youth from the darker America of the city, eventually leading to an extreme existential location in the Negro, offered the imaginative possibility of living beyond existing categories in some deep and immeasurable night. It was the chance, however fleeting, to break with inherited limits. The hope, the symbolic gamble, that behind the accumulated mirrors of a nullifying common sense there must be something else, came to be identified in the imagined US underworld of the gangster, the hustler, the Negro, and associated urban 'cool' styles of talk, body gestures, clothing and music. These were disparate, deliberately exotic, options for white British working-class youth. The arrival of rock 'n' roll and the formation of a youth oriented pop music, both 'made in America', promised to stitch them even more closely into a comprehensive synthesis.

The sense of isolation in which British culture was immersed in the immediate post-war years is often forgotten. These were the cramped years of rationing, few books or magazines: a period of dull prospects clothed in old institutions and confronting an uncertain future. It was in this situation that Hollywood film, American comics and rock 'n' roll seemed so alluring. They offered the 'sense of limitless possibility about American life which does not exist in England' (John Russel, in Russell and Gablik, 1969, p. 33). This was also the imaginative side of what elsehwere was underwritten by a commonsensical understanding of the United States as the symbol of 'progress', 'mobility' and the future (Hoggart, 1958).

America was by no means the exclusive property of the juvenile imagination. It was also the blatant model for post-war commerce and industrial life – the British record industry and entertainment world included. When rock 'n' roll arrived in Britain in the winter of 1955–6 it discovered a tightly controlled native popular music field. The British record industry, including in its ranks EMI, then the biggest record company in the world, was in the hands of four major companies: EMI, Decca, Pye and Philips. There was BBC radio with its Light, Third and Home services. The only alternative radio was Radio Luxemburg, transmitting from the Continent. The time allowed for playing records on the BBC each week ('needle time') was restricted to twenty-two hours. There were two national musical weeklies: *Melody Maker* and *New Musical Express*. British pop music existed in a cultural field of notable institutional inflexibility.

In the United States, an enthusiastic disc jockey like Alan Freed could promote black R & B and take a New York radio station to the top of the audience polls. While at 706 Union Avenue, Memphis, an equally enthusiastic white record producer, Sam Phillips, was reputedly looking 'for a white man who had a Negro sound and a Negro feel' (Guralnick, 1978). He came up with Elvis Presley, to be rapidly followed by Carl Perkins, Jerry Lee Lewis, Roy Orbison and Johnny Cash.

Although destined to have a profound impact on British popular music, these new American sounds were forced to intersect with the existing patterns of the British music industry. The commercial imperatives of the record companies led to a quick accommodation: if rock 'n' roll was selling, they would sell it; and they dragged an initially reluctant musical commentary in their wake. Elsewhere, opposition could often afford to endure for far longer. The combination of monopoly and non-commercialisation left the British radio network as probably the clearest barometer of official resistance to rock 'n' roll and the changes represented by pop. This was particularly significant for pop – a music almost completely formed inside the relations of an electronic medium.[7] Live tours continued to promote singers and records, but it was radio airplay and, increasingly, television exposure that encouraged people into the shops to buy the sounds.[8]

In this context, the virtual monopoly of radio airplay by the BBC had important consequences. Radio Luxemburg, being sponsored by British record companies, did play a substantial amount of pop and consequently enlarged its audience. But the BBC resisted rock 'n' roll and pop for a considerable time. It was only the striking confirmation of popularity achieved by the pirate radio stations in the mid-1960s promoting beat and 'underground' music that the BBC relented. It has meant that the importance of radio in the development of British pop has been rather marginal, and certainly not comparable to its importance in the USA. In Britain, new proposals in pop have often acquired a rather underground, grass roots, style, usually located in different types of clubs. It was not the Sun recording studio and local airplay around Memphis, but the Two I's coffee bar in Old Compton Street,

Figure 5. Elvis, 1956

Soho, that became the mythical site of British pop. Just as later it would be the Cavern, Liverpool; the Crawdaddy Club, Richmond; the Club Go Go, Newcastle; and the Nashville, Kensington, that hosted successive British developments.

In other parts of the popular music field, an 'American model' gained ground with more ease. The new importance of the singer, encouraged by the portable electrical microphone which permitted a personal, intimate, 'crooning' style, was one. Singers were now no longer *in* a band but accompanied *by* a band. The effect of this change was to free popular singing from strict dance tempos. This encouraged a switch in focus to the 'individual' style of the singer. It announced a new phase in popular music. It would be media accessibility to the particular singer, rather than the song, that would become crucial. The pioneers – Bing Crosby and Frank Sinatra – spawned a countless offspring: Tony Bennett, Dean Martin, Buddy Greco, Al Martino, Perry Como. But, by the early 1950s, the dramatic populariser of musical personalisation – in some respects anticipating the hysterical reification of rock 'n' roll's idolatry – was the 'Nabob of Sob', Johnny Ray. Famous for the outbreak of tears during his performance, Ray was a singer who 'leapt from obscurity to world-wide fame by baring his emotions in public', as the *New Musical Express* acidly described him in 1953.

In Britain, meanwhile, the dance bands did not disappear. Ambrose, Jack Parnell, Eric Delaney, Ted Heath and Cyril Stapleton continued to maintain a position in popular music, particularly dance music, right up until the arrival of pop in the mid-1950s. But that in no way hindered the British reproduction of the US fashion for solo singers: Dickie Valentine, Ronnie Hilton, Anne Shelton, Denis Lotus and Joan Regan. It was to continue, with the addition of the voices of Frankie Vaughan, Ronnie Carrol, Michael Holliday, Shirley Bassey and Matt Monroe, through the 1950s and 1960s, leading eventually into the up-dated international show business styles of Tom Jones and Engelbert Humperdinck.

Elvis Presley's unprecedented success in Britain was also bound up with a rich and overall sense of 'Americanness'. A suggestive combination of Latin good looks, cowboy speech and manners, Negro sartorial taste and performance, and their musical equivalents in ballads, country music and R & B, produced in Presley 'a point in which separate attitudes could merge' (Nuttall, 1970). In musical terms it was not a purely fortuitous combination. It had its own biographical specificity and individual stamp. 'Rockabilly' was happening, rock 'n' roll was coming together, but without Elvis it might well have taken on a different shape. It was Presley who stamped upon this fledgling musical synthesis its inaugural authority. It was the force of Presley's voice and performance on the combined features of the musical material that meshed white gospel, country music and black rhythm and blues in a new musical and cultural code.[9]

Listening to the recordings that Elvis made for Sam Phillips in Memphis in the mid-1950s and comparing them with those made a little later for the same Sun label by Carl Perkins, the magisterial power of Presley's performance is unmistakable. With Perkins there are similar musical currents at work, but the respective country and blues elements remain less integrated; his voice tends to cut across and over the instrumental backing. Presley's voice, however, has a 'voluptuous' presence within the music. This is particularly evident if we compare the two singers respective recordings of 'Blue Suede Shoes' (see Discography). It indicates Elvis's greatest debt to the blues. It is an aural difference that permits us to appreciate both Presley's fundamental importance in white popular music and Roland Barthes' point that in the 'grain' of the singing voice it becomes possible to locate a cultural sense. What emerges from Presley and rock 'n' roll is the Atlantis of a previously largely unknown musical continent.

A British repertoire

While there were few American singers who could claim a 'voluptuous' presence in their music, in Britain there were none. Rock 'n' roll's hi-jacking of the blues, R & B, country and white gospel music was always a highly attenuated affair even in the USA. In Britain it was a non-starter. All the first wave rock 'n' rollers came out of the rural, southern states, and had, within the deep tensions of its segregated and racist cultures, imbibed a multiplicity of cross-cultural musical influences. Their urban British counterparts – Tommy Steele, Marty Wilde, Terry Dene, and later, Cliff Richard, Adam Faith and Billy Fury – had no experience and little awareness of the explosive combination that rock 'n' roll rested upon. And as for the transatlantic harmonies of street corner 'doo-wop' or the black music of Fats Domino, Little Richard, Bo Diddley and Chuck Berry, it was completely beyond their ken. The exposure of rock 'n' roll in Britain, on records, in films like *Blackboard Jungle*, *Rock Around The Clock*, and later live tours, conjured up for British audiences not the peculiarities of specific cultural realities but quite simply, to employ a Barthian neologism, 'Americanicity'.

Later, the discovery of what lay behind rock 'n' roll was to have the most profound consequences on British pop. But in the mid-1950s there existed few other possibilities than imitating a barely understood American style. In fact, rock 'n' roll hits in the British charts continued to be made by Presley, Little Richard, Jerry Lee Lewis and Chuck Berry. British singers, apart from one or two stabs at rock 'n' roll that verged on the pastiche in the case of Tommy Steele's 'Rock With The Caveman' or Cliff Richard's more successful 'Move It', quickly reverted to being up-tempo teenage pop singers.[10] British pop, despite the inital shock of rock 'n' roll and the discovery of the 'teenager', continued to move in the grooves of show business and the established entertainment world. In this case, following hard on Elvis's heels, British male pop stars – Tommy Steele, Cliff Richard, Adam Faith, Billy Fury – all made films: *The Tommy Steele Story*, *Espresso Bongo*, *Beat Girl*, *Play It Cool*, *The Young Ones*. Tommy Steele eventually embarked on a full show business career. The nature of the popular music industry, together with a monitored acceptance on radio (*Saturday Club*, *Easy Beat*) and television (*Oh Boy!*, *6.5 Special*, *Juke Box Jury*, *Thank Your Lucky Stars*), combined to pull pop music into the orbit of what David Jacobs, the avuncular chairman of *Juke Box Jury*, referred to as 'excellent entertainment for all the family'.

After the brief irruption of rock 'n' roll a rapid return to an updated musical and cultural conformity seemed almost compulsive: 'Before, I was a rocker, only acceptable to the kids. 'Living Doll' brought me an audience that was far more family, it brought mums and dads along to see what the apparition was on about' (Cliff Richard). But the omens had been there right back in 1956 when John Kennedy, Tommy Steele's manager, moving even faster than Presley's Colonel Parker, had decided that it was necessary to 'smarten up' rock 'n' roll and give it 'class' in order to attract a wider audience.

Rock 'n' roll had signalled an important shift in popular music, but for the moment it remained an allusive possibility, a peripheral musical revolt. In 1956, the best selling single in Britain was Pat Boone's 'I'll Be Home'. The highest position achieved by a rock 'n' roll record that year was Elvis's 'Hound Dog'. It was tenth. In 1957, Pat Boone, again sold the most singles with 'Love Letters In the Sand'. It was followed by Paul Anka's juvenile lament 'Diana'. Elvis occupied third place with 'All Shook Up'.[11] Despite the uproar at the time and such examples as Bill Haley and the Comets heading the charts with 'Rock Around the Clock' for two months solid between November 1955 and January 1956, rock 'n' roll did not swamp the British Hit Parade. Throughout this period, the heart of British pop was drawn from the more assimiliable American developments. It resulted in a teenage sound that was largely divided between ballads, up-tempo numbers and instrumentals. There were some peculiar British inflections such as skiffle, even hints of the music hall (Tommy Steele, Lonnie Donegan, Joe Brown), and a little later the commercial success of Trad jazz, but the principal tendencies in British pop were encouraged by the comfortable prospects set by the US music industry. When Adam Faith and Billy Fury were launched in 1959 they found themselves in a stable music scene in which pop had clearly become an integral part of the calculated world of the major British record companies.

The US contribution to the British charts, which was large and extremely important can be divided into several areas. First there was rock 'n' roll: Bill Haley, Elvis, Chuck Berry and the others. This was succeeded in the period 1957–8 by what is often called 'High School'. Meant to indicate juvenile sentimentalism, 'High School' is actually a blanket term for a whole series of different musical strands, including later developments in rock 'n' roll. In the wake of Presley's success, his most easily imitated side – ballad singing – led to a school of teenage warblers: Fabian, Tommy Sands, Paul Anka, Ricky Nelson. However, the rural America that had produced rockabilly, Elvis, and the first wave of white rock 'n' roll did not disappear. Often tending more explicitly towards country music, hence softer in tone, the music of the Everly Brothers, Buddy Holly and the Crickets, and Eddie Cochran, continued to refine and extend the rock 'n' roll tradition. Elsewhere, there were the influential black 'doo-wop' city R & B sounds of Frankie Lymon and the Teenagers, the Coasters, and the Drifters. They were supplemented, in an important studio extension of black urban pop music, by the numerous and imaginatively produced female groups: The Chiffons, The Ronettes, The Crystals.[12] Finally, there were the instrumentals (Duane Eddy, Johnny and the Hurricanes) and the dance records (Chubby Checker, Little Eva, Rufus Thomas).

The 'death' of rock 'n' roll in 1958 and the rise of 'High School' is widely understood as the obvious replacement of rock 'n' roll's 'wildness', its disturbing appeals to the body, to sexuality, by an innocuous adolescent sentimentality. This 'cleaning up' being the moment when the American popular music industry finally puts the brakes on the careering vehicle of juvenile sounds and direct them into more docile pastures. In part, this is no doubt true, although sentimentality has always played an important role in pop. It was there right from the beginning in Elvis ('Love Me Tender'), Jerry Lee Lewis and other rock 'n' rollers. But 'High School' also had important internal tendencies; while its various sounds may well have been interconnected through a general emphasis on teenage angst, it was never homogeneous. Further, with its growing exploration of studio production procedures – the work of important producers like Phil Spector, Ahmet Ertugun and Bert Berns – it also represented a new chapter in an increasingly urban sound. So, while British ears certainly extended their hospitality to the inspid sounds of Johnny Tillotson's 'Poetry In Motion' and Bobby Vee's 'Rubber Ball', there was also the Drifters's 'Save The Last Dance For Me', Eddie Cochran's 'Summertime Blues', and Buddy Holly's 'Oh Boy!'.

None of these particular styles were chronologically marked by extreme breaks, although 'High School' certainly dominated the late 1950s. It also encouraged a further crop of British teenage balladers with such singers as Craig Douglas and Mark Wynter. But at the same time, the musical immediacy and emphatic beat introduced by rock 'n' roll was not lost. It persisted in some of the faster songs of Cliff Richard and Adam Faith, in the music of Buddy Holly and Eddie Cochran, in the instrumentals, and in the black R & B harmony groups whose work was soon to modulate into the urban soul tradition of the 1960s (see Discography). These various tendencies led, both directly and through their long-term effects, to the laying down of a basic pop music repertoire in Britain; one quite distinct from previous commercial popular music. Much of it was sustained by a constant demand for teenage dance music.

Out on the dance floor

In the temporary 'freedom' of Saturday night, drink and dance, sex and fashion, fun and fantasy, are chained into complex chains of meaning. Pop music enters and seals together much of the romantic syntax of youth pleasures that emerge from these events. At dances, at youth club record hops, in draughty church halls and rural community centres, pop music, only weakly present on the radio, found a privileged space.

While dance halls provided a public stage for male postures, with the dancing itself it tended to be the girls present who cast the sounds of pop into a further social act. Dancing involved rigid ground rules that had been persuasively laid down elsewhere, outside the walls of the dance hall or youth club. Consequently, girls tended to arrive in groups and couples and danced amongst themselves, while the majority of boys lounged around the walls, talked and smoked, stared down alien males, and conserved their masculinity.

Scattered around the hall are clusters of boys in curious aggressive stances: heads thrust forward, backs arched like longbows, arms folded in front of their bodies. They will

gaze at the girls but rarely ask them to dance. Occasionally
one will burst into rapid movement, then, dissatisfied, lope
off to a new station on the floor. Simultaneously three or
four others will rise up like a flock of birds and follow him.

(Mabey, 1969, p. 67)

Inside the adult and parental horror generated by rock 'n' roll
and couples jiving in cinema aisles in the later summer of 1956
when *Rock Around The Clock* was regularly being expelled from
Britain's cinema, was the fear of unbridled instincts, of sexual
licence. The explicit references to the body in musical performances was verified in the gymnastic explosion of the
dancing. In reality, the frenzy of jiving couples was rarely
allowed by dance hall managers. Dance halls were anxiously
guarded as 'respectable' institutions with a 'good name', and
dancing and dress were expected to conform to a sense of
propriety. Spontaneity could only be regarded 'as the potential hand-maiden of rebellion' (Mungham, 1976, p. 86). The
same writer goes on to note that the project of installing
dignity in the halls led to the 'bouncers' on the door being
transformed into 'attendants', while the place itself became a
'ballroom' or a 'suite'. Not, it needs adding, that such
developments and their 'smart' aspirations were necessarily
antithetical to youthful tastes, particularly those that germin-
ated in the narrow prospects of a working-class experience.

The sexuality that was stamped on the public sentiments
and postures of rock 'n' roll was predominantly masculine in
shape. There were few girls who could embrace the rough
'street' inconography and unpolished directness associated
with the music and hope to escape the crippling censure of
their family, friends, neighbourhood and school. While from
boys 'toughness' and 'high spirits' was only to be expected,
from girls such extra-domestic activity could mean only one
thing: moral breakdown and all the negative connotations
that accompany female involvement in 'street life'.

Yet girls were deeply involved in pop music, just as they
had been in its immediate predecessors. From Frank Sinatra's
'bobby soxers' to the near hysteria of Johnny Ray's fans and
the juvenile empire that followed Elvis, a female presence has
often been determinant. With other options discouraged or

Figure 6. Bedroom girl

barred, the girl fan was encouraged to organise her commitment around a romantic attachment to the star. The result:
for the majority of girls, the sounds of pop were deeply
associated with a largely hidden female 'bedroom culture' of
pin-ups and a Dansette record player. For girls, dancing
proposed a charged public extension of a culture, where,
enwrapped in the romantic sonorities of pop, 'true sexuality
was only achieved within the context of reproducible
marriage'.[13] It was this domestic space that was permitted
rather than the public areas of streets, clubs, coffee bars and
amusement arcades (McRobbie and Gerber, 1976).

It is a slightly paradoxical footnote that there were more
women singers in pop in the 1950s and early 1960s than there
were to be in the two decades to follow. However, whether it
was the glamorous 'show-biz' personality with permissible
hints of sexuality (Shirley Bassey, Cleo Laine), better still the
'girl next door' (Susan Maughan, Helen Shapiro, Brenda
Lee), or, more simply, the Saturday night dancer and fan,
women were still largely considered marginal adornments in a
music that was apparently dominated by public male cultures.

In the margins of pop

The response of the British record industry to rock 'n' roll and
the success of US pop music – launching each new male singer
as 'Britain's answer to Elvis' – was the more obvious side of
the pedagogic effects of an American dominion in popular
music. To the other side were the connections activated in the
working-class youth culture of the period which, together with
complementary developments elsewhere, formed part of a
lengthening journey into the heartlands of US popular music.
By 'complementary developments' I mean the small but
significant links that were established through the 1950s in
Trad and revivalist jazz, in the folk song movement (much of
its material re-imported from the Appalachian regions of the
United States), and a growing interest in rural and urban
blues. Many of these interests involved a conservative nostalgia for the 'authentic' or 'folk' music of some imagined

yesteryear. Yet it was the eventual mixing of these more exotic American sounds with rock 'n' roll and pop that led to the British variety finally coming of age and finding its own 'inner voice' (Hall and Whannell, 1964) in the next decade.

Between pop music, the Hit Parade and a minority trad jazz following, there existed for a brief period a significant bridge: skiffle. In many ways skiffle was the first popular attempt undertaken to appropriate parts of American popular music that were not drawn directly from the US charts or show business. Rock 'n' roll had transmitted some unknown dimensions of American popular music. The British revival of New Orleans style jazz (1885–1914), which began in the 1940s and a decade later was a notable minority presence, offered another, although backward looking and largely static, view. Similarly, the blossoming folk song movement, although increasingly concerned with the 'purity' of a national heritage, did in its early days encourage an interest in American folk music, and not all of it white.

It was skiffle which clearly helped to transform these varied musical possibilities into a more popular and accessible form. Skiffle singing involved strictly imitative mid-Atlantic accents. The songs were about the 'Cumberland Gap' (Lonnie Donegan, The Vipers), gambling in Maine, fighting the battle of New Orleans (Lonnie Donegan), and freight trains (Chas McDevitt and Nancey Whiskey). Skiffle's instrumentation, consisting of acoustic guitar, and a largely home-made rhythm section of washboards and tea-chest string bass, with optional guitars, kazoo, banjo and piano, was a duplication of the New Orleans's 'Spasm Bands' of the turn of the century and the black Memphis bands of the 1930s (The Memphis Jug Band, The Mississippi Sheiks). Between 1956 and 1958, it popularised many of the elements of US white and black popular music in Britain for the first time.

In the hybrid forms drawn from the 'common stock' of black and white rural folk music, skiffle drew out a music stripped down to the essentials. The number of keys and chords employed were few, and the instrumentation tended to be concentrated in a strong rhythmic support for the vocals. Although deeply despised by the purists in both the jazz and

Figure 7. Home-made rhythms: the skiffle board

folk worlds, and largely excluded from the Hit Parade by the increasingly professional organisation of pop music, the popular format of skiffle was an important sign for the latter's future.

Above all, it offered a major democratisation of music-making. With little money and limited musical skill it became possible to be directly involved in a popular music. By 1957, there were numerous amateur skiffle competitions being regularly held everywhere in Britain and literally thousands of groups. Individual members of groups as diverse as the Shadows (Hank Marvin and Jet Harris in The Vipers) and the Beatles (John Lennon and Paul McCartney in The Quarrymen) had their musical baptism here. Slow musical apprenticeships and professional training in show business, or the teenage star's 'lucky break', no longer represented the two extreme entrances into pop. With skiffle a third way seemed possible.

Lonnie Donegan's first skiffle hit, 'Rock Island Line', was a folk song taken from the repertoire of the black singer Huddie Ledbetter. Ledbetter, or 'Leadbelly', during the latter part of his life had moved in the musical circles of Woody Guthrie, Pete Seeger and the post-war American folk song movement. In his youth he had led the blind itinerant bluesman Blind Lemon Jefferson around. The flipside of Donegan's 'Rock Island Line' was 'John Henry', a ballad common to both the black and white folk traditions. In its own way, this American folk song mix of white and black provided, in its British skiffle appropriation, a sort of weak but significant counterpart to the more decisive contemporary making of rock 'n' roll in the southern USA. The analogy is probably more suggestive than real. However, skiffle was very influential, and its effects were certainly not contrary to the tendencies indicated by rock 'n' roll. Apart from reinforcing the centrality of the guitar as a musical instrument, and thus marking the first step towards eventual electrical amplification, it also encouraged an interest in rural and urban blues.

British skiffle actually emerged out of the folds of traditionalist jazz. 'Rock Island Line' and 'John Henry' were both cut in an LP session by the Chris Barber Group. Donegan was then the group's banjo player. Traditional jazz, the music of a pre-First World War New Orleans, played in strict ensemble, employing march times and containing no instrumental solos, had its high priest in Ken Colyer. His jazz band began in 1949. Trad jazz grew out of a deep aversion to 'swing' and its 'decadent commercialism'. Modern jazz as it appeared in the late 1940s in the pioneering Kansas City and New York sounds of Charlie Parker, Thelonius Monk, Dizzy Gillespie and Charlie Christian was never considered. Besides, it would have involved the embarrassment of coming to terms with a new, black militant musical consciousness; something that could be conveniently overlooked when nostalgically evoking a mythical New Orleans of around 1900.

The debates and acrimonious disputes that raged in British jazz in the 1950s completely excluded any modernist tendencies. The struggle was between 'trad' and 'revival' jazz. The latter being the jazz of the 1920s following its migration north to Chicago. It was most widely associated with the music of Louis Armstrong's Hot Five. In both cases, a stern morality scorned the subsequent commercialisation of a one-time 'folk' music and insisted upon the 'authenticity' of the respectively championed musics. In a similar vein, skiffle was for Lonnie Donegan 'a genuine development of folk music' which had 'a legitimate position within the Jazz Movement', and was 'the music of the people' (Bird, 1958). Naturally, all these musics were frequently contrasted with the assumed commercial manipulations of rock 'n' roll. But while it was possible in the folk song movement to enforce the criteria of 'authenticity', to the degree that Ewan McColl insisted that singers sang only material coming from their own national repertoire, the paradoxes of white men seeking to reproduce faithfully a black folk music, of Britishers slavishly imitating a now largely extinct Afro-American cultural form, drew it up short of such artificially purist closure. Further, whatever may have been the private desires of individual musicians, the musical policies of most jazz bands remained fairly flexible. Outside the clubs, it was these bands that provided much of the music for dance halls up and down Britain in the first half of the 1950s.[14]

Now all these musical styles – skiffle, Trad jazz, folk song – were also, in differing degrees, the cultural signs of the expanded post-war presence of popular music as a mass medium. For it was often largely due to the availability of records and the success of American popular music in general that the further diversities of a musical America came to be known. This, in turn, subsequently revealed sources and styles upon which British tastes and interests could be built. The fierce rearguard action of those intent on defending 'authentic' folk musics against the commercial machinations of Tin Pan Alley and such US 'fads' as rock 'n' roll, was the most telling symptom of the irreversible change that had occurred in British popular music. Ironically, such reactions, largely constructed on borrowed Afro-American music, eventually provided much of the musical impetus that was to translate this 1950's 'traditionalism' into a 1960's 'hip' (Nuttall, 1970).

The final irony was that the *coup de grâce* of Trad jazz was the brief commercial boom it enjoyed at the beginning of the 1960s. It was the moment in which, in George Melly's words, 'an increasingly dull noise' was crossed with the Edwardian music hall in the person of Mr Acker Bilk ('Stranger On The Shore') and the whole ensemble nailed to the cross of its imaginary past, briefly hailed and then forgotten. But by this time, in the clubs that had formed the jazz band circuit, other sounds drawn from the USA were being played and experimented with.

The sounds of the steamy Crescent City – New Orleans – of half a century previously were about to give way to the contemporary timbres of a brasher, urban grip: R & B and soul music. Early British white R & B was largely nurtured by Alexis Korner and his Blues Incorporated (among his protegées were Cyril Davies, Charlie Watts, Mick Jagger, Davey Graham and John Mayall). This music and the eventual formation of young R & B groups like the Rolling Stones and the Yardbirds, were initially interventions in the London jazz scene as fervently 'anti-commercial' as the music they were supplanting: 'I hope they don't think we're a rock 'n' roll outfit' (Mick Jagger, in *Jazz News*).

At this point the web of musical intersections becomes further complicated as the effects of rock 'n' roll and US pop music in general overlap with the more esoteric musical practices spawned in and around the Trad jazz world. It was this combination, briefly anticipated by skiffle, that was to lay much of the basis for the particular tones of British pop in the decade to come.

Chapter 3

Britain's 'Inner Voices', 1963–66

'A strange bedlam was taking over which had nothing to do with anything we had previously known.'

Lonnie Donegan

With the opening years of the 1960s American pop continued to set the prevalent patterns for native musical efforts. Despite adverse medical advice warning of the dangers of slipped discs and muscular contortions, the latest dance fashion, the Twist, was in full swing. Chubby Checker, a corpulent black singer from Philadelphia, was the centre piece, but Sam Cooke ('Twistin' The Night Away'), Joey Dee and the Starliters, and a series of imitative British twist records by Frankie Vaughan, Bert Weedon and Susan Maughan, all found varying degrees of Hit Parade success.[1] To coincide, the Chubby Checker film *Twist Around The Clock* was released. Several British film comics – Peter Sellers, Charlie Drake, Bernard Cribbins – took their revenge and made records.

On 8 December 1962, sandwiched between Frank Ifield's 'Lovesick Blues' and Del Shannon's 'Swiss Maid', Elvis Aaron Presley, 'the King', entered the British charts for the fiftieth time in his career with 'Return To Sender'. Coming in immediately at number 2, a week later it was number 1. That same week, at number 19, there was 'Love Me Do', the Beatles' first record. Within six months, under growing headlines, escalating hysteria, and an unprecedented commercial interest, this Liverpool group had seized the crown of British pop. Cliff Richard survived as top pop singer, but he

50

was no longer 'Britain's No. 1 pop star'. However, he was a rare exception. Lonnie Donegan, previously among Britain's most successful singers, obviously spoke wistfully from the other side of the divide: 'Had they [the Beatles] known what the aftermath would be, I wonder if they would have done it in the same way. I admire their musical integrity, but at the time, I was resentful of the change. The whole of conventional show business had the same resentment' (Palmer, 1977, p. 231). Meanwhile, advertisements offered collarless 'Beatle style jackets' and Cuban-heeled (2½" heels) 'Mersey boots' – 'specially constructed height now in fashion with "beat" trends'. The Anglo-American Chewing Gum Company launched a 'Beat Mint' gum.

The interest and excitment that the Beatles and 'beat music' generated was without precedent in British pop. Elvis had never appeared in Britain, but it was not simply that vacuum which the Beatles filled. They represented, largely unknown to the enthusiastic record company executives and tour organisers, the vanguard of an internal remaking of British pop music. Frequently, as was the case with the Beatles, it had involved a slow apprenticeship beginning back in the days of skiffle: John Lennon and Paul McCartney, later joined by George Harrison, had formed the Quarrymen in 1956. In London, white youngsters in and around the bohemian enclaves of the metropolitan jazz world may have seen Muddy Waters on his British tour in 1958 playing electric Chicago urban blues. Certainly, they knew of Cyril Davies' All Stars and Alexis Korner's Blues Incorporated. This, together with a subterranean blues record culture fed by US servicemen and students, seamen and specialist record shops, largely nurtured in and around the art schools and often fuelled by an initial enthusiasm for rock 'n' roll and skiffle, eventually led to a confident musical proposal; one previously unheard of in British pop and largely unknown to the US pop music of the day.

During the course of 1963, the monumental impact of the Beatles and the continual expansion of the beat boom started to bring about the musical and cultural reorganisation of the face of British pop. At the outset, this unexpected triumph appeared destined to encounter the very predictable symbols

of British show business success. In November 1963, the
Beatles appeared at the most prestigious event in the British
show business calendar – the Royal Variety Show. The
following year, their film *A Hard Day's Night* opened with a
royal première. Then in 1965, the self-proclaimed architect of
'New Britain', Prime Minister Harold Wilson had the MBE
conferred on them. But these traditional tokens of public
achievement, however much appreciated by the Beatles'
manager Brian Epstein, were hardly the real story of the
success and innovative energies of British pop in those years.

When the Beatles and beat music began to monopolise
public attention at the beginning of 1963 there were frankly
few shock waves in the musical press. There was no replay of
1956. Record companies were soon busily scouring Liverpool's clubs and dance halls, anxious to tap the seemingly
inexhaustible gold mine of the 'Mersey sound' (see Discography). Nine months later, with 'Beatlemania' triumphant,
pre-release reviews of the next Beatles' single were solely
occupied with whether or not the phenomenon had run its
course. 'Beat' music was fully accepted. The critical outrage
and rejection that had once surrounded the mysterious
menace of rock 'n' roll was no longer in vogue. Only in the
margins with R & B, that distant cousin of both pop and jazz,
was it still voiced. But 'beat' was quickly accepted as a
speeded up version of popular show business. There were the
stars, styles and passing phenomena, all usually subject to
short lives and with rare exceptions – Elvis, Cliff and the
Shadows – rapid turn over.

Critical discussion of pop in the musical press no longer
employed terms like 'taste' and 'musicianship' (shortly to
return with a vengeance once pop found a new respectability
in the wake of the Beatles). The capitulation to a market
rationale was complete. It was commercial viability and
staying power that counted. The Hit Parade, not aesthetic
canons, firmly dominated the common understanding of pop
music. Now safely divided off from the rest of popular music,
from the universe of ballads, folk music and jazz, and reduced
to the assumed innocuity on an uncomplicated consumerism
(the choice of television set, record or washing machine was,
and is, an indifferent sign in this type of logic), pop apparently

served to provide for crazy teenage enthusiasms and rampant commerce.

'Affluence' and 'modernisation'

'It was like we were taking over the country.'
(18-year-old mod, in Hamblett and Deverson, 1964)

A hooter for a 'miss' and a sharp ring for the record voted to be a future 'hit'. Around these two stark sounds *Juke Box Jury*, the BBC's weekly Saturday afternoon showcase of pop music in the early 1960s, was organised. You did not, unlike ITV's *Thank Your Lucky Stars*, also late Saturday afternoon, see the music performed.[2] Sometimes there would be a singer on camera whose crestfallen reactions we would follow while the three-person 'jury', unaware of this presence in the adjacent room, discussed the merits of the record. After twenty seconds or so of listening a 'verdict' was passed on the song's commercial viability. The smirk on chairman David Jacob's face as he pressed down on the hooter was always a rather irritating reminder of a sober-suited, short-haired, responsible, adult 'No'.

The 'higher objectivity of the market' (Laing, 1969, p. 27) was what most apparently orchestrated the spectacle of *Juke Box Jury*; the same rationale as that displayed in the confident public handling of pop music in such Cliff Richard films as *Wonderful Life* and *Summer Holiday*. Behind these well-ordered commercial arrangements were also those buoyant arguments that elsewhere found the Conservative government of the day extolling the benefits of 'affluence'. Meanwhile, the Labour Party was left traumatically reassessing who it should be addressing now that economic prosperity threatened to become a permanent feature of contemporary Britain. Still, it was a very confusing moment, and one that could be easily misread by its participants. When Harold Macmillan resigned as Prime Minister in 1963, Conservative inner party politics revealed itself to be strangely out of joint with Britain's wider currents. In the publicised world of beat music, Pop Art, Concordes, hovercraft and a promised 'white heat technology', the grouse-shooting 14th Earl of Home appeared a perilous throw back as the new leader of the Conservative Party, a peculiar anti-climax after the flamboyant style of 'Supermac', a false note in the rising crescendo of meritocracy.

'Affluence' and 'modernisation' were the two major themes that, in varying guises, dominated public discussion through-out the first half of the 1960s. What 'modernisation' largely implied was economic growth and a rate of expansion that came nearer to Britain's European competitors.[3] Britain was clearly slipping down the economic and political league tables. General de Gaulle's recent veto on the Conservative government's Common Market application had been the latest sharp reminder. Returned to office after 'thirteen years of Tory mis-rule', the real sense of excitement and optimism that initially surrounded the 1964 Labour government was, however, rapidly deflated by the chameleon politics of the new Prime Minister (a man who smoked the humble pipe in public but really preferred cigars), and the deferential ideas that the Labour leadership brought to the government of the day. But, for a brief spell, while Mr Wilson blustered on about clearing 'dead wood' out of the nation's board rooms and dismantling the dynasty of Tory society, his rhetorical flourishes produced unsuspected echoes in a 'perverse nationalism' (Jeff Nuttall) that ran from the official 'I'm Backing Britain' campaign to the Union Jack suddenly becoming an icon of pop culture. Just what sort of 'Britain' was being backed remained suitably vague in both cases.

If 'modernisation' was a symbol of economic growth it was destined for a paradoxical career in British life. In April 1964, although illegal under British law, Radio Caroline went on the air. Its promoter, Ronan O'Rahilly, one time manager of The Scene club in Soho, a favourite mod haunt, succinctly caught the spirit of the moment: 'Youth was bursting out all over. There was a lot of money to be made'. (Frith, 1978, p. 104). Radio Caroline, backed to the tune of £500,000 by City businessmen, proved to be the first of many pirate radios broadcasting from rusting hulks in various fog-bound reaches of the North Sea. It was an unmitigated success. It has been claimed that in their brief life span (1964–7), pirate radios accounted for up to 20 million listeners a day.

While the BBC operated with its limited 'needle time' and programmers who gave extremely short shrift to pop music, the pirates offered an uninterrupted diet of pop, and one by no means limited to the state of the current Hit Parade. Not only were these stations far more closely attuned to the tastes of the clubs and dance halls (at least the London ones), they also went further and provided specialist programmes covering the cultural and musical fringes of the pop world. John Peel's *The Perfumed Garden* show on Radio London, and its mixture of poetry, pop, classical and folk musics, was an important anticipation of what around 1966–7 would become known as the pop 'underground'.

Elsewhere in the music business, 'modernity' meant keeping up with the trends, particularly those that had mushroomed after the outbreak of the 'Mersey Sound'. In technical terms there was little that was new.[4] Stereo was still in its infancy and stereo LPs offered as an optional luxury. Only with a drastically changed attitude towards the LP format, accompanied by a major growth in its sales and the availability of economic Hi-Fi systems, did stereo successfully supplant mono records towards the end of the decade.[5] Also, it should not be forgotten that the ubiquitous password of 'authenticity' was still an extremely influential idea, both in music – 'authentic' folk, blues, jazz – and recording studio ideology. On their first LP, recorded on a two track machine, the Beatles went out of their way to indicate the rare occasions when they had employed 'double-tracking' (i.e. the 'artificial' studio inflation) of their voices.[6] It was principally the 'curvilinear' American and American inspired guitar designs of the late 1950s that most obviously embraced an unashamed futurism. The 'streamlined' Vox Phantoms, Fender Stratocasters, Guild Thunderbirds and Hofner Futuramas – soon to have their electrical sonorities dramatically extended by the fuzz box and wah-wah pedal – were unambiguously plugged into the theme of modernity.[7]

'Affluence' was an altogether wider and more complex motif. While there were disturbing signs that poverty, that 'forgotten Englishman', had never really disappeared, it was temporarily tucked away between the sheets of the hire purchase agreements and overshadowed by the bright lure of consumerism. The myth of a classless, affluent society had by now become extremely persuasive. For a time the iconography of 'affluence', daily circulated by television, advertising and journalism, became more powerful a reality in the field of public representations than the contrary state of affairs it regularly obscured. This myth co-existed with other realities, they intertwined. When, after the mods and rocker battles on southern English beaches in 1964, a mod offered to pay his £75 fine to Margate Magistrates Court with a cheque, the fact that he has neither a bank account and has never signed a cheque in his life is no longer important. The gesture had already entered another symbolic domain: the mods were obviously 'affluent hordes whom "fines couldn't touch" (Cohen, 1973, p. 33).

A mod's defiant gesture or the outrageous behaviour of the Rolling Stones and their manager Andrew Loog Oldham – writing deliberately offensive LP covers (*Rolling Stones 2*), thrown out of hotels and restaurants for not wearing ties, fined for pissing against a garage wall, refusing the show business chore of going on the revolving stage at the end of the televised *Sunday Night at the London Palladium* to wave at the audience – was a novel and disturbing form of deviancy. Working-class delinquency or gang fights was one thing, but this disdainful refusal not of the fruits of the consumer society but of the traditional means – hard work, servile gratitude, sacrifice and dedication – for obtaining them, was something else. Physical surliness and rude grudges were to be occasionally expected, widespread ideological disaffiliation was far more serious.

The 'affluent society' had seemingly overriden the earlier boundaries between individual effort and retribution, class and social position. Cracks in the traditional façade had been the Profumo scandal, rumours of an orgy involving eight High Court judges, and Kenneth Tyan on the television programme *BBC 3* coolly stating, 'I doubt if there are rational people to whom the word fuck would be particularly diabolical, revolting or totally forbidden' (Wheen, 1982, p. 95). The limbo of affluence apparently permitted new possibilities. However, the 'faces' who finally came through were rarely examples of a 'rags to riches' success story. Behind the noisy arrival of the Beatles, Michael Caine, Twiggy and Terence Stamp was a widening sense of revitalised entrepreneurship.

It was this dynamic that directly fed into the myth of 'classlessness', although it was more accurately evidence of changed practices – ones that were faster and invariably sharper. This was as true of the new, hustling managerial style in the record industry (Brian Epstein, Andrew Loog Oldham, Kit Lambert, Tony Secunda) as in other, frequently notorious, business practices: Emil Savundra's Fire, Auto and Marine Insurance Company, John Bloom's Rolls Razor washing machine company, the Slater-Walker property empire. Meanwhile, on television the reassuring solidity of Cliff Michelmore was overtaken by the speedy, cosmopolitan, transatlantic style of David Frost (who 'rose without a trace'). Ultimately, however, as Tom Wolfe's 'Mid-Atlantic' British advertising executive discovered, to tie oneself to the modernistic allure of 'New York' offered no real escape from the prescribed order of London company life: the old British hierarchy – 'class, to call it by its right name' (Wolfe, 1972) – remained irritatingly intact. But, for a brief moment, the boisterous enthusiasm that surrounded Mr Wilson's new Labour government seemed to point elsewhere.

Around 1964–5 there occurred a decisive shift in the economy of public imagery surrounding pop music. Pop stopped being a spectacular but peripheral event, largely understood to be associated with teenage working-class taste, and became the central symbol of fashionable, metropolitan, British culture. It had moved from being a show business mutant to becoming a symbolisation of style. In select clubs like the Scotch of St James, the Ad Lib, the Cromwellian, a glittering caravan, photographed by David Bailey and Terence Donovan, dressed by Mary Quant, Ossie Clark and Angela Cash, hair styled by Vidal Sassoon ('Camus is my favourite writer... very few people turn me on like he does'), rubbed shoulders with John Lennon, Jean Shrimpton, Mick Jagger, Dusty Springfield, Roger Daltrey, and Twiggy, and pursued their magazine copy life-styles to the imperative rhythms of pop. However illusory and restricted was this image of a supposedly classless breed of 'New Aristocrats', it certainly fed the ravenous eye of the press, offering the British people a voyeuristic peep into the concentrated image of recent, rapid, and confusing change.

Figure 8. Talking about a generation

The spectacle of easy money and a classless amoralism also
provided stimulating copy for the new colour supplements of
the Sunday newspapers. On 4 February 1962, the first issue of
the *Sunday Times* colour supplement appeared.[8] Its cover was
composed of a series of photographs (by David Bailey) of a
model (Jean Shrimpton) in a grey dress (by Mary Quant).
Two years later and it was writing of the Liverpool beat boom:
a 'thunderously amplified music', 'full of wild insidious harmonies', played by the Fourmost, the Mindbenders, the
Undertakers, who at 'night... flood out into the raw mistral

that rips in from Liverpool Bay' (Booker, 1970, p. 210). The romance between pop music and the 'quality' Sunday press was now under way. The glossy pictures and cosmopolitan phraseology of the colour supplements provided a fitting mirror in which the young 'actors' and 'actresses' of this 'classless' advertising agency world 'performed'.

While the consequences of Britain's growing economic problems and the exhaustion of adequate political responses had been temporarily displaced by the bold language of the new Labour administration, this failed, however, to suppress the emergence of more morbid symptoms. But it was not so much the obvious satire and public irreverence for political leaders of *Private Eye* and the BBC's *That Was The Week That Was* that marked what has come to be seen as the real beginnings of the 'exhaustion of consent' (Hall *et al.*, 1978). A rapid succession of scandals involving housing, rent rackets, spys and public morality, had already set Britain's tabloid imagination running in high gear. It also stirred up more disquieting currents. A public breakdown in 'values' was connected to the jamboree of consumerism unleashed by the Conservative government in the late 1950s and early 1960s. Mr Macmillan's famous dictum began to turn to ashes in the mouths of many as *The Times* and other pontiffs of public morality suggested that the British had 'had it too good'. Rattling its prescriptions, prophecies and lurid pessimism, a moral crusade launched by Mrs Mary Whitehouse and Mr Malcolm Muggeridge ('the Savonarola of the Sixties', as Bernard Levin pithily described him), set off on its bitter pilgrimage through the 'permissive' wastes of a consumer-bloated Britain. In the incestuous juxtaposition of youth, consumerism and sex, this growing army of reaction was to feel increasingly confident that it had discovered the true malevolence of recent social change.

For the moment, however, these were vague misgivings. Public opinion was apparently elsewhere. In November 1963, the *Daily Mirror* published an editorial which began: 'You have to be a real sour square not to love the nutty, noisy, happy, handsome Beatles.' Five months later even the *Daily Telegraph*, hardly a paper noted for its radical tastes, began publishing the 'Top Ten' each week. The isolated signals of

long-haired males, the mod and rocker invasion of Britain's
beaches, and the teenage 'weekend kit, purple hearts and
contraceptives' (Margate police chief, in Cohen, 1973, p. 56),
had not yet been processed through the catalyst of 'swinging
London', after which they would emerge, in a distinctly
different light, rolled together into a far wider menace, ripe
for a 'moral panic'.

British sounds

'We started off by imitating Elvis, Buddy Holly, Chuck
Berry, Carl Perkins, Gene Vicent... the Coasters, the
Drifters – we just copied what they did.'

(Paul McCartney)

In 1958 when Cliff Richard, aged 17, had his first hit he was a
year younger than John Lennon. Cliff, and many members of
groups like the Shadows or the Tornadoes, were of virtually the same generation as the Beatles and the Rolling
Stones. There, of course, the comparison ends. The difference
between the 'Shads' and the Stones was not one of simple
historical succession so much as a distinct division between
two quite different musical cultures. It is true that both groups
looked to a musical 'America' for their inspiration and style,
but in one case this was largely limited to what American pop
had declared legitimate, in the other it was an altogether
different, 'unauthorised' connection that was sought. The
former path led to the aseptic embracement of a teenage pop
music (despite the earlier wilder promise of rock 'n' roll) by
Britain's show business; the other, needless to say, elsewhere.

The Beatles, and the wave of male beat groups that
emerged in their wake, represented something extremely new.
The presence of dancing music, while not necessarily important for the Hit Parade, was an imperative for the Saturday
night crowds who filled the clubs and dance halls in search of
local excitement. The music had to be fast with a persistent
beat, a few slower numbers towards the end of the evening for
the 'smoochers', and loud. Its energy constantly sought to
recapture the initial excitement and shock that rock 'n' roll

had once represented. Skiffle had also suggested to many young British males that it was no longer necessary to be either American or supported by London's Tin Pan Alley in order to recreate that musical excitement at a local dance. A male camaraderie formed at school, on the street corner, at art college, or in a gang, was frequently translated into musical shape.[9] It seems hardly incidental that the beat music boom proposed a lower degree of female participation in pop than at any time previously or since.

In clubs like the Iron Door, the Mardi Gras, the Cavern (Liverpool); the Oasis, Three Coins, Twisted Wheel, Kingfisher (Manchester); Club A Go Go, Guys and Dolls (Newcastle-upon-Tyne); Discs-a-Gogo (Cardiff); Lindella Club, La Cave Club (Glasgow), the weekly, and sometimes nightly, output of dancing music was supplied by local musicians. When Little Richard appeared at the Tower, Liverpool, in October 1962, the supporting bill gave a good idea of the local musical scene that was on hand. Apart from the Beatles ('Love Me Do' had been released eight days previously), there were The Big Three, The Mersey Beats, Billy Kramer and the Coasters, Lee Curtis with the All Stars, Pete Maclaine with the Dakotas, Rory Storme and the Hurricanes, Gus Travis and the Midnighters, The Four Jays, and The Undertakers. But outside Liverpool, which also boasted its own local pop paper, *Mersey Beat*, the development of a new style of British pop music, profoundly American in inspiration, was widespread. There were the future Animals, then the Alan Price Combo, in Newcastle; Wayne Fontana, the Hollies, the Statesmen, Freddie and the Dreamers in Manchester; Dave Berry and the Cruisers, the Sheffields, the Debonaires, all from Sheffield; the Beachcombers, Carl and the Cheetahs, Mike Sheridan and the Night Riders, and the Rockin' Berries in Birmingham. The innumerable Mecca, Top Rank and Locarno dance halls dotted around the country hosted the national package tours of Top Twenty stars when they passed through; but for regular Saturday night dancing and sounds it was to local groups and their loud rhythms that dancers bent their limbs in the Hully Gully, the Madison, the Mashed Potato and the Twist.

Listening to the songs on the first Beatles' LP provides an

idea of the repertoire used by groups in the Saturday night northern dance halls and clubs during the early 1960s. There is one important qualification here, however: the Beatles were almost unique by virtue of the fact that they had begun to write a lot of their own material. Still, listening to those songs today, their location within the wider context of the beat boom is not difficult to trace. Between May 1963 and December 1964, the Beatles released four LPs: *Please Please Me, With The Beatles, A Hard Day's Night, Beatles For Sale.* The majority of the songs were by John Lennon and Paul McCartney, but there among the non Lennon–McCartney material was 'Twist And Shout' (previously recorded by the Isley Brothers), 'Please Mr Postman' (written by Berry Gordy, head of Tamla Motown records, and recorded by the Marvelettes), 'You Really Got A Hold On Me' (recorded by the Miracles), 'Roll Over Beethoven' and 'Rock And Roll Music' (both written by Chuck Berry), and 'Money' (again written by Berry Gordy and recorded by Barrett Strong, another future stalwart of Tamla Motown). All these songs underline the Beatles' fundamental debt, later reaffirmed in John Lennon's LP *Rock 'n' Roll* (1975), to largely contemporaneous black pop music.

At the same time, with their royal premières and MBEs, the Beatles had seemingly been absorbed into the cushioned category of 'family entertainment'. Later, with 'flower power', drugs and mysticism surrounding their music, this cosy adoption was slightly distanced, but it was never fully shaken off. To some who held deeply entrenched views on musical 'values', the Beatles may have constituted an aesthetic threat of sorts, but hardly a moral one. The same could hardly be said for the scruffy R & B groups or the largely hidden association of the new 'mod' subculture with certain exotic black musics ('Mods were not Beatle fans... Richard Barnes): it was an important distinction.

The lasting success of the Beatles is as much symbolical as musical. The sticky *mythology* surrounding the group – four mop-headed, working-class, Liverpool lads, who defied the grey prospects of a northern seaport town to compose the most successful music in the history of pop – stubbornly absorbs every other part of their story. Their impact upon the public imagination, and their demonstration of the success that was possible for British groups (particularly in the USA), returns to dominate every discussion of their musical importance and cultural effect. The continual revival of their attractively crafted, but rarely innovative, songs is perhaps our surest explanation. The scale of the Beatles' success, not unconnected to their rapid acceptance into the existing canons of taste, was built upon a tangential jolting of the public musical cliché. They did not dramatically tear up Tin Pan Alley and previous popular music. Their music was described as 'fresh' and 'exciting', not 'alien' and 'offensive'. Masterfully working through black and white pop traditions they offered a novel, synthetic focus: an altered perspective, not a foreign landscape.

Why this musical mixture should come out of Liverpool at the beginning of the 1960s has led to some ingenious speculation. A decaying port town, populated by various immigrant communities and shifting musical cultures, linked to America courtesy of the Cunard liners – these, and other cosmopolitan traces, supposedly turned Liverpool into Lancashire's equivalent of New Orleans. The less glamorous truth is probably that Liverpool's clubs drew upon the fairly typical late 1950s cultural symbiosis that occurred between young white boys and pop music encouraged by the participative simplicity of skiffle. There may well have been other local conditions up in Lancashire, although these are now difficult to interrogate. But while from afar it seemed that Liverpool had decisively stamped its accent on the music, in reality the new sound was by no means restricted to that city alone.

Throughout their brief period of success the majority of Liverpool groups (the Searchers, the Swinging Blue Jeans, the Mojos) continued to look to black American pop, or even Britain's Tin Pan Alley (Gerry and the Pacemakers), and in some cases the Beatles themselves (Billy J. Kramer and the Dakotas), for their material. The enormous success of the 'Fab Four' – by December 1963, Richard Buckle, writing in the *Sunday Times*, was calling them 'the greatest composers since Beethoven' – obviously exposed other Liverpool groups to an unheard amount of record company interest and resultant signings. But, remove the Beatles and the Liverpool scene takes on a different complexion – important, but not so

different from what was then happening in Manchester or
Birmingham.

The new music was neither an anonymous dance rhythm
nor simply the copy of black sounds. Between the imperatives
of the former and the example of the latter, a novel musical
synthesis, recognisably British in tone, was produced: 'I
Wanna Hold Your Hand', 'Can't Buy Me Love', 'Day
Tripper'. It is this which sets the Beatles' first rather rough
recording 'Love Me Do' (1962) a continent apart from the
smooth, sophisticated sound of Cliff Richard's 'The Young
Ones', released earlier in the same year. The already noted
musical humus of the Beatles' music was the then developing
sounds of Tamla Motown and the black girl groups associated
with Phil Spector's production: the Ronettes, the Crystals...
These were crossed with rock 'n' roll and parts of white pop –
Elvis, Little Richard, Carl Perkins, Chuck Berry, Eddie
Cochran, Buddy Holly, the Everly Brothers.

The adoption and reworking of these transatlantic influences, both black and those filtered through country and
western music and rock 'n' roll, produced a significant tension
between two musical worlds. European classical harmony,
however simplified, still remained at the centre of white
commercial popular music. It drew attention to linear musical
development: a recognisable tune, an attractive melody. Black
music concentrated its sonorial powers elsewhere, in the
vertical interiors of the song: varying the tone, pitch, pulse
and rhythm. As a bridge between these two musical continents, beat music displayed, with varying emphases, tendencies, taken from both traditions. So, guitar sounds were
frequently 'full' (often further underlined by the use of an
organ) and employed highly 'coloured' chords that pointed to
the previously unsuspected levels and timbres of a song. Yet
such techniques were rarely so developed as the guitar leads
and shifting rhythms of complex chords employed by black
musicians. The solo guitar in a song like 'Can't Buy Me Love',
for example, has an unmistakably bluesy feel, but it remains
disciplined by the melodic shape and linear pull of the song. It
is not permitted the searching, dismembering tone of the city
blues and soul.

The characteristically relaxed singing style of the Beatles, occasionally offset by the rasp of Lennon's voice, together with their harmonies and sometimes almost singalong choruses ('From Me To You', 'She Loves You'), while all American derived, also revealed strains that were culturally far nearer to home than the stark outpost of undiluted soul and blues.[10] The use of the voice as a rhythmic instrument ('Yeah, Yeah, Yeah'), the call and response patterns between the lead singer and the others harmonising behind, all recently revitalised in the then contemporaneous black pop of the Ronettes, the Isley Brothers and the Miracles, can be traced directly back to the famous corner singing 'doo-wop' black groups of the early 1950s: the Orioles, the Ravens, the Dominoes (with Clyde McPhatter), the Penguins, and later the influential Coasters. In this more familiar environment the darker timbres of the blues were softened by the more 'innocent' hues and sentimentality of juvenile pop music. However, the smoother harmonies and sweeter melodies of the latter did not completely forsake the deeper 'ambiguities' of Afro-American music, particularly in evidence in the vocal slides, slurs and jumps that betrayed the lurking presence of the 'illegitimate' musical ladder of the 'blues' scale.[11] The edge of the Beatles' music and the heart of black American sonorities were ultimately linked to this disturbing shift in a musical 'centre', to a sense of songs being 'out of tune' and rhythmically erratic. This, and the resulting clash with official, 'legitimate', musical languages (the 'Do Re Mi...' scale of European harmony, for example), were the obvious offspring of a 'forbidden' exchange. Such a renewed public bringing together of the surbordinate cultures of black music and the rebellious tones of white pop, once associated with rock 'n' roll, was largely due to the unprecedented success of the Beatles in Britain and the USA. The indiscriminate reproductive powers of recording, permitting white youth to directly absorb the blues, R & B and soul, had made this initiative possible, but it was the Beatles and the groups that followed who successfully shaped that possibility into an effective cultural form.

Soon after the Beatles and northern beat music there emerged a terser, more neurotic, musical combination with the music of the Rolling Stones, the Animals, the Yardbirds, the Pretty Things, and other white English R & B groups. Where the Beatles could in a certain sense be said to have come out of the long cold ashes of skiffle, the Stones were more immediately challenging the vestiges of the Trad jazz movement for the throne of a white played, 'authentic', black music. It was here that the real polemic against beat music in general arose. Jazz musicians having seen many of their provincial venues whittled down by the popularity of beat music, now found themselves challenged on their own turf. Young white R & B groups were pounding on the doors of their traditional London strongholds. 'Rhythm-and-blues? It's nothing but rock-'n'-roll without the movements' (jazz band leader Micky Ashman, *Melody Maker*, 2 February 1963).

Both the Stones and the Beatles shared a common interest in rock 'n' roll, particularly in the crucial figures of Chuck Berry and Buddy Holly (listen to the Stones' very 'Hollyish' recordings of the Beatles' 'I Wanna Be Your Man' and Bobby Womack's 'It's All Over Now', alongside their recording of Holly's 'Not Fade Away'); but the Stones dug much further and more directly into the urban blues and contemporary soul scene. The group also drew on contemporary black pop: the Drifters's 'Under the Boardwalk', the Coasters's 'Poison Ivy'. But the more influential examples found throughout their early music was the Chicago urban blues of Muddy Waters and Howlin' Wolf, and the developing Detroit and Memphis soul sounds of Solomon Burke, Marvin Gaye and Otis Redding. The sometimes rather frantic playing of this urban black music by the Stones (listen to their version of Muddy Waters's 'I Just Want To Make Love To You' on their first LP, *The Rolling Stones*) indicated some of the problems involved in translation. Initially not counterbalanced by their own material, the 'excess' involved in this musical appropriation, later more effectively carried over into the textures of their own songs, provided an important contrast with the increasingly revealed musical 'balance' of the Beatles.

The music of the British R & B groups was, for the existing standards of pop, extreme. It was certainly not welcomed and accepted in the manner that the Beatles had been. The 'sartorial' style of many of these white groups – long hair, scruffy clothes, an unkempt and 'lived' appearance – was also understood to be the manifesto of bohemian sentiments. Now the rhetoric of a previously restricted enclave, and its social, moral and political disaffiliation, begins to enter popular culture. The expression of a select few was now transposed to a wider screen where it would connect to a far broader pulse than ever before. The electric media reproduced the individual gesture as a thousand possibilities, magnifying the proposal and supporting its imitation and extension. It would contribute to the public establishment of deliberately contentious style.[12] The surly stare of the Who caught in the photographer's lense, and the monosyllable replies of Mick Jagger and the rest of the Stones when they slouched on to *Juke Box Jury*, only served to confirm responsible fears.

The inward-looking, self-sufficient image of these groups, apparently fed by their fierce loyalty to the blues, had quickly acquired the edge of male rebelliousness. Most obviously, the blues-indebted Stones' sound, and the socially provocative stage and public personae of a Mick Jagger and Brian Jones, marked an important breaking away from the traditions that ruled pop and popular music in general. It tended to take the form of reducing the ironic cast of the blues to a blatant obsession with male sexuality. This was the heart of the musical and cultural outrage represented by a group like the Rolling Stones. In one sense, this seemed to raise the barriers even higher for white women singers anxious to abandon the sentimental roles pop persistently endowed them with. Only Dusty Springfield's soulful voice managed some sort of escape. Lulu with 'Shout' (1964) got by on youthful energy but was then absorbed into the rituals of show business and television shows. The public display of white female sexuality in pop was still restricted to the shady musical fringes of jazz and cabaret. However, as the shock effect of parading a blatant male sexuality (although frequently crossed with the then contradictory signs of long hair and 'effeminate' dressing) sank in, existing conventions were everywhere affected. Proposing music as the direct extension of a sexual body, white R & B became a potential instrument of cultural revolt. The translation of black R & B and soul into white pop thus involved – particularly in the Stones's case – an explicit sexual strategy intent on dismantling the prevalent sentimental and romantic ties that dominated pop and Tin Pan Alley.

Refusing pop music's central cultural referents has always been the first sign of rebellion. This had been the case with rock 'n' roll and was to be so with punk. In all three cases, anti-sentimentalism was mixed up with strong hints of misogyny, none more clearly so than in the case of the Stones. But it also indicated the first, contradictory steps away from a certain numbing naïvety. The titles of the Stones' songs speak for themselves: 'The Last Time', (I Can't Get No) Satisfaction', 'Get Off My Cloud', 'Under My Thumb', 'Stupid Girl'. Where the Beatles had begun experimenting in the popular song tradition, and offered a deprecating humour in their music and films that still left room for sentimentality ('Michelle', 'Yeserday', 'Eleanor Rigby'), the Stones, in the best blues tradition, mumbled disturbing lyrics over neurotic rhythms and a jarring sound that promised no compromise with earlier pop music. There were exceptions – 'As Tears Go By', 'Ruby Tuesday' – but their rarity was shocking. The 'black beam' (Richard Merton) of their music illuminated the powerful 'erotic narcissism' of the blues. The acceptance of this style of music in England around 1963, at least by some, meant that 'erotic narcissism becomes a possibility in English life, rather than remaining something that one reads about in Paul Oliver or listens to on Chess Records' (Beckett, 1968).[13]

Involving such potentially high stakes, the distinction between the Rolling Stones and the Beatles – Britain's top two groups by the end of 1963 – quickly congealed into cultural battle lines. There were, as we shall see, other important options, but this remained a significant choice. The rapid adoption of the Liverpool group, as a symbolic embodiment of the healthy, zany, exuberance of British youth, by the national press, parents, Prime Minister Harold Wilson, and the Establishment, could only mean one thing to many of us. The contradictory musical and cultural outrage represented by the Stones was destined to transform them, first in England and subsequently in the United States, into the decade's sonorial metaphor for white metropolitan youth rebellion.

'All aboard... the night train'

'He took my music. But he gave me my name.'
(Muddy Waters speaking of Mick Jagger)

The curt, onomatopoeic, rasping, 'choo-choo' rhythm is set in motion by the brass players, and James Brown, 'Soul Brother No. 1', is on his way, swooping along the nocturnal tracks of America: 'Miami, Florida... Atlanta, Georgia... Raleigh, North Carolina... night train, night train'. Released by James Brown and the Famous Flames in 1962, 'Night Train' was one of a selection of black American sounds produced by Brown, Solomon Burke, Marvin Gaye, Rufus Thomas, Martha and the Vandellas, that resounded nightly across the dancing floors of urban clubland. The dearth of dance records in the official Hit Parade, and consequently on the radio, not only provided the important opportunity for many groups to fill local dance halls and clubs with their sounds, it also promoted a deepening of the channel that connected British pop to black music.

The blues, urban R & B and contemporary soul music, initially found their early audiences on the fringes of the folk and, more importantly, jazz club world. These musical interests were often intersected by an art school bohemia, an area that was particularly important for preserving the musical exotica of the blues in Britain after the collapse of Trad jazz.[14] The factional warfare conducted in the British jazz world of the previous decade (between the New Orleans 'traditionalist' and the Chicago 'revivalists') for custody of an 'authentic' black music was passed on in the missionary style with which young white zealots now followed R & B. By late 1963 the letters page of the musical press was truculently occupied by the debate on R & B, what exactly it was and the preoccupation with whether whites could play the blues.

At the same time, the success of a group like the Rolling Stones, and the subsequent extension of the connection with soul music, indirectly encouraged by the contemporaneous establishment of independent record companies (Tamla Motown, Atlantic, Stax, Volt) in the USA specialising in contemporary black music, led to a radical reorganisation of

Figure 9. Tiles

the London club scene. Old jazz haunts such as the Marquee,
the Flamingo and Eel Pie's Island rapidly reduced their
offering of live jazz, replacing it by R & B groups. *Melody
Maker*, which until then had devoted over 50 per cent of its
coverage to jazz, was forced to drastically rethink its policy
and similarly reduce its jazz contents. Between 7 and 9 August
1964, the National Jazz and Blues Festival was held. On the
bill were the Rolling Stones, Ronnie Scott, Tubby Hayes,
Manfred Mann, Chris Barber, Memphis Slim, Long John
Baldry, Jimmie Weatherspoon, Kenny Ball, Georgie Fame,
Graham Bond, Humphrey Lyttelton, the Yardbirds, Mose
Allison. It was almost certainly the last blues- R & B -native
jazz agglomeration to be held on such a scale and with such
apparent integration.

On any night in 1964 there would be the Yardbirds at the
Crawdaddy Club, Richmond; Georgie Fame and the Blue
Flames, Zoot Money, Chris Farlowe, at the Flamingo Club,
33–7 Wardour Street; Graham Bond at Klooks Kleek; John
Mayall at The Scene, Great Windmill Street. The central live
London venue, however, was the Marquee Club, after 1963 at

90 Wardour Street. The Marquee acted as a launching pad for innumerable groups. With its promise of metropolitan acceptance and perhaps commercial recognition, it was a beacon for aspiring British groups everywhere. There was also the 100 Club, ironically once the home of the London Jazz Club. As a discothèque it provided the narcissistic environs (boutiques and mirrors adjacent) for the lunch time mod culture of London's 'noonday underground' (Wolfe, 1972).

Both the Marquee and the Flamingo adopted fiercely parochialist musical policies. The Marquee tended towards the Chicago style R & B (Muddy Waters, Howlin' Wolf, Junior Wells, Willie Dixon) of the blues 'purists', while the Flamingo leaned towards the more contemporary urban black music of Ray Charles, early soul and Tamla Motown.[15] By 1964 both clubs had gone as far as to feature regularly Jamaican ska sessions with Syko and the Caribs, the Exotics and Mickey Finn. This more esoteric musical experience was not only restricted to Soho. Prince Buster ska songs like 'Thirty Pieces of Silver' and 'Madness' also swept through South London dance halls, becoming crucial, along with the ska style of dancing that was later transformed into the 'shake' and the 'jerk', to the developing aesthetic of the exclusive mod world.

It was in the clubs, late into the nights and early mornings, that the inner connection between black Afro-American musics and British popular culture was progressively constructed. It is now that the predominantly black roots of rock 'n' roll, that hidden American heritage of the 1940s and 1950s, comes to be absorbed both directly and on an increasingly larger scale. The musical trinity of Trad jazz/skiffle/folk music had provided various jumping-off points, permitting some young Britons to go behind the more obvious appearances of American popular music. These sometimes isolated, but then mutually encouraging, probes – stretching from blues guitar experimentation in the Soho folk clubs (Davey Graham, Bert Jansch) through the fringes of the jazz world and into pop – led to an irreversible appropriation. It was particularly within the bohemian inheritance of the jazz venues that these musical connections were initially made, but the newly opened discothèques and clubs increasingly offered similar possibilities.[16] Elsewhere, outside the capital, closely super-vised youth clubs and dance halls – 'NO JIVING. NO ROCK 'N' ROLL' – were not so accommodating.[17] But black music continued all the same to obtain a wider hearing. In 1964, Millie Small had a hit with the ska song 'My Boy Lollipop', followed later that year by a white ska version of 'Mockingbird Hill' performed by the Migil 5. Tamla Motown, with a special debt to the Supremes, was increasingly becom-ing a regular part of the British charts. The more uncomprom-ising music of James Brown, Wilson Pickett and Otis Red-ding, on the other hand, entered more infrequently.

To hear live music, raw R & B interspersed with the latest US releases, it was to clubs like the Flamingo and the Marquee to catch Cliff Bennett and the Rebel Rousers, Jimmy Powell and the Five Dimensions, the Downliner Sect, Chris Farlowe and the Thunderbirds, that you went. Geno Washington, a black ex-USAF serviceman, sweated nightly to songs like 'Up Tight' and 'Ride Your Pony' in an effort to bring live soul music to provincial mods. He attracted an almost fanatical following: the charged communion of his show can be sampled on the 1966 LP, *Hand Clappin 'Foot Stompin' Funky Butt – Live!*.

For dancing to the febrile sounds of Wilson Pickett' ('In The Midnight Hour'), James Brown ('Out Of Sight', 'Papa's Got A Brand New Bag'), Otis Redding ('Pain In My Heart', 'Respect'), Sam and Dave ('Hold On I'm Coming'), there was The Scene club, Soho; the Hammersmith Palais; the 100 Club, Oxford Street; the Streatham Locarno. Meanwhile, already in 1964, Long John Baldry and the Hoochie Boochie Men were playing all night sessions at Manchester's Twisted Wheel club, setting a precedent and connection to the late 1960s Northern Soul circuit.

By the end of 1963, with the success of the Rolling Stones, the Animals and other R & B groups, rhythm and blues was becoming a household term. So it tended to be in the thickness of sound and sentiment of US soul and Jamaican ska, occasionally augmented by a new native mod group such as the Who, or later the Small Faces, that many young whites now found the sonorial pegs on which to hang their selective 'coolness'. Anxious to discover an alternative to the palid

'Americana' represented by the more established tastes of British pop, the earnest 'all-white Soho negro of the night... living on the pulse of the city' (Pete Meaden, in Barnes, 1979, p. 14) was irresistibly drawn to the promise of soul and ska: both musics simultaneously offering a symbolically charged rhetoric and an exclusive image.

The secret style of black jazz musicians Charlie Parker, Theolonius Monk and Miles Davis stalking the New York nights of the late 1940s in berets, dark glasses, goatee beards, and smoking 'reefers', an image that had been so revered by the white bohemians or 'beats' of the 1950s, was now set to another beat. A 'funky' roots music, drawing on the blues and gospel, and pioneered in different ways by Charlie Mingus, Bobby Timmons, Horace Silver and Cannonball Adderley, had begun to hint at such change. This musical bedrock was subsequently further exposed in the experimental modes of 'free jazz', in the music of John Coltrane, Ornette Coleman, Archie Shepp, Albert Ayler and other young black jazz players in the 1960s. But it was above all in black popular music that the fire of gospel and the gritty, secular rootedness of the blues was most clamorously crossed. It resulted in soul music.[18]

Singers like Ray Charles ('I Gotta Woman', 1955; 'What'd I Say', 1959) and James Brown ('Please, Please, Please, 1956; 'Try Me', 1958), introduced the screams, shouts, sobs and grunts of the preaching and testifying singer. The gospel 'choir' was substituted by the brass, the 'church' replaced by sustained chords on the piano or organ. The perpetual cycle of the blues was broken up into short, staccato rhythms and phrases or 'riffs', with the instrumental chorus responding to the meandering cries of the singer. This 'secular preaching' broke down previous structures and the 'rules' of popular song in general, resulting in a far greater freedom for the voice.

But it was the apparent accessibility of this music, its obvious excitement and dancing rhythms, that held its innermost secret. The vertical shifts of the growls and falsettos, the downward tugging brass, the shock of religious fervour translated into secular musical excitement, all marked a step beyond the stoical resignation of the blues into an active affirmation. The music, like the singer, like the song, was no longer held down, but was consciously moving on up and rising. Soul music was a self-controlled communication system between 'soul brothers' and 'sisters'; the potential fragmentation of its volatile elements were disciplined and formed by the continuing construction of a black identity and the distillation of this labour into an irrepressible *style*.[19]

No matter how hectic the rhythms, how frantic the voice, the music was property of the 'soul community', it was forever *cool*. The tight public connection between the singer and the wider black experience of racism, the general run of ghetto life, and economic and political discrimination, brought together and aired in the black singer's hip ghetto dialect and adoption of the latest black dances in the stage show, meant that a singer like James Brown was 'his audience writ large' (Haralambos, 1974, p. 106). 'This', in the words of a black disc jockey, 'is soul' (ibid). 'Coolness' and 'soul' are elusive qualities. They seem so 'natural' to urban black poise and posture, yet they require a revealing amount of dedication and attention when their white counterparts are attempted.

Ska, which was also popular in the London clubs, particularly in the Roaring Twenties club in Carnaby Street, was an even more esoteric choice although it clearly found a ready audience in London's West Indian communities. It was widely known as Blue Beat after the label which distributed it in Britain, and it represented a Jamaican appropriation of black American R & B. So it was transfused with local Jamaican inflections: a pinch of 'mento' (the Jamaican variant of calypso), a touch of Pocomanian (a fundamentalist Jamaican religious cult) dance and drum rhythms. In Britain in the early 1960s it was probably most widely known through the records of Prince Buster and Laurel Aitken. Large black attendances at clubs like the Flamingo brought it and its dance styles to the eager attention of the white soul boys.

Black music had also provided much of the impetus for the dance music performed by the Merseyside and Manchester groups who had first broken the British beat boom at the beginning of 1963. But that particular appropriation had tended to be restricted to either the fringes of earlier rock 'n' roll (Little Richard, Chuck Berry) or contemporary American pop (the Miracles, the Contours). The eventual musical development of these northern groups, best represented by the Beatles in these years, was culturally distinct from the stricter, more 'academic', R & B school and its later variants, soul and ska, for which London became the centre.

It was to London that the Animals (Newcastle-upon-Tyne), the Spencer Davis Group (Birmingham), Them (Belfast), and countless other groups, migrated during the period 1963–5. London's record companies' headquarters, now alerted to new developments in the wake of the northern invasion, were clearly crucial. But what was immediately more important in terms of day to day musical survival was London's extensive and eclectic club circuit (experiencing a boom in group turnover as British pop grew nationally and internationally more successful), a large bohemian catchment area that had adopted the blues and which was also wired into the national art school network, and finally the public and imaginative endorsement of the R & B and soul scene by the metropolitan male mod subculture. The coming together of these elements brought the pulse of British pop music activity, and, for a brief moment, apparently that of the rest of the industrial world, back to London.

From modernists to fashion cycle

'London's streets are making a massive anti-establishment statement every Saturday night.'

(Pete Townshend, 1965)

'Life is the best film for sure, if you can see it as film.'

(Colin MacInnes, *Absolute Beginners*)

Ready, Steady Go! ('The weekend starts here'), Rediffusion's Friday evening television pop show began broadcasting in August 1963. Between it and the *Juke Box Jury – Thank Your Lucky Stars* versions of television pop there was an obvious abyss. *Ready, Steady, Go!* gave out the appearance of a club populated by sharply dressed teenagers dancing to hip sounds. It was compèred by a breathless Cathy MacGowan: her gushing introductions to the groups appearing on the programme betrayed a true fan. The live feel of *RSG!*, its apparent fusion of spontaneity and style, made it the weekly showcase of British pop culture.[20] It was possible to see not only the Stones, the Animals, the Who and the Kinks perform, but also their often little known and certainly unseen musical and cultural progenitors: John Lee Hooker, Solomon Burke, James Brown. When *RSG!* advertised for new dancers to supplement those hand-picked every Friday afternoon, the aspiring teenage modernists were so numerous as to lead to a riot in the Wembly studios.

Nicknamed the 'Mecca for Mods', *RSG!* seemed the unique television programme, both then and since, to have had its finger on the pulse of an important part of contemporary teenage Britain. The bland greyness of the adult world so obviously in control of *Juke Box Jury* was temporarily displaced by the imposition of a decisive youth style, Pop Art decor, sharp camera work, sweating performances and dedicated dancers. It was as though it were there, right now, between the 'Supers' and 'Smashings' of Gathy's sentences, that it was all happening.

To that select breed, the full-time mods, *RSG!* was as much a window dressing to the subculture it proposed to represent as Carnaby Street fashion and advertisements in *New Musical Express* for 'Mod shirts' ('Paisley, Plain Tabs, Polka Dot, Long John, Kildare', all retailing for around 35 shillings). But what was there for those who could not manage it to the 100 Club each lunch-time, or the Marquee every Wednesday and the Flamingo on Sunday? Aspiring 'mods' who were geographically cut off from that big city scenario and had neither the pills, energy nor company to transform 'Welwyn Garden City... into Piccadily Circus' (Hebdige, 1976, p. 90), and for whom even the closer material possibility of that mod icon the scooter was a pipe dream, could still struggle for the symbolic ties. They took from *RSG!* about as much of the metropolitan mod myth as the programme had itself absorbed from the young London stylists.[21]

The mods' music was strictly black in inspiration: rhythm and blues, early soul and Tamla, Jamaican ska. It was these rhythms that were synchronised with the nuanced steps of The Block, The Ska and the weekly turnover in other dance fashions. When not spun by a DJ – discothèques were now opening: there was La Discothèque in Wardour Street in this period – the chosen sounds of James Brown, the Miracles, Prince Buster, Mary Wells, John Lee Hooker, were recreated by Georgie Fame and the Blue Flames, Chris Farlowe and the Thunderbirds, Long John Baldry and the Hoochie Coochie Men, Ronnie Jones and the Night-Timers. Not long afterwards, a more local 'Londonesque' sound, also influenced by R & B and early soul music, appeared. The Who were probably the nearest thing to a mod group. Their first record, when they still called themselves The High Numbers, was fittingly titled 'I'm The Face'. The music was altogether more edgy, more nervous, more distinctly white and English than the earlier British R & B groups. Pete Townshend's chopped guitar chords, the manic drumming of Keith Moon, and Roger Daltrey's waivering vocals – whether by intention or association – neatly caught the 'pilled up' London night life of the mod mythology in a series of effective anthems: 'My Generation', 'Can't Explain', 'Anyhow, Anywhere'.

But while the mods' taste in music often served to introduce new styles, in clothes it worked consistently to establish them. A sharp, cosmopolitan, sartorial fashion, if we are to believe Colin MacInnes's reports (1959, 1961), had been in the making for some years prior to the full public emergence of the identifiable 'mod'. These earlier modernists or stylists were working class and overwhelmingly male. They were obsessed by clothes, and in particular with an 'anglicised adaptation of Continental Europe (particularly French and Italian) and of American styles' (MacInnes, 1961, p. 153).[22] The more immediate geographical locale of the mods, as befits their flashing, floating, mythology, is not so clear. According to most accounts they either started in Stepney, East London, or in the Shepherds Bush area of West London. It was through the summer and autumn of 1963 that a distinctive mod style rapidly established itself in the metropolis.

A shared sartorial regime, the patronage of particular clubs and musical venues, the purchase of certain records: all these activities formed part of an indivisible continuum, a world

within a world. Dancing to the persistent bass of black R & B,
soul and ska, dashing from tailor to record shop aboard stylish
Italian scooters and fuelled with amphetamines ('purple
hearts', 'French blues', dexedrine), this frenzied activity –
whether actual or not is secondary – stretched the mods'
weekends and nights to that imaginary point where it released
the cool, timeless 'reality' of perpetual style. In the frozen
reaches of mythology, the Blue Beat hat worn just at *that*
angle, the three-button, two-vent jacket and 17-inch bottom
trousers, together with the imitation crocodile round-toed
boots, remained forever fixed, immortalised, and immune
from the dull work hours and school days of adult
supervision.[23]

While doubts were to be heard about the so-called benefits
of the 'affluent society', and in some quarters its very existence
being queried, its public iconography was triumphant. Television, film, advertising and journalism continued to indulge in
the glossy collage of a commercially successful popular culture. James Bond, Carnaby Street boutiques, white E-type
Jaguars, on television *The Avengers* and *The Man From UNCLE*,
youthful go-getting entrepreneurs, Sunday colour supplements – all firmly suggested that the power of 'affluence' was
far from over.

None knew this better than the mods. Frequently tied to
menial jobs, forced to pay for their clothes on weekly instal-
ments and their scooters (if they had one) on hire purchase,
they nevertheless made 'furious consumption' (Richard
Barnes) the conspicuous motif of their style. To 'live' took on
an added, unsuspected, dimension in the manic imprinting of
their own style upon the flux of consumerism as they rewrote
the surfaces of sounds, clothes and transport in their own
image. They created themselves as 'mods', living their lives in
that most public of theatres – the market-place of commodities
– as self-proclaimed 'artists' or 'actors'. The adult world was
locked out not by fashions that went 'ricocheting off every
eyeball' (Tom Wolfe), but through an exaggerated *neatness*
and consumerism which adults could only dimly understand
teetered on the edge of parody.[24] The recognisable bric-à-brac
of affluence – continental fashion, records, clubs and scooters
– each marked with secret signs (it had to be *two* vents in the

jacket, *The Scene* club in Soho, US soul and Jamaican ska music, a personalised *Lambretta TV 175*), were transformed into the inscrutable image of mod.

Eventually, however, this stylised 'teen arrogance' became overexposed. It had been constructed upon borrowed time. The sustained commitment to the Continent, and to a mythologised America that reached its most authoritative moment in the far 'Other' of black urban 'cool', involved the mod in a losing battle. This brief imaginative gesture was doomed against the accumulated boredom and routines of English urban existence; the imaginative possibilities of the myth were eventually forced to wander without a residence until ground down or dissipated by the pressure of external events.

The magical 'otherness' of black city style, suitably translated into the sounds of soul and ska, had offered the mods a tangible but 'forbidden' reality. But this radically symbolic assertion by a section of white working-class youth ultimately involved a cultural distance that no amount of amphetamine frenzy could ever hope to cross.[25] The deadly attention that the male mod devoted to this stylistic labour could only finally lead to the frozen frame of the narcissistic stare. Lost in the mirror, and pursuing an 'otherness' that could never be his and whose experience he could barely comprehend, he threatened to become an empty fashion icon.

In 1964 the mods had come fully under the public gaze following a series of Bank Holiday battles on the beaches of Margate and Brighton with opposing groups of 'rockers (a motor-cycling mutant of the earlier teddy boys).[26] The mods' own symbolic gamble against the constraints of time and place led them to see in the rockers, stuck in their hair grease and leather like so much nostalgic memorabilia from another decade, a symbolic insult to their felt sense of the possible. But when finally the mods' own 'moment' began to slip away, one alternative was to acknowledge with a vengeance the limits of the daily reality. This was the trajectory that went through the 'proletarian' wardrobe (boots and braces, closely cropped hair) of the 'hard mod' style and on to the skinhead. Another possibility, one sometimes chosen by the more metropolitan followers, was to attempt to step even further into the imagination, eschewing 'speed', soul music, and their buzzing connection to the everyday for the even more exclusive 'reality' of LSD and the psychedelic music 'trip'.[27] Naturally, there was also the more likely conclusion of confused compromises signposted by regular employment, creeping responsibilities, and a family.

But for a brief moment (1964–6), the divulgation of the productive tensions so sharply outlined in the mod style became the hub of a far wider cultural configuration; one that most succinctly stamped on British pop music the image of its clamorous success: 'swinging London'.

The mods' intense celebration of male narcissism bequeathed a complex inheritance to the wider metropolitan British pop culture of the mid 1960s. The mod style, organised and sanctified by male obsession, spoke 'in the accents of [its] sex' (McRobbie, 1980). This had clearly been central to the manner in which a group like the Rolling Stones explored a potential fascination with the male 'self', particularly in evidence in the use of Jagger's voice in Solomon Burke's 'Everybody Needs Somebody To Love', or the Stones's own composition 'Heart Of Stone'. Males preening themselves in public was no novelty, but in its scale and effect it now seemed to outrun more traditional, particularly working-class, codifications of male sexuality. That Mick Jagger could launch 'a new vision of male beauty' (Cohn, 1970), and go on to become a 'classless, androgynous, and ultimate social *star*' (Hoskyns, 1982), represented a notable extension in the then public constructions of 'maleness' and masculinity.

The generally vaguer fashion silhouette of the mod girl, in contrast to her precisely tailored boyfriend, and her widespread successor, the 'dolly', remained one step behind the male definers. Still, the previously rather static position of women within the spectrum of public style began to demonstrate some movement. Mod girls did put together their own styles... and the contradictory appearance of the mini skirt (the male gaze, the pleasure of female assertion...?), together with the new valorisation of the female fashion model (Jean Shrimpton, Twiggy), augured a change in the social production of female sexuality. If, for the time being, pop music continued to remain largely immune to this new female activism, the successful marketing of mod fashion by Mary Quant, Biba's and innumerable boutiques in London and the provinces, at least introduced a new tone into the public recognition of the female 'I'.[28]

The purchase of particular types of clothing, cosmetics, magazines and hair styles, while frequently less fastidious in choice than the male mods's finicky consumption programme, all the same did represent a possible *public* construction of an effective imaginary relationship to daily life; in this case, through an increased insistence on the active production of female sexuality. As Janice Winship has pointed out, it was in the greatly expanded consumer production of the 1950s and 1960s that female sexuality 'provides the reason for the kind of consumption that is indulged in and is constructed by that consumption' (Winship, 1981, p. 23). This contradictory 'widening' of the commodity, as it were, to acknowledge the feminine, together with the growth of more effective forms of birth control, 'opened up more decisively the possibility for the incorporation of the active, if male-defined, sexuality of women into the repertoire of public debate...' (Weeks, 1981, p. 260).[29]

The subsequent, masculine-informed, 'eroticisation of modern culture' (Weeks), brings us back to the shallow metaphor of 'swinging London', to 'kinky' fashions, and to the connection of pop music, popular culture and the emerging theme of 'permissiveness'. By 1966 the growing song writing sophistication of the Beatles (listen to the *Rubber Soul* and *Revolver* LPs) had turned pop music into an object of serious comment. But while certain Sunday papers and colour supplements indulged in hyperbole, pop stars filled the tabloids with their faces and exploits as they passed over from the narrow, musty, and unwelcome, confines of stolid show business into the social flurry of the world's temporary fashion centre.

In the brief whirlwind of 'swinging London', between the newly opened bistros and boutiques, among the Mini-Mokes and mini skirts that defied the British climate, there occurred some unexpected, but not accidental, encounters. Up in Soho's Ad Lib club, in front of the very large window that looks out over central London, the bohemian diaspora of

Britain's art schools – pop groups, fashion designers, painters
– met up with those who had more simply just 'made it', film
stars Terence Stamp and Michael Caine, photographers
David Bailey and Terence Donovan; together they celebrated
their conquest of the capital. The more exclusive concerns of
both the 'Art' world and the mod life were now expanded into
a prosaic combination of music, fashion and the visual arts.
The gallery gesture of American Pop Artist Jasper Johns' flag
paintings was translated into the media effect of a Union Jack
jacket hanging from the skinny shoulders of Pete Townshend
of the Who. Old hierarchies were disturbed, disrupted by
images drawn from daily life. 'Art' was absorbed within the
profane languages of the popular media. Derek Boshier's
barber poles and Peter Blake's targets formed the weekly
decor of *Ready, Steady, Go!*. The Pop Art lesson that the
'synthetic' and the 'artificial' are 'real', that they 'count', now
began its aesthetic life in popular culture and pop music (well
caught in the Who's paen to interchangeable, 'plastic',
appearances: 'Substitute').

But the growing worldliness of British pop, the first signs of
fracture induced by success, both in Britain and increasingly
in the United States, and the hint of a darker reality tinged by
drugs, 'decadence' and breakdown, also had the air of a guilty
connection between public prosperity and the suggestions of
social and moral collapse.[30] When style no longer displaced
generational antagonisms but only paraded them; when
youthful spirits apparently passed over into moral abuse and
an explicit disregard for older values; when there was too
much leisure, too much money, and a dangerous 'boredom'
seeping through the pores of British society, the full political
metaphor of 'permissiveness' began to take on a harder shape.

The seeds for a conspiratorial explanation of growing moral
decline had already been sown by the Vassal affair in 1962: a
spy trial shrouded in homosexual blackmail. The following
year, a melodramatic cast consisting of call girls, a Soviet
diplomat, an osteopath, the Minister for War – Mr John
Profumo, a property racketeer, country house connections,
were assembled into a public scandal that sent the Macmillan
leadership of the Conservative government tumbling. These
dramatic denouncements of the lax morality of official life,

and what seemed the unnecessary 'liberalisation' of legislation in such sensitive areas as prostitution and homosexuality, began to swell into a deep undertow of reaction. There were many who felt external to the sentiments of liberal reform and who were beginning to express the opinion that the negative costs of 'affluence' were becoming too high a price to pay.

The connection of this dark theme to the 'frivolous' world of pop music and London night life was not yet fully clarified. But the enthronment of a bohemian corpus at the pinnacle of British pop, some of whose most revered members – the Rolling Stones – owed their popularity to a politics of public outrage, did mean that pop would become increasingly susceptible to being publicly netted in the widening casts of a moral panic. It required a further twist in the cultural scenario before the unholy alliance of pop, public polarisation and moral breakdown finally fell into an identifiable menace. Then, and only then, would yesterday's 'nutty, noisy', heroes be transformed into tomorrow's 'folk devils'.

Chapter 4

The Dream That Exploded, 1966-71

'People who talk about revolution and class struggle without referring explicitly to everyday life, without understanding what is subversive about love and what is positive about the refusal of constraints, such people have a corpse in their mouth.'

(Comite Enrages – L'Internationale Situationniste)

Once simply viewed as the raucous manifestation of working-class teenagers lounging around in coffee bars feeding garish juke-boxes, by the close of the 1960s pop was to be as much at home in fashionable urban residences as late at night on BBC 2. While public attention in the latter half of the decade was often attracted by the music's place among the disrupting signals of a 'youth revolt', pop was also being quietly absorbed into parts of official or 'respectable' culture. A nonconformity, previously associated with the twilight world of beats and jazz – longer hair for men, sexual promiscuity, extravagant dress, the smoking of 'pot' – was translated into the 'radical chic' of a 'thinking' person's music. Those parts of pop appropriated were pointedly rechristened 'rock' or 'progressive' music by its recently enfranchised grammar school, student and 'hip' middle-class audience. It was also now that the professional 'rock critic' appeared to legitimate the whole affair.

Accompanying this rearrangement, the packed and heterogeneous energies of the earlier beat and rhythm and blues boom gradually began to separate out. By 1970, distinct publics, often hermetically sealed off one from the other, were

84

established. The most striking evidence of this change was the dissolution of the once central interplay between white pop and various forms of Afro-American music. Black music was exiled to the far reaches of the white rock world. There it was hidden in unrecognised cultural relations and histories. These will be considered apart in a later chapter. For the moment we are confronted by separate histories, diverse cultures, distinctive musics.

This important remaking of British (and American) pop which goes under the label of progressive rock made a deep incision into the body of pop, dividing rock off from the rest of the field. The effects of this operation were to last the best part of a decade. The principal signposts advertising this new phase are, on one side, the increasing sophistication of British pop. This was widely associated with a succession of Beatles's LPs (*Rubber Soul, Revolver, Sergeant Pepper*), but fundamentally nurtured by the London 'underground'. The other, equally crucial, dimension was the profound influence of Bob Dylan and West Coast rock music. The overall change in cultural tone was explicitly broadcast in the alternative life style proposals of the 'counter-culture', and most precisely located in the utopian figure of the 'hippy'. As we shall see, British traits by no means disappeared, but the textures of these developments is fundamentally American in feel and inspiration.

American horizons

After a three-year interregnum of British beat music, the cultural gravity of pop unmistakably moved back to the USA. New British groups continued to emerge (Spencer Davis, the Small Faces, the Move), and experiments in the London 'underground' marked out new musical extensions, but British 'voices' were now increasingly involved in an American-derived spectacle. California had become the principal source of a revitalised American pop music: the surf music of Jan & Dean and the Beach Boys. Subsequently transformed into the El Dorado of a highly publicised hippy life style, California – as fits its mythical post in the European imagination – became the pole around which an important segment of British pop began to orbit.

After 1964, the cosmopolitan success of British groups and the promise of American culture, and money, encouraged a cultural shift westwards.[1] Meanwhile, US pop, alerted by the 'British invasion' to the further reaches of its own musical landscape, embarked on the task, boldly proclaimed in the title of one of Bob Dylan's LPs, of 'bringing it all back home'.

It is always surprising the degree to which a single, individual voice manages momentarily to sum up the complex body of a major musical shift. Yet the cultural constellation that so clearly circulates around the tone, timbre and delivery of Elvis Presley's voice in the mid-1950s, and Mick Jagger's less than a decade later, do just that. The same can be said for Dylan.

Dylan's entrance into the British record charts in 1965 with the prophetic 'The Times They Are A-Changin' was a striking event.[2] A 'flat', nasal voice, drawn from the rural singing styles of white American folk music, coupled with hints of the blues, and self-penned songs that were literary in the extreme, produced an abrasive combination. Alongside both mainstream pop and the Afro-American derivatives of the British boom, it was a decidedly extraneous sound. Supported by a simply strummed acoustic guitar and reedy harmonica, Dylan's almost spoken delivery emphasised the lyrical contents of the song. The adenoid tones of his intrusive voice and verbal 'message' tug at our attention in a manner quite distinct from the equally compelling lyrics of the Stones' 'Satisfaction' (1965).[3]

The structure of 'The Times They Are A-Changin'' is borrowed from the white Anglo-American folk tradition, but its biblical tones and apocalyptic metaphors pile up to undercut finally that tradition's narrative form. Freed from the constraints of a sequential tale, the song is propelled into the regions of poetic statement. Now all this stands in stark contrast to both the lyrical simplicities of much existing pop and to Afro-American modes of singing. There is a potential clash here between treating lyrics as 'sonorial signs' (Simon Frith) or as explicit semantic tokens. Certainly, Dylan and the other folk singers – Joan Baez, Donovan – who encountered popularity in this period, pitched the sense of song in a quite distinctive direction. They embraced the studied affects of writing almost with a vengeance after the shouts, slurs, mumbles and screams of rock 'n' roll, beat music and R & B.

Dylan, however, a self-declared 'trapeze artist', remained a complex example. The widening range of his voice as R & B and pop timbres were absorbed, and his often blurred delivery, once coupled with the regular electric rhythms of a rock band – *Highway 61 Revisited* (1965), *Blonde On Blonde* (1966) – exchanged the directness of folk song for a more distanced, urbane cool. In the meantime, the shimmering collage of literary metaphor, alliteration and imagery, well illustrated in Dylan's 'Mr Tambourine Man' (the first 'folk-rock' hit for the Byrds in 1965), had a momentous effect on both US and British pop. A new set of cultural accents had now established their place.

The idea of valorising the word in popular song and folk music had an important precedent. In the 1930s and 1940s, American radicals had set about appropriating American popular oral culture in their protest against the Depression, poverty, racism and social deprivations. This tradition went on to form the backbone of the US folk song revival of the 1950s which was celebrated in the folk festivals and 'hootenannys', in magazines like *Broadside* and *Sing Out!*, and in the figures of singers Woody Guthrie, Leadbelly and Pete Seeger. The organising themes behind this post-war revival were 'truth', 'sincerity' and 'authenticity': the universal clarion calls for the critics of mass industrial society at the time. The resulting music was hooked to the faith that there existed a lost 'community' out there awaiting its recall to a genuine, popular, 'organic' American experience.[4] The vagueness of such sentiments and its surrounding aura of rural nostalgia was naturally open to many interpretations. But in the 1960s, under the pressure of fresh and urgent events, the prospects of folk music were driven into a precise shape.

By the early 1960s, the development of Civil Rights struggles by southern blacks and the birth pangs of campus radicalism (the Port Huron statement of the Students for a Democratic Society was issued in 1962) had greatly extended

the radical resonance of the folk song movement. Folk music
came into the universities, into the bohemian circles and
coffee houses of New York's Greenwich Village, and into a
vastly widened folk song circuit. Black agitation for civil rights
in the South also pulled northern white students into the
'freedom rides', protest and general support. It contributed,
especially after British R & B had pricked up their ears, to
many young, middle-class, northern whites listening in to
black radio stations and absorbing blues, R & B and soul.
Protest, and the binding together of the radical community by
the gesture of song (i.e. 'We Shall Overcome'), was likely to be
most easily moved by the claims of the sounds of other
subordinated Americas: by the 'truth' of the blues ('telling it
like it is') and the roooted, home-spun values of white country
music. It was these musical strands, with the explanatory
gloss of 'authenticity' and echoes of rural populism separating
them off from the 'shallow' sentiments of commercial popular
music (both white *and* black), that became central to the
establishment of American rock music and its ideology in the
second half of the 1960s.

The appearance of 'folk–protest' music in the British and
US charts of 1965 – Dylan, Joan Baez, Donovan, Barry
McGuire – was, in fact, only the foretaste of a more extensive
current. The American folk music scene, especially in New
York's Greenwich Village, while putting together various
elements of native folk music with certain pop influences (R &
B, British 'beat' music), invariably mingled with a marginal,
and predominantly, literary, bohemia: the survivors of the
white hipster and beat generation of the 1950s. In Britain,
native beats and the radical fringes of CND (the 'Ban the
Bomb' movement) were also by this time flowing into the
makings of a British 'underground'.[5]

To move from the beat poet Allen Ginsburg to the singer
Bob Dylan, or from the road novels of Jack Kerouac to the
acid rock of the Grateful Dead, often required a remarkably
short step.[6] This aura of radical artistry was to be crucial in
the successive rock culture. The 'sincerity' earlier revealed in
Dylan's singing and the folk song idiom now proved more
complex, less clear cut. It permitted a passage from an
assumed shared communal 'authenticity' to an individual,

personal, one; from 'social' concerns to poetic ones. It was the preliminary announcement of the later introduction of self-conscious aesthetic strategies into rock music.

'Protest' turns into proseity, and the 'truths' of the individual 'artist' replace and refine vaguer populist sentiments. It was to be this later existential radicalism, this 'uncharted journey into the rebellious imperatives of the self' (Norman Mailer), as much as the sharpened impact of race and student politics on American campuses, that ended up woven into the cradle of the 'alternative society' and its counter-culture. Musical 'authenticity'; now suggested a new project, one that was simultaneously 'political' and 'artistic'. It meant that rock was destined to be quite consciously distinct from other parts of pop music.

'California dreaming'

> 'Dreaming of utopias
> where everyone's a lover
> I see San Francisco from my window.'
>
> (Lawrence Ferlinghetti)

In 1964, Doctors Timothy Leary, Ralph Metzner and Richard Alpert published *The Psychedelic Experience: A Manual based on the Tibetan Book of the Dead*. Leary was soon to be widely associated with the slogan 'Turn on, tune in, drop out'. He and his associates were sacked from Harvard University and subsequently hounded by the US and Mexican authorities for their public endorsement of the hallucinogenic drug Lysergic Acid Diethylamide (LSD). Parallel to these events, concerts at San Francisco's Longshoreman's Wharf and Avalon Ballroom were mixing music, light shows, dance and poetry into a potent brew that was shortly to be baptised 'acid rock'. Translating hallucinatory effects into a disorienting public spectacle, these mixed media encounters offered temporary bridge-heads to another order of experience, one considered to be somehow more 'real', more 'genuine', than the surface rationalities of daily life in the American mainstream. Loud electric music and strobe lights distorted the patterns of sound and sight, shifting shapes and colours projected on large screens jumbled up normal perception ('messed up your mind'). Subtracted from the narrow strictures and goals of 'straight' society, you were delivered up – 'freaked out', 'a blown mind' – to an alternative 'reality'.

The frequent recourse to cerebral metaphors, recalling both drug and cultural effects, were by no means accidental. The quest for a deeper 'reason', whether through the new Californian music, LSD, or an alternative life-style – all profoundly interconnected, if not simultaneously embraced – revealed a powerful intellectual existentialism in action among white, American middle-class youth. Official culture, choked with the passive objects of respectable status, was increasingly spurned · for the symbolic activity of transforming non-respectable forms – pop music, bohemian dress, drugs – into a widely imitated alternative. Popular culture, particularly the popular youth culture of music and generational style, experienced a new and important input. This took place, though in diverse fashion, in both the United States and Britain. But it was the original American example that was to provide the persuasive model.

In the West Coast urban conurbations of San Francisco and Los Angeles, musics considered to be firmly apart from the discredited centre of US pop and free of its blatant commercial blight were welcomed and incorporated into the repertoire of the likes of the Grateful Dead, Jefferson Airplane, Country Joe and the Fish, Big Brother and the Holding Company. The more 'authentic' sounds of white folk (and later country) music, rural and city blues, filtered through the example of the British groups and often injected with a Dylanesque literary gloss, made up the major musical architectue of what was coming to be referred to as the 'counter-culture'.

At the outset, black American music was fundamental to the making of this new West Coast sound. Going back behind the Beach Boys' example of employing Chuck Berry riffs it was the blues that provided the anchorage for drawn out songs and lengthy guitar solos to accompany the extended 'high' of the dancers. But the contradictory context of the counter-culture, its decisive shift around 1967 from direct protest to alternative life-style, from folk and blues to psychedelic or acid rock, from the student world of Berkeley to the urban bohemia of Haight–Ashbury, was also to effect deeply the nature of the music. Dance rhythms became less imperative – the body had discovered other ways to be 'transported' – and musical effect was increasingly concentrated in the 'head', in mental sensationalism. Rhythms were absorbed into an endless flux, the sense of 'beat' was replaced by that of 'vibrations'. Afro-American music was increasingly submerged in a spreading eclectical musical spectrum.

In 'San Franciscan Nights' (1967), Eric Burdon, former singer with the Animals from Newcastle-upon-Tyne, eulogised a reality composed of hippies, LSD, Hells Angels, Red Indians and malignant policemen ('pigs'): all caught up in the warm glow of a new 'American Dream'. During the 1950s, white beat writers and poets had compounded an exotic cosmology of jazz, drugs and Zen Buddhism to guide their frenzied chase of the sensory freedom of America's promise. Such a select bohemian journey into the margins of American life was now overtaken and absorbed by a public 'freak out', a mass participation trip towards 'something wilder and weirder out on the road' (Tom Wolfe).

The arrival of the hippies in the midst of Californian abundance, and their symbolic attempts, through drugs, mysticism, rock music and communal living, to rediscover the honest poverty of a simpler, more 'authentic' America, rendered a dramatic tear in the fabric of white American youth culture. Rebellion had been no novelty to the tone of earlier American pop music and youth cultures. But the brief scandal of rock 'n' roll, the influential iconography of Marlon Brando and James Dean, the irruption of street gangs or leathered bikers, or the peculiarly esoteric West Coast youth cults that built shrines to surfing and custom cars, faded in scale alongside the articulate and self-conscious refusal of the 'status quo' that the hippies and the subsequently wider formation of the counter-culture represented.

The explicit political and aesthetic dimensions of the counter-culture existed in a complex symbiosis, each part of the formula subject to redefinition by the other. The more traditional politics of its beginnings, nurtured under the generational umbrella of the 'New Left', formed the nucleus of campus struggles for intellectual freedoms, the movement against the escalating war in Vietnam, and attempts at an alliance between white radicals and a new, autonomous, black militancy. After 1967–8, however, it was overshadowed by a wider metamorphosis. The proclaimed hippy ideal of constructing an alternative society, involving, in the words of the beat poet Gary Snyder, an attempt to 'kill the white man, the American in me', proposed a far more dramatic utopia to that found in 'normal' politics.

It was a historical paradox that the outright rejection of American industrial society and the 'system' it supported discovered its 'alternative' in that most American of themes: the Westerner. The search for a 'lost', rural American community, like the earlier radicals's representation of American folk music, projected a fresh frontier mythology. As cowboy, beat, hipster, hippy or surrogate Indian (all popular countercultural sartorial styles in the late 1960s), it is this white, predominantly male, figure who falls 'not merely out of Europe, but out of the Europeanised West, into an original and archaic America' (Fiedler, 1972, p. 23). Beyond Kerouac's hipster heroes of *On The Road* (1957) and their borrowed Negro 'cool', there now beckoned the rich identification of an even vaster alternative: the 'authentic' soul of the 'original American'.[7]

The city was abandoned, even if only symbolically (its technology – record players and electric guitars – usually retained), for the more 'natural' horizons of the country, while LSD offered 'a ready window on the Zen eternal', 'a short cut back to the organic life' (Nuttall, 1972, p. 190). Middle America was transcended by the 'trip'. Hippy or, more aptly, 'head' culture played with a new series of symbolic cues that mocked the utilitarian logic of 'normal' society and substituted it with a dislocating 'freak out'. This could range from the central referents of psychedelic rock and drugs to the far reaches of mysticism (in Britain there was a renewed interest in the magical connotations surrounding Glastonbury and Stonehenge), the extra-terrestial dimension of science fiction (a favourite motif with both Jimi Hendrix and the Pink Floyd), and even sorcery. This 'revolution' – spiritual/cultural/political – was 'total', it had to be *lived* in order to be made; revolution became life-style.

But the experiential textures of this 'living' were also highly cerebral. 'The first revolution (but not of course the last) is in your head' (Tuli Kupferberg of the Fugs). Physical sensations, induced by music, sex and drugs, were measured against a new intellectual order. The 'authenticity' of these experiences was discovered using other maps, ones that referred to territories outside the entropied consciousness of contemporary industrial society: the Orient, the rhythms of 'Mother Earth', inner, and sometimes, outer space.[8]

In the mythical theatre of these new frontiers a metaphorical reversal of American affluence and the imperatives of its political economy was enacted. A complete alternative was sought in a 'state of nonordinary reality' (Carlos Castaneda). LSD and the drugs of the New World – marijuana, peyote, mescaline, cocaine – were increasingly married to a novel life-style and, across the ubiquitous cultural contract of rock music, offered the symbolic tools with which to undo the 'American way of life'. On the West Coast, Ken Kesey and the Merry Pranksters set off in a motorised entourage to 'zap' American with acid, music and 'happenings', while everywhere the 'best minds' in US higher education 'turned on' to rock and directed their attention to the counter-culture.[9] The green promise of an American Arcadia, echoed in folk and country music and their passage into American rock, was busily rehearsed in the beads, buckskins, headbands and moccasins of the pioneers of the 'alternative society' camped out in university campuses and the bohemian quarters of the American metropolis.

The massive bombing of Vietnam which had commenced in 1965, the subsequent draft, and live television coverage of the war, brought protest at home against US military involvement in South-East Asia to a new pitch. This, plus race riots in major American cities (the firing of Watts, Los Angeles, occurred in 1965), a new defiant black militancy, being busted for drugs, and the resulting police brutality against public dissent in general – the Chicago Democratic Convention demonstration in 1968, the manhunt conducted against the

Black Panthers – also brought parts of the counter-culture into far sharper outline. The Yippies (the Youth International Party) put the hippy ideal of simply opting out of 'Amerika' into reverse. 'Doped, they stumbled into politics backwards' (Neville, 1971, p. 32), and facetiously intervened in the conspicuous public arenas of US society – distributing free money in the New York Stock Exchange, for example – in an attempt 'to establish a new frame of reference', and 'put the country on an acid trip' (Jerry Rubin, in Neville, ibid, p. 116).

In this climate an important segment of West Coast rock music – the Jefferson Airplane, Country Joe and the Fish, the Doors – vibrated between the harsh edges of American politics and the utopian gestures of an alternative America.[10] Political slogans – 'They've got the guns but we've got the numbers' (the Doors) – set to white rock rhythms were, however, only the most obvious part of what turned out to be a far deeper transformation. Querying the accepted 'disassociation between the political and the non-political' (Henri Lefebvre), the non-conformity of educated white youth threatened the apparently seamless web of existing cultural and political fabrics from within the cocoon of abundance and well being.

After this initial step, the 'introduction of the aesthetic into the political', through the counter-culture's imaginative adoption and patronage of rock music, certain life-styles, particular sexual and social arrangements, took the idea of revolution and placed it in 'its authentic dimension: that of liberation' (Marcuse, 1972, p. 11). The personal had become political. Just what all that might mean has only slowly come to be appreciated after the first flush of enthusiasm subsided. It was only later that a sexual politics led by the Women's Liberation Movement was able to revalue the counter-culture's vaunted sexual liberation and discern in it a freedom largely restricted to male needs.[11] But the full import of the concept of 'personal politics', again the example of the Women's Movement is pertinent, remains the most lasting and undoubtedly the profoundest inheritance of the youth politics of the late 1960s.[12]

Between 1966 and 1969, when the US rock magazines *Crawdaddy*, *Creem*, *Fusion* and *Rolling Stone* were founded, the situation remained extremely fluid; the indications were multiple, although often confusing and contradictory. There was the fresh, interventory 'surrealistic' politics of the Yippies, the graphic and journalistic inventiveness of the underground press, and the presence of rock music everywhere. At the other extreme was the sealed quiescence of the self-concerned 'freaks' for whom anything beyond personal gratification was just 'too heavy'. Stretched out between these poles was a wide range of political, cultural and spiritual options bursting with optimistic energies.

Representing the 'extreme variant of American individualism' (Hall, 1969), the hippy proposal percolated down through the counter-culture into West Coast musical practices and into rock music in general. It provided an important passport ('Do your own thing') for innumerable musical experiments to flourish. The biting edge of the electric blues guitar remained essential, but it came to be understood differently – a point of departure rather than arrival; it was rapidly overlain by other musical languages, many completely foreign to pop's previous tradition.

The music of Frank Zappa and the Mothers of Invention can be treated as a highly personal but influential summation of this rearranged musical sense. His knowing execution of previous pop styles (the high school 'doo-wop' of *Reuben and the Jets*, 1966; and the parody of the Beatles on *We're Only In It For the Money*, 1967), augmented by his jazz and classical influenced work on *Lumpy Gravy* (1968) and *Hot Rats* (1970), represent some of the principal musical boundaries of counter-cultural experimentation. Zappa, who in some quarters was considered a musical guru, combined eclecticism with musical mastery and an ironic ear. He produced collages of musical quotes that, drawing equally on jazz, rock 'n' roll and contemporary avant-garde music, mocked the commercial imperatives of the record he was producing by 'mirroring contemporary culture – from Sinatra to Varèse – as a giant scrap heap of disposable consumer trash' (Paddison, 1982, p. 215).[13] At the same time, the pronounced nods towards jazz and classical motifs, further underlined by the introduction of lengthy instrumental *compositions* and the insistence on improvisation skills as a major instance of an individual's musical 'authenticity', were distinct signs of a heterogeneous musical and cultural sophistication quite distinct from the rest of pop and set well apart from the earlier social configurations of the music.

From the first pop festival of Monterey in 1967 to the mammoth Woodstock Festival in August 1969, rock was neither a simple 'background' nor dancing music. It had become a central 'experience' in the counter-culture, refracting its deepest investments and contradictions. The subsequent variety of the music – from the country sounds of the later Dylan to the strangely garbled blues of Captain Beefheart and the jazz–rock of Blood, Sweat and Tears – called for close attention and *listening*; these were not mere sounds, but cultural 'texts' as rich and solid as any book.

For every generalisation it is immediately possible to add a list of exceptions, but there is no mistaking the alteration in cultural referents that can be discerned here, nor much doubt about their wider origins. Although American commentary is frequently silent on this aspect, the class, race, and even gender specificity of the counter-culture's articulate musical programme was no mystery. It was educated, white, middle class, and overwhelmingly male in character. Superficially, it was also perhaps inevitable that the spreading 'head' shops, health food stores, artisan merchandising, mounting sales of rock LPs, and the selling of Woodstock (the film and the triple album) to the rest of the world, produced a new variant of stylised consumerism. Later, in Britain, this cultural coterie would eventually also find a rather mundane niche alongside the Habitat furniture and the Laura Ashley patterns. In the United States, much of the counter-cultural scenario slipped back into the mainstream of college life and post-college 'hip' status in the early 1970s, taking with it a notable part of rock music, longer hair, some dope, and the suitably accommodating *Rolling Stone*.[14] These developments were not, of course, by any means the ultimate limits of the counter-culture's proclaimed 'revolution'. Its contradictory drives were not necessarily so easily placated.

For on the opposite side, rock music and the counter-culture of the late 1960s can, with hindsight, be understood as a particular cultural option that posed probing questions about previous distinctions between music and everyday life, between politics and experience. The stylised moments of imaginative freedom that the mods had once snatched from the working week were now overtaken by confident ambitions that naïvely thought to establish a whole new way of life. The counter-culture proposed to abolish the taken-for-granted division between leisure and work time, between pleasure and daily routine. In its place it offered the programme, iconography and sounds of a 'total experience', a radical reintegration of 'culture' and 'society'. Rock and the counter-culture extended the scope and vision of pop music and its surrounding youth cultures. It was destined to remain, even if its appeal turned out to be less universal than was imagined, a persistent referent under these wider skies.

Meanwhile in Tottenham Court Road...

'The Negro hipster took his drugs for kicks. The Underground... took them as a means to the experience of something in which one could place something like belief and faith.'

(Jeff Nuttall, 1970, p. 164)

In Britain, the confluence of pop music and a native counter-culture, agitated by the American spectacle, was assiduously encouraged by the freshly launched 'underground' paper *International Times* (later *IT*) and recently opened clubs like the UFO in Tottenham Court Road. It was an *International Times* benefit – the 'Twenty-Four Hour Technicolour Dream' – held at Alexandra Palace in the summer of 1967, that was the first major indication that the American seed had taken root. Shortly afterwards, Britain's first pop festival was held at Woburn Abbey in Bedfordshire. Woburn was clearly not Monterey, California, nor the 'Ally Pally', the Avalon Ballroom, San Francisco; still, the public iconography of these musical events were remarkably similar. The 'summer of love' of 1967, and the spread of the 'flower children', seemed to have unleashed the promise of a transnational counter-culture – an electronic 'global village' (Marshall McLuhan) of the Aquarian Age.

Figure 10. The Summer of Love

The profoundest sense of an alternative cultural current in the field of British pop music after 1966 was produced in the predominantly London based underground. Here the links between pop music and London's drifting literary bohemia were drawn tighter and tighter. Dylan had, of course, been the influential trigger, pulling the vaguer links between 'Art' and pop music into a clearer prospect. The suggestive connection between the literary hobo songster and pop, even the Hit Parade, probably more than anything else, brought the obscure literary underground out into the light, into print, into the new clubs and recently opened Art Labs, and into pop. It would not be long before poet Pete Brown would be writing song lyrics for Cream (he later formed his own group), and record covers became the privileged canvas of underground art.

The initial strand in this reconstruction of British pop was, however, more public. It lay in experiments that had been conducted using existing pop forms and timbres as, for instance, by the Yardbirds (listen to Jeff Beck's Indian drone guitar work on 'Still I'm Sad', 1965). These novel elements were subsequently popularised and polished in the Beatles' recording between 1965 and 1967. By the time of 'Strawberry Fields' and the *Sergeant Pepper* LP (1967), elaborate harmonic structures, novel, sometimes electronically induced, timbres, and verbal intricacies – ' a deeply mysterious poetry of the commonplace' (Mellers, 1976, p. 82) – had expanded many of the existing conventions of pop to the maximum.

While the Beatles pushed against the limits of the pop and popular music canon, a substantial part of the underground moved out well beyond it. In venues such as the UFO, the Electric Garden (later renamed Middle Earth) in Covent Garden, and the Roundhouse in Camden Town, a series of the most startling musical syntheses started to emerge. All shared a sense of experiment, improvisation and free interchange between existing pop and non-pop musical categories. A frequently 'loose' musical structure, generally controlled by an introductory and concluding riff or motif, gave rein to more or less improvised sections often employing experimental electronic sounds. The music of the Pink Floyd, for example their second LP *A Saucerful Of Secrets* (1968), is an obvious

example. But it stretched from the most avant-garde tendencies such as the contemporary jazz-influenced Soft Machine –
notice that the group's name comes from a William Bur-
rough's novel, a telling sign of the times – to the fiery blue
electricity of Jimi Hendrix.

Meanwhile, after the success of the first wave of R & B
groups the commitment to the blues had still remained. Eric
Clapton, Peter Green, Mick Taylor and a host of other
musicians passed through the crusading ranks of John
Mayall's Bluesbreakers. But after 1966 the tendency was for
both the electric blues and sophisticated pop to be engulfed by
the West Coast example of 'psychedelic music'. 'Psychedelia'
explicitly evoked a drug induced dilation of time and senses.
In musical language it implied longer songs, often based on a
blues structure, and 'significant' lyrics: 'mind' rather than
'heart', 'sensations' rather than sentiments, were its principal
metaphors.[15]

The most important bridge between the blues guitar tradition, psychedelic music and electronic experiments was found
in the music of the expatriate black American Jimi Hendrix.
Hendrix's music and guitar style – the most influential of the
decade, if not in the history of pop – was drenched in the
blues, in his experience of playing lightning package tours
under Little Richard and the Isley Brothers before coming to
Britain in September 1966. But it was a blues sifted through
the electronic tissues of the present, through the controlled
extensions of electric amplification. Such is the dark emptiness
captured in his extraordinary onomatopoetic guitar – 'Loneli-
ness is such a dragggggggggg'/wah wah wah wah/wah wah
wah wah/wah wah wah wah/ wah wah wah wah/
wahwahwahwah – played on the wah-wah guitar pedal in
'Burning Of The Midnight Lamp' (1967).

The distortion, the presence/absence of the 'wah-wah', and
the prolonged moans, screams and growls of bent notes and
feedback, permitted Hendrix to turn the blues into a frenzied
electronic metalanguage. It was a loaded syntax that spoke
not only in the expected lexicon of sex and drugs, but also with
pronounced racial and cultural accents. For Jimi Hendrix was
a black guitar hero in a very white world; a favourite persona
in his songs was fittingly enough a gypsy.[16] As Richard

Middleton has noted: 'The fact that so much of his music has all the appearance of a "bad trip" confirms that it is not only – and perhaps not mostly – an autonomous cultural quest, but also an attempt at catharsis and escape' (Middleton, 1972, p. 232).

The electric scream of Hendrix's guitar, like the bitterly ironic silence of Sly Stone's 'There's A Riot Going On', was an anguished reminder of how much black music was being systematically expunged from the new cultural hierarchies of progressive rock. When the occasional performer like Hendrix or Sly Stone found acceptance, they were deified and, religiously distanced, permitted to perform like 'souls on ice'.

The telling singularity of Hendrix's music and cultural fate apart, the blues cycle was gradually transformed into the counter-cultural motif of expanding one's 'consciousness'. Cream, with the arabesque guitar solos of Eric Clapton, the virtuoso drumming of Ginger Baker and the soaring vocals and intricate bass patterns of Jack Bruce, represented the British musical epitomy of this idea (as well as setting the precedent for the concept of the 'supergroup'). Here in the blues-based soloing and improvisation there existed a musical laboratory for counter-culture experiments in spontaneity, free expression and self-development.

The mockery of 'normal' society implicit in the American hippy alternative, and then the more direct threat of militant student politics that emerged in a second moment in Britain, pointed to something that went beyond the previously disconcerting working-class dandyism of the mods, or the sporadic violence of the rockers. This articulate disaffiliation, symbolically announced in psychedelic rock, long hair, drugs, the ornamental clothing and spiritual withdrawal of the hippies, and then dramatically driven home by international youth protest against the war in Vietnam and university structures at home, was doubly shocking. For the breakdown in the institutions of higher education, this crisis in the 'social brain', this attack on 'the petrified city' (Tom Nairn) of the predictable estrangement and officialised boredom of middle-class adult life and its deferential culture, was led by the very sons and daughters of those habitually used to participating in the definition, control and curtailing of such social unrest.[17]

The spectacle of the chosen and carefully nurtured heirs 'dropping out' of their inherited places in the central lanes of British society and, wrapped in Afghan jackets and stoned beatitude, setting off for Katmandu, or, more modestly, the weekend pop festival, was profoundly disquieting. These suburban rebels, with their amorous arrangements, their music, drugs and exacerbated individualism, dared to put in question the very touchstone of the rest of society's own sense of 'reality': the work ethic, the nuclear family, reciprocal obligations between the 'citizen' and the state; in sum, the 'rational' and 'normal' rules of everyday life. It was a particularly unwelcome irruption, coming as it did precisely in the moment that the post-war boom and the rhetoric of 'affluence' was about to take its leave. When such cultural refusal was connected to direct political activities at the end of the 1960s, it became a 'treachery' destined to harden the hearts of public comment.

Amongst the psychedelic records, kaftans, Herman Hesse novels, hidden in the marihuana smoke of the inner city bed-sitter zones and campus burrows – the 'pads' of the counter-culture – there was something going on; even if to the outside eye and ear just what was not exactly clear. Probes were made. Talk of sexual licence, of drugs, of political agitation, was in the air. London woke up to the grey dawn of a soured permissiveness. *IT*'s offices were regularly subject to police raids. Mick Jagger and Keith Richards were arrested on drug charges in 1967 and given prison sentences (later quashed). The Regional Drug Squad was set up, and Jagger sent the revolutionary marxist paper *Black Dwarf* the lyrics of 'Street Fighting Man' (1968).

The attempts by the police – the 'Fuzz' – and the judiciary to come down hard on drugs and pornography, and to 'bust' the small change of cultural disaffiliation, proved to be the prelude to a far more intensive politicisation of such a sensitive area. Britain was not California. The public protest of students for greater democracy within the universities and against the war in South-East Asia never touched the temper of the US campuses, nor the pivotal intensity of the Parisian May in 1968. Still, official responses to the disturbances and sit-ins at the London School of Economics, at Warwick,

Figure 11. Suburban rebels. The Rolling Stones, *Big Hits (High Tide and Green Grass)*

Cambridge, Keele, Essex and other universities were revealing in their severity: students were considered 'sluts making love (if that is the word for it) in the streets' (Mr John Sparrow, Warden of All Souls College, Oxford). By now the nebulous rumblings of the counter-culture had taken on a more threatening form. The moment had arrived when the 'junction of the erotic and political' (Henri Lefebvre), when

Figure 12. '1968'

music, drugs, life-styles and political alternatives, had
apparently come together in a common assault on the old
citadels of political and cultural power. It goes without saying
that it was a highly charged moment for all concerned,
producing a nervous overkill in the official riposte.

University Vice-Chancellors, the police and the British
press, already encouraged by a similar ploy rehearsed by
Prime Minister Harold Wilson in confronting intransigent
seamen strikers in 1966, professed to find among the student
'agitators', with their 'foreign' ideas and their counter-culture
ambient, the diabolical social disease of 'anti-British' behaviour. Sections of white middle-class youth and its 'offensive' press – *IT, Oz, Black Dwarf, Ink, 7 Days* – not only offered
a radical critique of British society, but at the same time laid
on a practical demonstration (attacked for their clothes,
music, drugs, press and personal politics) that the oppression
they were contesting was not only about one's position in the
means of production; that, drawing attention to psychic and

sexual realities, it was also 'about more than economic exploitation' (Juliet Mitchell).[18]

Although this proved to be a movement that in Britain was often less frontal than elsewhere, and whose 'totalising' aspirations did not encounter ready success, it nevertheless quickly touched the conservative truths of British society. Disparate but disturbing signs – student agitation, pop festivals, drugs, squatting, women's liberation: all amongst the varied offspring of the counter-culture – were rapidly plotted on an expanding spiral of common signification. Once there, they, and other, even more ominous scenarios, such as the growing wave of civil unrest in Northern Ireland, militant strike action, and the spectre of Black Power, could be publicly admonished as the dangerous symptoms, if not the direct cause, of Britain's perilous decadence and decline.

The end of the trip

'British pop music is teetering on the edge of becoming art.'
(George Melly)

At the conclusion of Michelangelo Antonioni's film *Zabriskie Point* (1969), a luxury home perched in the American desert explodes. This imaginative representation of the bursting apart of the narrow materialistic perspectives of the 'American way of life' was, in reality, being cruelly parodied elsewhere. The very forces that had been expected to lay the charges for that detonation were themselves undergoing fragmentation. Whether at the level of symbolic choice and alternative, or literal application (the programme of the white urban guerilla group, the Weathermen), the counter-culture's attempt to 'make the continuum of history explode' (Walter Benjamin) was breaking up.

The 'American moment' (Stuart Hall), launched by the hippies in the mid-1960s, and since expanded into an international youth counter-culture, was turning bitter at the core. In the cold dusk of a free Rolling Stones's concert at Altamont Speedway, California, in December 1969, just four months after Woodstock, the alternative society began to snarl up in its own contradictions. The Hell's Angels – recently elevated to the status of motorbike outlaw heroes by such West Coast authorities as Ken Kesey, Allen Ginsburg and the Grateful Dead – irrupted in murderous fury, killing one of the few black citizens of 'Woodstock West'. A year later, Charles Manson's atavistic tribe came out of the desert of southern California and, demonically slaughtering the Hollywood actress Sharon Tate, delivered a mortal blow to the precarious symbology and libertine intentions of the 'alternative society'.[19] The journey through drugs, music, communal living, and more exotic referents to 'prefigure a new kind of subjectivity' (Hall 1969), was tipping over into a ghastly parody, an apocalyptic nightmare, and an extremely 'bad trip'.

The British media was quick to imprint these dark 'lessons' from across the water (adding them to US race riots and the rise in urban crime) on the popular mind. Their importance was further magnified when the turbulence of change began to surface at home and the tacky limits of an apparent affluence and public consent began to come undone at the seams.

Britain's perennial economic crises had been real enough since the early 1960s (the notorious 'Stop-Go' cycles). But more powerful in the short term was the expressed indignation of those who felt they had been cheated, overlooked, or simply felt apart from the disturbing currents of an inflation-ridden consumer society. Mr Enoch Powell darkly hinted at the 'enemy within', who, with the cringing connivance of the liberal establishment, had been permitted to take root. The new skinhead subculture violently reasserted a hard, ethnic proletarian mythology that was organised around an iron localism and savage attacks on 'provocative' outsiders: Pakistanis, gays and hippies. Mrs Whitehouse (Viewers and Listeners Association) and Lord Longford (Festival of Light) talked of a 'pornographic Britain', and argued that the country's moral body was being eaten away by a cancer of permissiveness.

A turn downwards into moral retrenchment, and the call for the requisite disciplinary proceedings, was now massing in the wings. The Kray twins, once the glamorous 'villains' of 'swinging London', rubbing shoulders with Mick Jagger and Terence Stamp in David Bailey's *Box of Pin Ups* (1965), were ignominiously jailed in 1969.[20] In the same year, the mild liberalising measures proposed in Baroness Wooton's report on drugs was howled down in the press as the 'Junkie's Charter'. Elsewhere, pursued for drug abuse and obscenity, the insular hedonism of London's underground was increasingly forced into confronting some bleaker political realities by the continual pressure of 'the Fuzz'. The 1970s open, as they will close, seated on that eternal political work horse: 'law and order'.[21] As the boundaries fell back, persistent sores again emerged: black immigration, Northern Ireland, unemployment, poverty, inner city decay, the fall in public services, the polemic on education 'standards'. The once optimistic promise of the 'Welfare State' was now grimly besieged.

As a cultural practice whose skin had been bathed and sustained by the warm currents of the counter-culture, British rock music resonated with this change in climate. The full wave of the alternative politics of the 1960s had now crested. In its wake it had beached a music, now robbed of this central referent, that increasingly sounded 'loudly within... and hollow at the core' (Joseph Conrad). The music, like many individuals in the counter-culture, began 'to strike a bargain for survival on purely personal terms' (Thompson, 1980, p. 416). The complex association of progressive rock music with the politics of a rich, heterogeneous cultural moment sundered, the concept of 'progressive' came to be increasingly identified with the restricted deployment of narrow musical criteria and the subsequent awarding of formal aesthetic merits.

Perhaps the best way to pick up this strand and the alteration that occurred in the nature of progressive music between the late 1960s and the early 1970s, is to look at two distinct examples: Van Morrison's 'Astral Weeks' (1968), and 'The Knife' by Genesis (1972). Van Morrison's song begins with a languid rhythm carried by a double bass, maraccas and acoustic guitar. The pastoral spell and pulse is anchored in the cross-rhythms set up between these instruments. Then, Morrison's voice enters. Coaxing and teasing each word, syllable and sound, his vocal style casts the sonorial mixture into a series of improvised flights. The evidence of black R & B and soul music is unmistakable. This, and the 'poetic' lyrics

('If I venture in the slipstream, behind the viaducts of your dream...'), is extended through scat singing and jazz timbres. The absence of drums further underlines the lack of a regular pop-style beat, encouraging a 'looser' structure, a polyrhythmic continuum, where in each instance something novel, improvised – the inflection of the voice, the shifting bass line, the bluesy guitar injections across the rhythms – is proposed.

With 'The Knife' we discover a very different type of musical construct. Both 'Astral Weeks' and 'The Knife' are over seven minutes in length. But while Morrison's song uses shifting timbres, rhythms and emphases to explore the multiple interiors of the simple song schema of verse/chorus/extended coda, 'The Knife' develops, through the calculated addition of one distinct musical cell to another, into a type of mini-suite. Preceded by a riff that echoes early twentieth-century Russian classical music, the normal verse–chorus arrangement gives way to a linear sequence of highly structured instrumental variations and solos. The internal musical details are not particularly interesting, but the overall shape of the piece is extremely significant. The example of 'The Knife' can be said to offer a musical paradigm for later progressive music after 1970, as much in evidence in Jethro Tull as Frank Zappa, in Emerson Lake and Palmer as Van Der Graaf Generator.

Writing in the marxist journal *New Left Review* in this period, Andrew Chester inadvertently hit upon the ideological shift at work here. Chester was attempting to identify the musical basis for an 'autonomous aesthetics' of rock music. He argued that the specificity of rock music, due to its insistent Afro-American inheritance, lay in the music building 'inwards', as it were, to explore the vertical sonorities and rhythmic possibilities of the musical form (Chester, 1970). This strategy he contrasted with that of the European classical musical tradition which, with its insistence on sequential harmonic structures, sacrificed rhythmic subtleties for melodic shape, vertical richness and ambiguous harmonies for clear linear developments. The unintended irony is clear. In the very moment that Chester was seeking explicitly to establish rock's 'autonomous aesthetics' on such grounds, progressive music was in practice deserting those criteria for others that were in musical and cultural formation diametrically opposed. It is the sequential addition of musical unit to unit that makes 'The Knife' musically 'complex' (in the accepted 'classical' sense) in a fashion very different from the richness of 'Astral Weeks'.

This ulterior musical reworking of the idea of 'progressive' music was, in part, further encouraged by technological possibilities that had become available in the recording studio. The studio had rapidly become the privileged, if not unique, compositional space for pop. Technological factors, due to their integral role as productive musical elements (echo, double-tracking, phasing, editing, etc), have never been external but always 'within' pop music's history; there at the 'interface where the economies of capital and libido interlock' (Wollen, 1982, p. 176). In fact, the full flowering of progressive rock at the end of the 1960s was directly involved in the second major turning point in the post-war history of sound recording. After the introduction of recording tape and the ensuing flexibilities that were increasingly exploited in pop through the 1950s and early 1960s, it was the introduction of multiple track recorders that led to a further revolution in recording in general, and producing pop music in particular. These new machines were initially four track, but there quickly followed in rapid succession, eight, twelve, sixteen, and a little later twenty-four, track recording studios.

Balanced between increasingly sophisticated electronic hardware and a cultural impetus to establish the LP at the apex of pop music recording, the recording studio further advanced its importance in the making of the music. Record producers and engineers like Jimmy Miller, Shel Talmy and Glyn Johns rose to become the equivalent of recording stars in their own right. Even the peculiar sound characteristics of particular studios acquired their own individual fame and clientele. All this was deeply stimulated by the now widespread availability of relatively inexpensive hi-fi equipment and the universal adoption of the stereo LP by the end of the 1960s.

Employing a sixteen track recording studio, a four-person group had the possibility of producing the musical equivalent

of sixteen individual musicians mixed together into a contemporaneous sound. Clearly, musical ideas and their execution
could become more ambitious and complex. If a mistake
cropped up during a difficult passage, a good 'take' could be
selected or assembled from previous recordings of the passage,
or else be 'dubbed on' later. Vertical complexity – the
employment of all sixteen tracks – could also be matched by
lengthier, horizontal developments, especially if there were
sixteen 'voices' to follow and develop. Segments could be run
together and a lengthening set of combinations explored. The
emergence of concept albums, pop operas and extended
instrumental suites, was almost inevitable. But, as always, it
was hardly a matter of simply technological pulls and shoves
that led to such musical forms and ideas being adopted in pop.
In isolation, many of the musical options that recording
facilities offered might never have been taken. It was a
particular cultural framework that finally suggested and
encouraged them.

By the end of the decade there existed in pop a substantial
and influential grouping of musicians, and an accompanying
public, who explicitly refused the 'artistic' limits of the Hit
Parade-destined, sub-three minute, single. It was a rejection
that, with the undeniable commercial success of the LP
format, also met with record company acquiescence. The
larger ideas that the space of the LP and developments in
recording suggested to these rock 'artists' were pursued with
little interference. The robust, frequently scratched and
abused, 45 rpm single was now both commercially and
culturally overshadowed by the more delicate and protected
hi-fi stereo LP. The increase in audio sensitivity (from microphone to record-playing equipment) was also accompanied
by a far greater attention to auditory details. Pop's indiscriminate mobile soundtrack, criss-crossing leisure and turning
up unexpected senses everywhere, from the Saturday dance to
the poster-covered bedroom walls of a temple to Elvis, was
now replaced by the concentrated attention of the 'discrimi-
nating' rock listener.

In the mid-1960s, the Animals with 'House Of The Rising
Sun', 'Story Of Bo Diddley', and the Rolling Stones with their
eleven-minute opus 'Goin' Home', had already begun to

indicate the potential of longer recordings. The allusive song narratives of Bob Dylan's 'Like A Rolling Stone' (1965) and 'Positively 4th Street' (1965), linking the impetus of lengthy literary compositions to a corresponding musical spread, further advanced the claim. Contemporaneously, the counter-cultural motif of expanding one's consciousness and expression ('let it all hang out'), found a direct musical echo in the concept of having a 'blow', of improvising, and associated itself with the 'freedom' from constraint that jazz – the bohemian '*art*' *par excellence* – symbolised. This was significant for musics as diverse as that of Cream, Traffic, Van Morrison, Family, and the short-lived 'supergroup', Blind Faith.

But these vaguer referents were gradually overtaken and refined. Attention moved towards the more precise focus of musicianship, and frequently bowed in the direction of the official canons of European 'art' or classical music. Some attempts – Deep Purple, Procul Harum – were even made to orchestrate rock. In these successive phases, the names of jazz musicians and classical composers not only began cropping up regularly in pop critics' prose, but also in the comments and practice of many pop musicians willing to be associated with this process of aesthetic legitimation.[22]

Behind lengthy improvisations such as Cream's 'Spoonful' (found on the *Wheels Of Fire* album) lay the theme of individual spontaneity, exploration and extension. The musical basics of pop now thoroughly mastered, rock was apparently ready for greater things. Its 'authenticity' was to be discovered in the 'natural' expresion of an artistic autonomy freed from commercial restraints. The counter-culture's project had once provided an extensive claim for both this and the rest of rock's claims on the future. But as that vision contracted, the music tended to seek residence in the abstract refuge of the artist intent on separating his (it was rarely 'her') artistry from 'vulgar commerce'. The confused but fruitful energies surrounding rock in the late 1960s were transformed into the stilled, but highly marketable, waters of 'Art'.[23] Paradoxically for its declared aesthetic claims, it also represented the removal of the music into a fairly unambiguous wealth and success.

The financial fruits of progressive music were revealed after it had carried the sales of LPs over and beyond the 'commercial' single. This change was then registered in the increased capital investment laid on for studio time and technology, tours and promotion, necessary to reproduce the position that progressive rock had now gained in the institutional field of pop music. For rock music was also deeply involved in the search to maximise profits. Only in its case this occurred through different expressive/aesthetic/ideological avenues from those employed elsewhere in pop. As has been recently observed, rock is not a genre but an ideological category (Taylor and Laing, 1979). With the wider cultural and political memories of the late 1960s now dispersed or abandoned, progressive music moved almost ineluctably into the security of a 'politics' of the aesthetic. But then how could it be otherwise when this extremely successful music claimed to be based on artistic 'authenticity', as opposed to the commercial crassness of pop?

Chapter 5

Among the Fragments, 1971-6

On the cover of the LP *Space Oddity* (1972), the slightly dazed terrestial David Bowie gazes out from tufts of orange hair into the middle distance.[1] Turning the record over we find Bowie's slight frame clothed in a silverish jump suit slashed open to the waist. The singer regards us with an interrogative look, raised chin and arched eyebrows. Around his neck hangs a necklace terminating in a large glittering pendant that rests on his ivory chest. Seated, his hands pressed between his thighs, legs splayed out from the knees and tapering floorwards inside bright red boots, Bowie offers himself to the camera's eye as an image of artful disturbance. His 'feminine' pose and extravagant attire speak an indeterminate language, an androgynous code. But the narcissistic atmosphere this image invokes is in turn richly ambiguous. The object of our surprised stare, Bowie is yet simultaneously the constructor of the 'shocking image'. Such a public display in self-fascination gestures towards the possibility of |loosening the sexed male subject from previous, more predictable, moorings.

'Glam' or 'glitter' rock's inroads into the public figure of male sexuality, in which the chameleon figure of David Bowie was seminal, seemed to crack an image brittle with repression. Yet various commentators insisted that all that was really involved was a commercial manipulation of sexual ambiguities, a shallow contortion. Understood in that key, glam rock simply becomes a conspicuous part of a general retreat by pop music from more committed concerns: from the wider aspirations of the counter-culture, or the instinctive assertions of working-class habits and tastes. What this view overlooks is that *within* the cultural economy of pop playing with sex and the erotic imagination – with its imagery and possible senses – can hardly be considered a retreat: more a return with a vengeance to the music's central social referents. Like several other tendencies coming out of the tail end of the counter-culture, it highlighted that 'development which has made sexual characteristics a major organising element in our culture' (Weeks, 1981, p. 287).

But this is a description of glam rock which is usually only accepted with some reluctance. It was elsewhere that it was considered to be more innovatory. In its sophisticated reaches (Bowie, Roxy Music, Lou Reed), glam rock offered an aesthetic prospective that was markedly different from that of progressive music. Its 'artistry' went beyond traditional European aesthetic canons, and, like 'Pop Art', looked to the shiny ones of modern industrial life and its continual reproducibility. The rhetorical gesture of progressive rock which had sought to separate commerce from conscious, artistic poise was brusquely abandoned. The two were now indiscriminately mixed together on the same palate. In this fashion, the objects of everyday life – the sense of music, of sex, of art, of pleasure – were disturbingly rearranged, and unexpected suggestions able to emerge. Inside that process, 'good' and 'bad' taste were superseded by the disturbance of 'kitsch' and journeys towards the frontiers of excess: out there where 'a-lad-insane' (David Bowie, *Alladin Sane*, 1974), could continue a perverse research for new extremes. The reception of this music was not organised through the appeal of an abstract aesthetic. Its futuroid imagery – an exaggeration of the present in anticipation of the future – celebrated a tangible technology, stardom and commerce. The invasion of psychic and social spaces by these realities was not refused, as had been the case with the counter-culture and progressive rock, but accepted, absorbed, investigated.

However, the 1970s opened preoccupied with other prospects. It is 'art' and 'musicianship', rather than explicit tamperings with sexuality, the pleasures of 'kitsch', and disruptive avant-gardist theories, that set the tone. It was the abstract chimera of 'art' surrounding the music of such groups as Yes, Jethro Tull, Genesis, Emerson, Lake and Palmer, and the Moody Blues, that continued to exert a disproportional influence on the direction and sense of much pop music, distributing judgement and dividing the musical field into frequently quite rigid divisions. And, up until the autumnal triumph of the progressive music ideal with Mike Oldfield's *Tubular Bells*, it remained the most privileged sector of critical attention.[2]

Between the distinctive intentions of progressive rock and sophisticated glam, pop's more predictable elements reproduced themselves. Variations on the electric blues format even enjoyed something of a mini-revival in the early 1970s. The Rolling Stones were joined by other blues-tinged sounds, as diverse as Rod Stewart and the Faces or Free. But it was the loud pummelling beat and flamboyant guitar antics of 'heavy metal' that most decidely occupied the centre of blues-riffing. Alongside heavy metal and electric blues there was a recall to pop styles that pre-existed the geological shifts of the late 1960s: the Saturday night rock 'n' roll euphoria of Creedence Clearwater Revival, and the wistful pop lyricism of Elton John.

What appears most clear about this moment is the new arrangement within pop. Under the umbrella of progressive music all the above mentioned styles constituted a rock 'mainstream', set apart from the rest of pop. Although the boundary was often decidedly hazy, rock in general considered itself separate from the pop-show business world of television variety shows, Radio One and Engelbert Humperdinck. This meant that while glam rock star Marc Bolan, or even Bowie, might remain uncertain cases, Deep Purple was 'in' and Tom Jones definitively 'out'.

Rock music was increasingly occupied with its own internal affairs. The more open, experimental, atmosphere of the late 1960s had evaporated. Rock was now taking itself 'seriously'. This self-conscious reality was fittingly caught in the rise of the professional rock critic: the writer, working not only in the musical press, but also on 'alternative' (*Time Out, Rolling Stone*) and 'quality' papers, who is paid to expound views and theories on rock as a particular body of musical work. While this was going on, pop's long standing affair with modes of

sexuality and the extravagancy of male style experienced a
compensatory inflation. Glam rock, certain parts of heavy
metal, and teenybopper pop, with their diverse economies of
the corporeal image and its possible sexualities, suggested a
very different set of concerns from those embroiled in the
rock/pop demarcation dispute.

'Art', 'authenticity' and 'roots'

Where British beat and R & B had drawn upon the immediate
environs of a peculiar blend of dance halls, urban clubs and
art school bohemia, progressive rock and its 'underground'
constituency had its feet firmly planted in a cosmopolitan,
white, Anglo-American counter-culture. It was correspondingly more 'global' and abstract in its scope. In a monument
to this latter tendency, *The Age of Rock* (subtitle: 'Sounds of the
American Cultural Revolution'), the editor Jonathan Eisen
confidently puts the case in firm teleological terms: '…by and
large the fifties were musically Neanderthal. You listened to
the music; you were not "turned on" to it. It wasn't a "total"
experience…'. By 1969, such a reality had been replaced by
the successful enthronement of 'rock': 'Born a hybrid of blues
and country-western. It is now a full-throated school that
incorporates everything from blues to Indian classical raga,
from Bach to Stockhausen' (Eisen, 1969, p. xi). Quite
obviously, a new and important legitimation had been consummated.

In October 1970, *Sounds*, a forty-eight page musical weekly,
was launched on an explicit progressive music platform. It
subsequently influenced both *Melody Maker* and *New Musical
Express* to alter their approach. *NME* brought in journalists
from the 'underground press' (Charles Shaar Murray and
Nick Kent), and both papers abandoned coverage of 'middle
of the road' pop. This occurred despite the fact that many of
the performers in the area of show business and the pop
mainstream – Tom Jones, Peters and Lee, Engelbert Humperdinck, Perry Como, the Carpenters – remained among the
most successful record sellers in both the LP and single charts
in the first half of the 1970s. Such a restricted attention on the

part of the pop journalists on these papers was semantically signalled in the quiet dropping of the term 'pop' and the adoption of the label 'rock' or 'progressive' music. The BBC continued to offer little on the radio that reflected this change with the notable exception of John Peel's Sunday afternoon broadcast *Top Gear* (in a second moment moved to *Night Ride*, late at night during the week). But on television, with *The Old Grey Whistle Test* – itself a child, via *Colour Me Pop*, of the arts programme *Late Night Line Up* – it did turn over a weekly television programme on the 'serious' BBC 2 to progressive rock.

This recognition of a particular area of pop was extremely revealing. It indicated the acknowledgement of a new public supporting rock music, and suggested that the field of pop as a whole had been successfully reorganised into distinctive fields and tastes. From this followed a whole series of wider consequences. Firstly, under its 'aesthetic' ear whole chunks of musical experience were now cast beyond the concerns of progressive music's critical attention. This was particularly applied to contemporary developments in urban black music. It was a tendency made all the more striking by the fact that Afro-American music at that time was neither of a strictly minority interest (the esoteric tastes of the 'Northern Soul' circuit was a case apart), nor of inconsequential commercial and public impact amongst a largely white working-class public. In 1969, during the triumphal heyday of progressive music, soul and reggae were a consistent feature of the British charts, and, more significantly, of British dance sounds, yet they were destined to be excluded from most critical concerns.[3] The telling absence of black sounds from the definition of progressive rock was well observed by Dave Morse at the time. 'Black musicians are now implicitly regarded as precursors who, having taught the white men all they know, must gradually recede into the distance, as white progressive music, the simple lessons mastered, advances irresistibly into the future' (Morse, 1971, p. 108). Contrasted with the 'natural' but technically limited talents of black music, progressive rock 'must now be considered as an art form' (Eisen, 1969, p. xii).

At this point one could be tempted to say that this direction simply represented the central clause of the progressive music programme: to separate its 'art' from commercial considerations. This would seem to be partly confirmed in the way its critical supporters set about recuperating certain white performers who had obviously remained close to an Afro-American sound. Employing the accusation of 'commercialism', black performers were compared unfavourably to what were referred to as the 'blue-eyed white soul singers': 'For today's soul, the REAL music, not the "sock-it-to-me" or "is everybody happy corn", is being sung by whites. The funkiness and feel is coming from Caucasians.'[4] The soul and R & B strains of Janis Joplin, Rod Stewart, Joe Cocker and Van Morrison were praised while Ray Charles and Aretha Franklin, not to mention the unredeemable Tamla Motown stable (with the precise exception of the 'progressive' Stevie Wonder), were accused of decaying in the swamps of a commercial jungle.

But that very operation ('REAL music' as opposed to black 'corn'), together with progressive music's extensive commercial success, warns us that its own version of itself is perhaps trickier than it initially appears. The circuit of rock 'superstars' who stalked the stadiums and festivals of the 1970s with their banks of speakers, sophisticated sound consoles and elaborate lighting rigs, were not only striking memoirs of another cultural epoch: jeans, long hair, the REFUSAL; they were also the material signs of an obvious wealth and investment. It was this contradictory platform that continued to command the consensus of what was considered 'significant' in British pop right up until the scabrous 'din' of punk broke up the arrangement.

Progressive music had by now become an important cultural option for an audience that tended to see its future as being set apart from the tastes and habits that had previously inhabited pop. This was well illustrated in the fortunes of dance. The marginalisation of black musics had taken with it stylised dancing, its inseparable partner. Dance music did not, of course, completely disappear; in many ways the passage of dance to the 'periphery' served to intensify its significance and successively deepen its relation to black musics in unexpected ways, i.e. 'Northern Soul', skinheads and reggae. But elsewhere the constellation of progressive

music existed apart from the more traditional loci of dance
halls, coffee bars and city clubs. In its use, progressive music
was either intensely private, locked away between the walls of
a bed-sitter, in the space between the headphones, or overwhelmingly a public manifestation: the mega-concert and the
open air festival. For pop music, once spurned by the majority
of white youth in higher education had now been appropriated and transformed into the new symbolic field of rock
culture. The attention paid to the university circuit by the end
of the 1960s for rock concerts, something unthinkable only five
years previously, was highly symptomatic. This, the international resonance of growing numbers of rock festivals held
each summer, and the critical tendency to set progressive
music down in the ranks of 'serious' comment beneath the
impassive totem of 'Art', demonstrated the successful occupation of pop by new cultural forces.

'Real' or 'authentic' music, opposed to the commercial pap
of pop, kept alive, if only inside an abstract aesthetic, the
'alternative society-music' themes of the late 1960s. Musics
that could guarantee this current, whether through their
'artistic' sincerity or 'roots', were welcomed. It was under this
canopy that country, country-rock, and singer-songwriters,
came into prominence in the early 1970s. Whether it was the
calculated artistry of Genesis, the lively 'southern boogie' of
the Allman Brothers, or the rugged country tones of Kris
Kristofferson, all apparently inhabited a shared universe.
'Art', 'roots' or 'authentic' simplicity were felicitously combined against 'commercialism'. This was the crucial unifying
denominator in an otherwise highly diversified musical bloc,
i.e. Merle Haggard, Robert Johnson and Bach against Tamla
Motown. Expressing extremely abstract criteria (that were
objectively in open contradiction with progressive music's
central role in the commercial strategies of the record industry
in those years), it seemed a rather dry, intellectual objection to
set against the visceral pleasures to be discovered in other
parts of pop.

But while, on the one hand, remaining firmly within the
rock fold, both the singer–songwriter and the various country
strains revealed defection from the potential bombast of the
more rococo aspects in later progressive music. Both, howev-

er, continued to be unquestionably tied to the progressive 'aesthetic unit' of the 'individual musician' (Christgau, 1973, p. 232). Meanwhile, country music proper – the biggest and notoriously the most conservative musical genre in the United States – was also experiencing some pronounced internal changes.[5] The emergence of a new levy of male country singers, Kris Kristofferson, Willie Nelson, Waylon Jennings, who were affected by certain counter-culture motifs, and the vicinity of Bob Dylan and numerous rock groups to country music in the late 1960s, connected country music to rock in a number of ways.

The 'outlaws' and 'honky tonk heroes' who sang the new country songs pointed traditional country 'common sense' towards a slightly more relaxed and liberal vision; one that unwound some of the tense immobility of 'southern ways' (these new accents are well in evidence on Kristofferson's first LP, *Me and Bobby McGhee*). The mythology of the male country singer is that he has travelled around, been to the city, tasted its drugs, drunk deep of modern life's ups and downs, but in the end remains sincere to the simple virtues: a rural seer who lays his battered emotions out on a gravel-lined voice. Apart from Dylan's place here (*John Wesley Harding*, 1968; *Nashville Skyline*, 1969), another important contribution, although at the time it went largely unnoticed, was the Byrds' *Sweetheart of the Rodeo* (1968). Leaving the Byrds after this project, Gram Parsons tried to promote country music as 'white soul', first with the Flying Burrito Brothers and then by himself before his premature and apocalyptic death: dying, in the tradition of the rebel country musician (*pace* Hank Williams), full of booze and drugs in the American desert. At times, it is a strange, unsettling picture full of unusual encounters. Both the 'straight' follower of Nashville's 'Grand Ole Opry' and the persevering hippy shared the potent theme of an individualistic rural populism and the promise of nature's refuge from urban life: a contradictory, cultural conservatism of the white 'American soul'?

The music of Dylan, the Band and a host of Californian groups like the Byrds, the Grateful Dead and Crosby, Stills, Nash and Young, not to speak of the open embrace of country in the music of the Flying Burrito Brothers, Poco and the

Eagles, were all deeply etched by rustic guitars and harmony singing.[6] A more vibrant version of country rock actually came out of the bowels of the South itself. Usually christened 'southern boogie', it sewed together white country music and black music into an unpretentious electric sound. The Allman Brothers, Lynyrd Skynyrd and the Marshall Tucker Band were its most noted exponents. They maintained the 'realism' of country music in rock rhythms intact from the increasingly aseptic West Coast school of the Eagles and Linda Ronstadt who were busily tapping the solid centre of white American pop and a vast 'hip easy listening' audience.

The other music with deep echoes in the folk 'authenticity' of country music was that of the singer–songwriters. Not surprisingly, when they were not country singers (for these penned much of their own material), most of the singer–songwriters came out of the white folk song movement of the 1960s. While in a certain sense part of a reflux from the gargantuan electronic spectacles that Woodstock had unleashed, these 'poets of the now' (Graham Nash) – Neil Young, Cat Stevens, Joni Mitchell, James Taylor – still fully participated in the cultural aura and 'unity' of rock music. Personal lyrics and the insecurities of a lone male, a man and a guitar, came to occupy certain positions more usually associated with female singing (self-doubt and self-pity). It also widened the possibility for a personal style among women singers. From the pioneering experiments of Judy Collins inside folk music (*In My Life*, 1967), through the acoustic biographies of Joni Mitchell and on to the urban sounds of Carol King, Lauro Nyro and Joni Mitchell's later work, the white female voice began to push against earlier constraints.[7] The quiet and unassuming category of the singer–songwriter, replete with the tranquilising mists of 'art', made it a particularly circumscribed space for women singers anxious to express new sounds and sentiments. But a literate and often highly sophisticated form of women's music did gradually begin to enter pop via this route. This was apparent to even male observers. As Robert Christgau noted of the persistent autobiographical basis of Joni Mitchell's songs: 'In a male performer such intense self-concern would be an egotistic cop-out. In a woman it is an act of defiance' (Christgau, 1973, p. 217).

It is largely against the precise artistic and musical proposals of progressive rock, rapidly turning into a new orthodoxy
in the early 1970s, that developments elsewhere in British pop
can be fruitfully defined. Some of these continue to enjoy an
ambiguous relation to the status and artistic command of the
progressive rock world, others fall decidedly outside. But all,
whether it involved the pubescent stirrings of 'teenybopper'
pop, the burlesque camp of a Gary Glitter or an Alvin
Stardust, the crude insistency of heavy metal, or the sophisticated claims of David Bowie and Roxy Music, can be viewed
as part of a firm objection against progressive music's more
ethereal claims. Still, progressive music continued to cast
influential shadows over many of these tendencies. It indirectly taught Bowie and Roxy Music, for instance, to combine
commercial success with a well-publicised 'artistry', encouraged pop to incorporate the 'authentic' sounds and sentiments
of country music, and provided the initial formulae for the
rough populism of heavy metal rock. More than this, it had
shifted the whole of pop, including the sense of a 'mainstream', out beyond earlier bearings. In the subsequent
readjustment and fall-out, pop music as a whole emerged
substantially transformed: notably wider in its musical heterogeneity, but tending for the moment to be more exclusive in
its internal divisions.

The fall-out: (i) heavy metal

Deeply endemic to the hippy and counter-culture life-styles
had been a particular mode of male romanticism. It drew
upon a masculine iconography of white rebellious Americana
– Kerouac and Dylan, James Dean and Jim Morrison. The
road was its central metaphor, and those 'born to be wild'
(Steppenwolf) adorned themselves in the street uniform of
denims and angular body talk, 'grass' and sidewalk argot: the
'street culture that fascinates the suburban young... a romantic version of the culture of working class peer groups' (Frith,
1981, p. 167). Nearly all the options collected together in the
progressive music bloc participated in this romance and its
harsh undertow. Along symbolic highways and in the cool

darkness of imagined bars, the 'laid back' country rock of the Eagles, or the musical muscle of Led Zeppelin, acknowledged women ('chicks') as so many signposts towards a barely disguised misogyny. But it was heavy metal that finally threw away the wraps and chopped down the ambiguities. Since it took 'balls' to play this music, as the musical papers continually reminded us, the complete celebratory rites of what some observers have bluntly called 'cock rock' were fully established.[8] Announced by the success of Led Zeppelin in the dying embers of the 1960s, and propagated by a host of similiar sounding groups as the new decade opened, heavy metal, despite the protestations of many rock critics, was unmistakably a mutant offspring of progressive music. Taking the latter's largely guitar based aesthetic (instrumental technique + complex/improvisatory pretensions = Art), it successfully transformed it into a loud and direct musical populism. The classic group line-up, derived from the urban blues, consisted of a powerhouse drums–electric bass combination laying down a bludgeoning beat as a base for the voice and lead guitar to narcissistically mix and mirror aggressive musical and sexual prowess (see the Discography for the relevant records).

Heavy metal also involved a crude extension of the earlier hippy legacy. For those unable or unwilling to entertain the utopias conjured up by 'California' or 'Katmandu', it proposed a more concrete life-style; one that was closely tied to the immediate emotions of loud music, beer and communal maleness. Its roughly hewn poetics unashamedly celebrated the basic powers of male sexuality. As the American critic Robert Christgau has noted, it was not 'sexy', simply aggressive. At the Reading Festival, Knebworth and other sites, contingents of long-haired, denimed males could be seen consuming large quantities of beer and playing imaginary guitar runs in sycophant homage to their alter egos performing on the stage. The heavy metal audience was (and is) composed of a popular alliance of scruffy students and working-class followers; it appears to represent an unexpected marriage of hippy and rocker culture. Since 1970, this music and its public has come to occupy a prominent and permanent place in the musical tastes of the provinces. Its 'wasteland' sound, seemingly untouched by the frenzied developments and transitory shocks of metropolitan change, has continued to recruit extensive support right into the 1980s. This is so much the case that it would not be inaccurate to refer to heavy metal as the true centre or 'mainstream' of recent rock culture. (The late 1970s saw the rise of a host of new, aggressively named groups: Motorhead, Iron Maiden, Whitesnake, Saxon. There were also some signs that the stiff male scenography was loosening up a little with the appearance of the all-female heavy metal band, Girlschool(?).)

For many critics, weaned on and now wedded to progressive music, heavy metal represented an important breaking point. Here the art of guitar playing, the aesthetic reach of progressive rock, and the communal commitment of the late 1960s, had been apparently exchanged for a 'mindless' display of inflammatory technique and a degraded populism. But the popularity that heavy metal encountered was undeniable. Its success, more than anything else, smashed the illusory barrier that rock music had professed to maintain between artistic merits and commercial imperatives. It left the ideologists of progressive music entangled in an unresolvable quandary.[9] The musical and cultural style of Led Zeppelin and the heavy metal groups that appeared in an uninterrupted regularity through the 1970s, had, after all, been forged in the very heartlands of progressive music. In particular, it rested on the triumph of the male guitar hero. Jimmy Page's apprenticeship in the Yardbirds alongside Jeff Beck, the influential model of Cream and their high-volumed electric blues organised around the guitar virtuosity of Eric Clapton, were, however 'vulgarised' they might become, all too much in evidence to be blithely disowned by the progressive rock fraternity. Heavy metal was not, as some would have liked to have believed, an extraneous development, simply one exit.

The fall-out: (ii) teenybopper pop

'I used to fall in love with pop stars, now I fall in love with people. When you're in love you ain't got no problems.'
                                        A teenage girl (Cowie & Lees, 1981)

A novel sign of the changed geography of British pop in the early 1970s was 'teenybopper' pop. This music, largely associated with the tastes of pubescent girls, had, of course, earlier precedents. In the 1950s, the Philadelphia based television show *American Bandstand* had launched local boys Fabian and Frankie Avalon into the female hearts of teenage America. In the mid-1960s, Hollywood had come up with the Monkees. This group had been put together as a calculated show business move designed to reply to the Beatles and capitalise on the kind of juvenile fan fever the British group had generated. Beginning in 1966 with their own television show, broadcast early Saturday evening in Britain by the BBC, the Monkees attracted a large following mainly distinguished for its tender age. The show tapped the specific responses of young girls to pop. It addressed these girls as a particular group and, however inadvertently, contributed to them seeing themselves as protagonists, actively imposing their tastes on pop. This has always been the case but now, with the decisive fragmentation that progressive rock was imposing on pop as a whole, it took on a sharper edge.

While teenage boys, particularly working-class boys, were out in the streets, in clubs and pubs, and sometimes making music together, their sisters were to be found elsewhere. Young girls coming from working-class families spend much of their leisure, at least until the brief moment of 'courting', that 'going steady' which is the prelude to married life, in the home. In this case, pop seems to be bound into a transitory freedom between childhood and the impending future of becoming wives, mothers and 'responsible' adults. 'Marriage was something you ended up with after you had lived' (quoted in Cowie & Lees, 1981). The underlying pathos in the teenybopper's romanticism comes from the acknowledgement that it cannot be permanent, it is only a moment in the passage towards adult sexuality. Although not necessarily the actual experience of all teenage girls, this particular narrative still remains a paradigm for many biographies.

In such a situation there emerge forms of female pleasures and fantasy constructed under constraints and in a reality quite diverse from that of the boys. This is not to suggest that female 'pleasures' at this point are automatic, as though teenybopper music was merely a conspiratorial vehicle for teaching young girls the required cultural cues of 'femininity'. Rather, it is the striking form of the teenybopper's style that throws into clear relief the struggle that goes on daily in pop music (as elsewhere) to distribute and position sexual powers according to prescribed cultural and social patterns.

For just what sort of pleasure young girls, gazing at the photos in *Jackie* or watching *Top of the Pops*, found in David Cassidy or the Osmonds remains an open point. By now we should need no reminding that the impact of pop revels in the ambiguous. However, in this particular case, there existed an important intersection of cultural intent and representations between teenybopper pop and the major weekly anchorage provided by such juvenile girl magazines as *Jackie*, *Mirabelle*, *Rave* and *Fabulous 208*. A concerted attempt to suck the ambiguities out of pop, and young girls' culture in general, is well in evidence in the moribund advice columns, the cautious fashion tips, and the interviews with male pop stars that inevitably conclude by underlining the stars's underlying moral 'normality'. This is not to mention the exemplary strictures of the romantic tales that are central to the paternalistic worlds of these publications.[10] Such a firm guidance through the blue eyes of David Soul towards the goal of 'normal' female sexual conduct (i.e. 'love' and marriage), and on to the desire for domestic happiness, suggests a quite precise set of pressures. Pressures that were moving in a very different direction from, say, those signalled by male ambiguities in parts of glitter rock, or the contradictory but explicit play of independent female sexuality found in soul and later disco music.

The musical pantheon of teenybop consisted of often extremely young, male stars: the Jackson 5, the Osmonds, David Cassidy, the Bay City Rollers, and in a more oblique relation, T. Rex, Gary Glitter, The Sweet. There was little unity of style except for a preponderance of sequined stage costumes. The Jackson 5 were unmistakably Motown, an exciting dance sound; the Rollers ('Scottish surf music' according to Gary Glitter) and The Sweet contemporary pop; the others tended distinctly towards nostalgia. Sometimes this simply involved reviving the ballads of a previous, more show business, epoch

and its comfortable connotations of the 'romantic'. Donny
Osmond dug particularly deep into this vein with a version of
'The Twelth Of Never', a Johnny Mathis hit in the 1950s;
'Young Love', a hit for Tab Hunter in 1957; and 'When I Fall
In Love Again', a success for Nat 'King' Cole in the same
year. Although clearly coming from an earlier moment in pop
these songs were not intended to represent a revival. What
they proposed were 'moments' suspended outside time,
beyond the narrow call of history: 'The Twelth of Never' did
not recall pop's past, only the external 'now' of romance.

The concept of 'romance' is obviously central to the *whole
cultural economy of pop*. It is important to realise this, and that
the romantic attachment of young girls to teenybop pop is not
in this sense exceptional. It represents a particular case
among others, where, as we have just seen with heavy metal,
boys are just as deeply involved. In all these cases, romanticism indicates a complex imaginary field. The teenybopper girl
was never simply the imposed product of cultural and commercial forces anxious to position her in a certain manner.
Such forces had to continue working through the ambiguous
passage of concrete female pleasures as much as on them.

The prospect facing many working-class girls remains
locked within the limited physical and symbolic horizons of a
localised culture consisting of neighbourhood school, the
parents' home, the estate or local streets, and, at the most, a
local youth club (McRobbie, 1978b). Outside this local
culture an increasing part of public rhetoric after 1970
revealed its intent to desexualise the representations and
consumption of pleasure. For many girls this fundamentally
conservative campaign offered (and continues to offer) a
paradoxical outlet. Invariably trapped between the sexual
brutality of boys their own age and the seeming unavoidance
of future domesticity, female teenage time makes the transcendental possibilities of romance its privileged territory in a
specific and unique way. It is this 'magic' dimension, together
with the concluding support of her girl friends, the pictorial
gallery of the stars, and the soundtrack of romantic pop, that
sustains many a girl to arrive finally at her only 'legitimate
expression of sexuality: marriage' (McRobbie, 1978b). There
she finds a permanent date, between the dishes and the baby,

with the dulled rhythms of Radio One. Somehow, pop's other possibilities seem to have been lost.

In this acute, but widespread, case – elsewhere, particularly in higher education, women often manage to explore more flexible options – the contradictory construction of female joy, excitement and pleasure ultimately remains extremely circumscribed. The external rings of social representations crushingly combine to carry the day, closing the circle of a traditional sexual and cultural location. For it must not be overlooked that, when the accounts are settled, after the negotiations and local victories noted, the wider choices and possibilities – from the macho heavy metal guitar hero through the glitter androgynoid to the gay disco star – stubbornly remained with the boys.

The fall-out: (iii) glam rock

'At the centre of the social space, stands the body. Upon it is inscribed the social order in terms of representation of masculinity/femininity, in terms of work and controlled leisure, and in terms of institutionalised objects of desire.'
(Jonathan Miles, 1981)

Around 1970–1, while the main body of progressive rock continued to inflate, glitter or glam rock appeared to propose a flight towards a sensationalist aesthetic of the 'strange'. Behind its disturbing theatrics, the masks, make-up, hair dye, platform heels and changing costumes, glam rock betrayed a wildly contradictory range of cultural motifs. Unashamedly caught up within the commercial meshes of the music industry, it also proved to be a sharp, mocking reply to the illusions of progressive rock. Further, it raised disturbing questions about male sexuality and styles from within a masculine universe. Apparently seduced by its own narcissism, sophisticated glam rock knowingly advertised the artifice and construction of the 'star'. It was quite clearly not lacking in some intellectual pretensions of its own. With all these intentions, glam rock became pop's most self-conscious expression. It tended to fragment older modes of reception, whether these were simply associated with 'fun' or the recently gained, but traditionally exercised, reign of 'art'. At the same time, much glam rock was itself simultaneously popular and yet, in its sophistication, often painfully 'artistic'. In this fashion, it held together a diversity of influences and heterogeneous publics. Perhaps its final significance lay in its rich and suggestive 'confusion of levels' (Ben Gerson).

For many, glam rock simply represented a novel twist in pop's public style and commercial stratagems: the latest fashion fad, encouraging an escape from immediate concerns and obvious commitment. Whether it was the glittering spectacle of Rod Stewart or the allusive communion of Bowie's show, it was considered simply to involved rhetorical stage costumes and commercial acumen. Behind this facade older musical and cultural rhythms apparently continued unperturbed. Examined in this manner, glitter rock signalled a return to a presumed 'golden age' of pop, when the mood was joyous, the beat insistent, and the music basically implied 'fun'. Here glitter frequently crosses tracks with the more precise focus of teenybopper pop. It is true that many performers insisted on the basics of pop music, on its beat (Slade), its R & B and soul heritage (Rod Stewart), and its lyricism (Elton John). Sometimes, there was a barely disguised revivalism, a glittering parody of rock 'n' roll and beat music (Gary Glitter, Alvin Stardust), elsewhere the synthesis was more subtle. When ex-mod, ex-underground, singer Marc Bolan took up an electric style in 1970 and launched T. Rex, his guitar echoed the immediate inheritance of Jimi Hendrix, but his riffs came straight from the US pop of the 1950s: Chuck Berry, Eddie Cochran and Ricky Nelson. Backstage, among the props and show business machinery, however, there was also another story; one that connected glam rock's 'camp' appearance to a more significant script.

Already in 1966, New York – increasingly the symbol of the modern city in crisis and breakdown – offered, with the music of the Velvet Underground, a bleak alternative to the open optimism of California's budding counter-culture. As a dark, isolated voice, oblivious of utopian release, the music of the New York group seemed destined to be only aware of the fragile prospects of defiance and snatched comforts in the 'mean streets' of the eastern metropolis.[11] If LSD and its promise of widening vistas was the West Coast cult drug, then New York was the habitat of the terminal prospects of heroin. It was as early as 1965 that the 'plastic' values and disposable aesthetics of metropolitan collapse issued their manifesto. 'Andy Warhol's Plastic Exploding Inevitable' opened in New York in November of that year. A multimedia event, it deployed the Velvet Underground, stroboscopes, the singer Nico, and such Warhol films as *Eat, Sleep, Banana* and *Blow Job*. There was no 'public'. Anyone who walked in off the street instantly stepped into the spectacle, everyone was temporarily a 'star'.

Warhol, and behind him Pop Art, became quite a momentous connection with a small but significant area of pop. At that time, Warhol's influence, apart from a short-lived and rather obscure co-operation with the Velvet Underground on their first LP (complete with Warhol banana cover), was minimal. But the exploration by the American and British Pop Art movement of the ironic expressive possibilities of the mass media and popular culture in figurative and iconic art was to be influential. Reproducing reproductions – Warhol's silk screen series of Campbell soup cans or Marilyn Monroe – was a celebration of the artist as 'thief', stealing and borrowing techniques, suggestions and images from wherever in contemporary culture. But it was productive 'robbery', and deeply instructive. It took and transformed the existing sign systems of popular culture (advertising, cinema, comics, photography) into fresh meanings, oblique messages about themselves and their place in the modern world: a soup can reproduced in a certain field becomes an art work. This, together with the deeply connected idea of the individual who *constructs* himself (or herself) as the 'self-referential object of his art' (Graham, 1981), became an important prosaic tendency in British pop after its introduction by sophisticated glam rock.[12] The lesson being that it is the gesture, the momentary perspective, that might be original, not the object.

The music of the Velvet Underground was part of this 'realistic', urban appraisal. It was a music stripped down to metallic guitar rhythms, electric 'noise' and inhuman vocals. The perpetual threat of cacophony was counterbalanced by

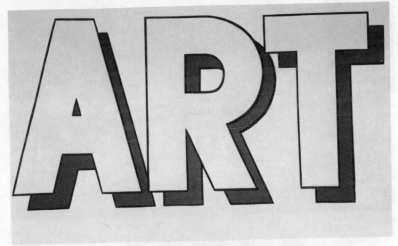

Figure 13. Roy Lichestein's *ART*

the harsh monotones and arresting associations of many of the songs: 'I'm Waiting For The Man', 'Heroin', 'Sister Ray'. These dark comments were later complemented by the theatrical violence of Iggy Pop and the Stooges from Detroit ('No Fun'), and the transvestite New York Dolls ('Personality Crisis', 'Trash', 'Pills'). The overall effect was that of a sleazy, East Coast, urban sound. A subversive musical snear that irreverently cast doubts on the 'authenticity' of the singer–songwriter confessionals or the 'sincerity' of progressive rock's 'art'.

In a twilight, urban imagination of fragmentation and moral crack-up, the trash aesthetics of the American metropolis turned out to have an important appointment with European 'decadence'; in particular, with the latter's morbid fascination in the stylised gestures of the extreme. To the vivid scenes of American 'street life' songs, Bowie brought the cold dramaticity of a dehumanised future, while Roxy Music proposed shiny projections and alluring icons – compare the music and record sleeve of *For Your Pleasure* (1973) – that ironically reflected nothing... but themselves. The 'flatness' of the artifice was paradoxically its profoundest statement: the

Figure 14. Seductive surfaces – *For Your Pleasure*, Roxy Music

construction was revealed, the borrowings exposed and mocked, the style shared.

It was above all Bowie who was the (self-admitted) master-
thief. His songs were miniature films, where the 'camera is the
eye of a cruising vulture' (William Burroughs). The resulting
song strips were full of startling images that apparently mated
Marvel comics with the eschatalogical vision of the American
writer William Burroughs. In the early 1970s, Bowie's songs
and personae were organised through a changing series of
sexually ambiguous protagonists (Ziggy Stardust, Alladin
Sane, the diamond dogs) who move through flashes of time

and disparate, colliding images, just like the adolescent homosexual warrior bands of the future that rove through Burroughs's novel *The Wild Boys* (1973). These songs emerge as a disturbing montage that spans Bowie's music from the early *Man of words, man of music*, 1969 (the original title of *Space Oddity*, reissued in 1973), to the moment in which he closes this part of his mannequined career with *Diamond Dogs* (1974) and swaps a sci-fi future for the uniform of white soul boy, neurotic funkster and a doomed dandyism.

With both Bowie and his protégé Lou Reed (Bowie produced *Transformer*, 1972), a musical mixture of the commonplace – orthodox pop song structures, frequently hard rock timbres and instrumentation – and the unusual (suggestive images drawn from the darker corners of the urban night) were provocatively focused on the ambiguities of male sexuality. Bowie, Reed and the android image of Brian Eno of Roxy Music, represented lives and habits out beyond the pale of the common imagination, they were 'extra-terrestial' in more senses than one. Embracing the ambiguities of the hermaphrodite, the transvestite, the bi-sexual and the homosexual, they appeared as 'forbidden heroes' whose 'walk on the wild side' (Reed) confronted pop's normal gallery with the subversive suggestions of an unstable male sexuality. Although already hinted at in Jagger's stage performance and the more relaxed, softer, male style of the hippies, it was Bowie and Reed who refined and concentrated this possibility to a sharp and shocking degree. The condemned melancholy of Weimar Berlin, or the harsh splendours of a decadent, futuroid New York, provided the dislocating backdrops that encouraged the emergence of a previously unspoken. It confronted male youth cultures with what to it was most disturbing: the shifting, sliding, but material, signs (it was there in the music, the clothes, the body) of an uncertain 'maleness' – the androgynous humanoids who 'fell to earth'.[13] A previously mute urban male romanticism began to speak in confusing and contradictory voices. The stability of a time-honoured sexual security was threatened by an ambiguous future.

Such 'ambiguity' appears to beckon us on to speculative ground, far away from the firmer footholds of explanation so far employed. Glam rock was, after all, a self-advertised refusal of 'reality', a glittering façade that perpetually slipped away from explicit contexts. Yet, on its inside, buried in its researched solipsism, its fleeting personae and studied vacuity, we can discover the tangible condensation of wider forces. In particular, Bowie and Roxy Music inadvertently exposed a certain cultural proximity to the counter-culture. Of course, the connections were tangential, disguised, subconsciously recognised, if at all; they remain lost in a bohemian fog. That is not important, conscious intentions are hardly the point here. What was significant was that the radical sexual and 'camp' styles found in metropolitan counter-culture and glam rock shared common ground when an apparently 'private' narcissism transformed itself into a public theatrics and took to a wider stage.

Public displays of sexuality – from advertising to cinema – had gone ahead by leaps and bounds in the 'swinging sixties'. It had been accompanied, encouraged according to malicious comment, by a series of liberal reforms relaxing controls on personal sexual and public moral conduct.[14] This development was now encountering mounting resistance. Encouraged by the rigorous climate of the Heath administration (1970–4), and the tightening of moral belts that invariably accompanies the observation of crisis clouds amassing on the horizon, public celebrations of sexual hedonism were decisively challenged. 'Permissiveness' was declared to have gone too far. The 'cost' of reproducing British society, by permitting the liberal movement of the citizen not only among consumer, but also moral, goods, was proving too high. With a world economic crisis rearing its head on an all too obviously unprepared Britain, the spaces for social experiments began closing down, earlier boundaries were pulled back and prospects retracted as the solid values of 'tradition' closed ranks.

Against these mounting prospects the 'frivolous' proposals of Bowie, Reed and Roxy Music are not merely light relief, but promise a 'dangerous affirmation' (David Bowie). The extraordinary attention paid by these glam rock performers to 'the outward appearances of role implies that roles and, in particular, sex roles are superficial – a matter of style' (Dyer, 1979a, p. 67). It was this seemingly hidden script that points to the possibility of a profounder sense in glam rock. To propose sexual ambiguities, and hence draw public attention to the details of sexuality, justifies some comment when precisely at that time a new, authoritarian morality was spreading over Britain's cultural landscapes, prosecuting for obscenity, 'cleaning up' television, campaigning against abortion, reasserting traditional views on sexuality, and swelling into a high wave of moral rearmament. In a tangential and distractive fashion, glam rock revelled in a display that was intent on demonstrating that the assumed 'privacy' of sexual matters, then being so fervently insisted upon by Mrs Whitehouse, was an illusion. Sexuality was as much part of the public domain as politics, class and subcultures. This often proved to be as equally uncomfortable to accept on the part of many radicals as it was for the moral crusaders.

It was Bowie, above all, who pioneered the shift of rebelliousness and images of resistance into the parade of male sexual ambiguities: in rock music (i.e. *Ziggy Stardust and the Spiders from Mars*, 1972), and then with disco *Young Americans*, 1975), before moving off into funk experimentation. Among Bowie's and glam rock's fiercest critics it was reluctantly accepted that the music's primary audience was made up of white, working-class teenagers. Glamrock was a '"focal cult" in working class youth culture' (Taylor and Wall, 1976, p.106). The same commentators also admitted that the imaginative 'night-life' that Bowie and his kind projected, 'provided working-class youth in general, and working-class girls in particular, with a way of participating in leisure consumption that has not been built into the traditional institutions of class' (ibid, p. 109). Actually this part of the spectrum of glam rock – Bowie, Reed, Roxy Music – also had a significant student and art school following. But what was important here were the new possibilities, particularly involving the public construction of sexual roles in youth culture, that glam rock held out. Strange as it may initially seem, the commodity on sale here, and glam rock blatantly represented a 'commercial sound', frequently offered greater expressive and imaginative potentials than the means found within the narrow cultural pathways and pinched perspectives of its varied publics.[15]

In everyday life, the cultural map of glam rock was destined to remain largely restricted to pop music's internal geography. Attempts made to translate its imaginative gestures into the more rigid performances of daily cultures often encountered vindictive male outrage:

> One evening on the Wall by Monmouth Estate, Tommy arrived looking like David Bowie, complete with make-up and streaked hair. Chorus of hoots, wolf whistles and jeers from the Wall gang. Then, Mick, who used to be a close friend of Tommy's but is now more involved with his motor bike, starts to have a go at him. 'Where's your handbag, dearie? Going out with your fella then?
>
> (Robins and Cohen, 1978, p. 81)

Such a turning to 'face the strange' on the part of male youth, particularly amongst working-class boys, had to settle accounts with some very settled patterns and attitudes. To play with 'masculinity' was still condemned to remain more an imaginary than a practical option for the majority of boys – 'involved with his motor bike' – participating in popular culture.[16] It had, however, widened the reach of the public imagination and become a permanent interlocutor in pop's future.

Contributing to such a sense of instability were Bowie's frequent public metamorphoses: Ziggy Stardust, Alladin Sane, white soul boy, Berlin émigré. Such characters underlined the continual sign production of the mass media, that possibility forseen by Warhol in which everyone would be a 'star' for fifteen minutes, a 'hero just for one day'. If all is 'falsehood', a media-induced 'illusion' of constructed images, then this, conversely, becomes the basis of a new 'reality'. At times the imagery seemed to take alarming directions: Roxy Music in Nazi uniforms, or 'Hitler was the first superstar. He really did it right' (David Bowie). But the disguises kept changing, their wider, historical associations perversely ignored. They were not so much statements about the world, as passing gestures of provocation. They did not 'represent' anything apart from themselves. For all was concentrated in the possibilities of the image; a careful construction revealed in the self-conscious deftness of the David Bowie or Bryan

Ferry persona. Bowie, in his dyed hair, make-up and leotard spider costume; Ferry in rakish evening wear and a late 1940s Dry Martini pose; Reed the trash poet, ashen faced behind dark glasses, topped off with peroxide hair: these were the 'artists' constructing their public 'selves'. The ultimate profanity of the star was ironically exposed through the sheer exaggeration of the image constructed.

In its music, this part of glam rock eschewed the simple continuities and revivalist spirit of more mainstream glitter rock for a brittle, shifting collage of researched musical effects. Both Bowie and Roxy Music scoured the post-progressive musical terrain with an impressive series of constructs, posing themselves as ironic commentators as they knowingly produced their own musical itineraries. Bowie proposed an aesthetics of musical and cultural fragmentation that moved from the hard rock sounds of *The Man Who Sold The World* (1972) through the 'plastic soul' (his definition) of *Young Americans* (1975) and on to the tortured funk experiments of *Station to Station* (1976). In a less intense, more whimsical, fashion, Roxy Music explored the inheritance of the 1960s. They produced a free wheeling musical *bricolage* of sounds, timbres and styles drawn from diverse sources. Synthesised together, the novelty, well exposed on their early records, lay precisely in the unusual juxtaposition and attenuation of already existing elements. Glam rock's fascination with the image and potential metamorphosis of the performer was a fitting phobia to accompany such labours.

Irony and image: these are highly familiar themes. Their undeniable centrality to the sophisticated play of glam rock's white aesthetic ultimately hinted at other cultural spaces and sonorities. Although it had been banished from critical concern by progressive music, modern soul had continued to pursue its own intentions confidently and coolly within pop throughout the late 1960s and early 1970s. By 1974–5, the young, white record-buying readership of *Record Mirror* was reading about and dancing to disco music. Meanwhile, the urban stylists at clubs such as Crackers, The Global Village, and other London spots were moving to the hottest soul sounds imported from the States. Up north, this music, was *the* sound of Saturday night (and Sunday morning in the case of the 'all-niters'), and everywhere, in one variant or another – Tamla, Stax, the 'Philly Sound', 'Northern Soul', disco – the music for dancing.

Set alongside the meticulous moves of Bowie through the icy reaches of stylised extreme, the sequined frenzy of contemporary American soul and disco seemed a world apart. But the release of Bowie's own 'avant-garde disco' (Peter York) record, *Young Americans*, in 1975, dramatically revealed an unsuspected connection. The LP, recorded at the Sigma Studios, Philadelphia – the headquarters of the 'Philly Sound', was influential in bringing disco music to Bowie's predominantly white audience. Occupying a position between a researched artistic pose and a mythologised black urban 'cool', David Bowie was one of the first white performers to open up an important passage between sonorial experiments in white music and the timbres of contemporary black musics. It marked the recognition of the return of the excluded and buried 'exotica' of the latter into the 'legitimate' considerations of white pop.

Chapter 6

The Release from Obscurity: Black Musics, 1966–76

'Africa? Africa? Africa? Just the mention of it, man, is like you call my name.'

Dennis Brown

'... there are no other stories to tell, it is the unique light that illuminates our obscurity.'

(James Baldwin)

Separate histories and discontinuous dimensions – to talk of reggae music in these terms, after more than a decade of halting exposure in the white pop world, seems justified even today; but soul music? Since the 1960s, soul has consistently supplied the turntable for dancing music in Britain. It has repeatedly enjoyed major commercial success with one or other of its styles. Surely it is only a rhetorical paradox that permits a reference to soul as though it was part of a hidden history. And yet, tangled up in the historical web of these musics, soul in one way, reggae in quite another, there is a buried sense of cultural semantics that consistently slip away from the superficial eye intent on the obvious.

Disc jockey John Peel once claimed soul to be Britain's

139

principal 'underground' music. He no doubt had in mind the
selective tastes and almost religious fervour of the 'Northern
Soul' enthusiasts whose existence was then barely acknowledged south of Birmingham. But soul music in Britain has
always been a multiple reality – running from the Hit Parade
success of Tamla Motown and Philadelphia Records to a
largely ignored regional cult. From the Supremes, the Jackson
5 and The O'Jays, through Millie Jackson and Bobby
Womack to the 'ultra-hip' (i.e. obscure) Northern Soul sounds
of The Prophets or Richard Temple, soul music has remained
a persistent, dark counterpoint to developments elsewhere in
British pop. Though often overshadowed by the glittering
pageantry of white pop (progressive music, glam rock, heavy
metal), throughout the decade 1966–76 it was soul that
monopolised dance rhythms, supplanting the earlier, short-
lived, Twist and anticipating the later disco explosion.

The dark imagination of soul, the sweet promise of the
neon-streaked streets of American nights and pleasures, filled
the Meccas, Locarnos and Top Rank suites and widened
weekend prospects. These were spaces and habits, found in
every British city, inevitably linked to a working week of
'soulless' labour, that progressive music rarely managed to
infiltrate. It was a striking allegiance, occurring thousands of
miles apart from the northern US ghettoes: the torrid production zone of contemporary American black popular culture
and soul. The mods had briefly charted out one symbolic
journey that ingeniously appeared to transport them closer to
the blatantly diverse reality of black America. But the carefully mustered white 'cool' and attentive style required in those
altitudes where stark dissonances are magically harmonised
eventually proved too much. Still, it had set an important
precedent, and one not lost on a wider audience.

Largely restricted to music, rare record collecting and
dance, the mod torch was carried on in a more restricted
fashion in certain cultish venues, above all in northern clubs
and dance halls. The later hard outgrowth of the mods, the
skinheads, attempted a similar exercise with Jamaican reggae
in the late 1960s. But, for its own internal reasons, reggae soon
turned into deeper and darker rhythms inside Britain's black

communities, leaving the skins prematurely stranded with their voiceless, white rage. Meanwhile, soul had travelled beyond the fragile screens of the earlier mod subculture into Britain's danceland; there to become *the* dance music in public places everywhere. If progressive rock was readily identifiable with a particular constituency, much the same could be claimed for soul. At student parties, individuals and couples moved vaguely through stoned, frequently self-conscious, motion to the Stones or Santana. On public dance floors, however, it was the 'speedy' but measured working-class step and judged foot movement of precise dancing patterns that investigated the inexhaustible paces of Major Lance's 'Ain't No Soul Left In These Old Shoes', or Archie Bell and the Drells exhorting 'Here I Go Again'.

Soul music, like the even more obvious case of reggae's indecipherable lyrics and disturbingly off-centred rhythms, came from 'elsewhere'. This was a crucial part of its attraction for its white adherents. Although apparently married to sharp clothes and explosive dancing at the Highland Room of Blackpool's Mecca or London's Countdown Club, soul music's cultural potency was also the evidence of a barely suppressed cultural 'Other', of the first continent of soul: black America.

The powerful continuity of black US soul music in the 1960s and 1970s rests on a tight combination of race and culture, appropriately designated the 'ideology of soul' (Charles Keil). The historical memory of US black popular culture that is distilled in the fervent testament of soul is a history apart; or almost. Dance, as Ian Hoare notes, is inseparable from the musical experience of black Afro-America (Hoare, 1975). It is also the fundamental transmission zone between black culture and the imaginative occupation of white popular leisure. But dancing is itself an obscure reality, the not so innocent refuge of many a social secret. It is therefore to the music itself that we must initially turn. Here we can hope to find some of the underlying 'textual' determinations that soul music has consistently exercised on unforseen and culturally distanced sections of white British youth.

Soul's two continents

'Sometimes I feel so nice. Good God!
I jump back. I wanna kiss myself.
I've got soul
And I'm superbad.'

(James Brown, 'Superbad')

'We didn't want anything to do with progressive music. So
we stayed with soul. And the kind of soul we wanted was
fast dance things. We work hard, bloody hard, and we want
to work hard on the dance floor. The faster the better.'

(quoted in Cummings, 1975a)

The persistency of soul music in the 1960s and the decade that
followed, for I understand disco to be a legitimate offspring of
soul, is a remarkable event that almost defeats analysis. But it
should not be mistaken for a monotonous musical output. A
fervent intermingling of US regional soul styles in the 1960s,
the stimulus of expanding technical possibilities in the recording studio, and fundamental changes in the 'ideology of soul',
combined to produce a complex, evolving, sonorial field.

Behind the confident musical styles of Tamla Motown,
Stax, Altantic, Philadelphia, and the hundreds of smaller
black independent labels that sprang into life in the 1960s, lay
the rich interweaving of the secular and religious souls of
black America. From the Negro church and gospel music an
internal solidarity and black cultural strength was taken and
grafted onto secular rhythms, producing the 'soul community'. Many R & B and soul singers, from Aretha Franklin to Al
Green, had a direct experience of gospel music from their
youth. Ray Charles took a gospel song like 'When I'm Lonely
I Talk To Jesus' and transformed it into 'I Got A Woman
Over Town'. In Big Bill Broonzy's noted phrase, he sang the
blues like 'they was sanctified'. Solomon Burke half-sang,
half-preached 'Everybody Needs Somebody To Love', while
the Staple Singers declaimed the secular gospel of 'Respect
Yourself'.

So, soul celebrated the marriage of the two great Afro-
American musical traditions: the blues and gospel. From

gospel, soul music took the use of a repetitive harmonic pattern which often employed only a pair of chords ('harmonic ostinato'). The song was perpetually threatened by a resolution which never arrived, the chords rolling to a summit and then falling away again. It often produced a seemingly 'timeless' structure, disciplined more by a shadowing pulse than any obvious sense of 'beat'. Simultaneously, the Afro-American tendency to 'spread' the music vertically was further accentuated by the practice of squeezing multiple notes into a single sung syllable ('melisma'). The consequence of these borrowings was that the earlier, 'closed', harmonic neurosis of the twelve bar blues and the tight fabric of the R & B format tended to be broken apart. A more open-ended, driving musical pulse was introduced.[1] Inside this structure the singer discovered greater possibilities to investigate the internal geography of his or her voice.

In 1956, the young James Brown and the Famous Flames recorded 'Please, Please, Please'. It was their first hit and consisted almost entirely of Brown repeatedly singing the word 'please'. Twenty years later, Gloria Gaynor's disco version of 'I've Got You Under My Skin' had a vocal largely made up of the phrase 'I've got you'. In both cases, the explicit relay of the word is subordinated to the physical and individual character of the voice, and the explicitly celebratory presence of the singer within the song. This, it may be objected, is true of all singing. It is what the French critic Roland Barthes once called the potential 'grain' of the voice: 'The "grain" is the body in the voice as it sings' (Barthes, 1977, p. 188). But the further complexity, and specificity, is that Afro-American musics are inherently 'vocalised' musics: the voice, the drum, the guitar, the piano, the bass, the saxophone, all are treated as sonorial extensions of the body. It displays an 'oral' approach to music-making, inadvertently revealing the profoundest retention of an African heritage and black oral culture. Its characteristic is to highlight a 'personalised approach to tone and timbre' (Vulliamy and Lee, 1982, p. 25).

The almost human sounds that Jimi Hendrix wrenched from his guitar, the 'talking' drums and 'replies' of the saxophone from Rashied Ali and John Coltrane (*Interstellar*

Space, 1974), the grunts, screams and shouts of Ray Charles or Millie Jackson, the wordless falsetto of Al Green, draw attention to and re-present the body within the tissues of music. As the primary producer of sound, pulse and rhythm, the body is not perceived as a secondary sounding board for musical stimulii elaborated elsewhere. On the contrary, it now shares the simultaneous status of being both the source and eventual destination of the music: the two moments being most significantly connected across the rich tension of dance.

In Britain, soul music experienced increasing exposure in the charts and leisure habits from the mid-1960s onwards.[2] Between 1964 and the early 1970s Tamla Motown records commanded an impressive proportion of British record buyers' attention. They were frequently joined by other soul offerings coming from Stax (Otis Redding, Sam and Dave, Arthur Conley) and Atlantic (Wilson Pickett, Aretha Franklin). In sheathed dresses and sequined suits, Diana Ross and the Supremes, The Four Tops, The Temptations, Junior Walker and the All Stars, proposed the glamour and emotional release of Tamla Motown's Detroit sound to British audiences with a striking regularity on BBC's *Top of The Pops*. Their glittering stage costumes and fussy dancing routines recalled the long obscured tradition of black performers competing for their place in the sun within the harsh limits of the black ghetto. Some managed to 'make it' in the wider world – but the stage gestures remained indelibly stamped with the 'entertainment' signs and flamboyant promise that might just produce that lucky break.

The sexual and emotional ambiguity (the 'pleasure' of the voice in communicating the pain) of high tenor and falsetto voices, the deep running bass, and the overall sweep of the enveloping pulse, provided a strong contrast to the generally more obvious sentiments and execution of white pop. Soul's immense popularity as dancing music further underlined the attractive peculiarity of its corporeal language. It was as though there was a 'god gone astray in the flesh' (Paul Valéry). Of the soul music available it was the Detroit sound of US soul that tended to prevail on British tastes; Tamla Motown usually ruling the Hit Parade while tiny Detroit

Figure 15. 'Northern Soul'

labels like Mirwood, Ric-Tic and Revilot unsuspectingly attracted the attention of the 'Northern Soul' enthusiasts.

'Northern Soul' was largely a male dominated, dance oriented culture, bound together by a common soul music philosophy. It existed, and continues to exist, as one of the unexpected testaments to the deep powers of soul music on British popular culture. Here, soul was a music for predominantly white, working-class teenagers who refused the passive acceptance and bombastic ritual of the rock performance. It was a self-contained, almost regional, culture, complete with its own music, dance styles, argot and sartorial rules.[3] Organised around lengthy dancing marathons and a devotion to rare American soul sounds, its musical criteria had little to do with existing soul chart successes, whether in Britain or the United States. In promoting rare American titles to a new significance on the dance floor, these white youngster produced their own hierarchy of stars.

> In their hometown of New York the Exciters are nowhere, forgotten by all save the mouldy oldie fraternity who recall 1962 when they were a three girl, one guy group who warbled ditties like 'Tell Him' and 'He's Got The Power'. Here in the sweating, heaving crush of the [Wigan] Casino the Exciters are superstars, here to bring alive their 'Northern Soul' smash of '72 'Blowing Up My Mind' and their monster sound of '75 'Reaching For The Best'.
>
> (Cummings, 1975b).

This particular northern musical culture had internal regional variants that moved from 'the ultra-cool, collecting purist of the Blackpool Mecca', to the 'handspringing, backdropping euphoric mass of the Wigan Casino' (ibid). Its specialist tastes were restricted to particular venues, although the 'Number One' club continually shifted locale. At one time it was the Twisted Wheel in Manchester, then The Torch in Tunstall, later the Dungeon in Nottingham.[4]

Elsewhere, soul music's more public developments shifted focus. In some cases, the musical timbres became even blacker, more 'funky', while other performers looked for a 'hip' sound that, following the example of Sly and the Family

Stone, drew on certain motifs developed in white progressive music. If James Brown and such 'street funk' bands as Kool and the Gang represented the former tendency, then it was the Norman Whitfield produced Temptations (listen to 'Papa Was a Rolling Stone', 1972) and the singer–songwriter Stevie Wonder who led the second. But both wings of the heterogeneous soul movement remained united in their conviction that the 'time for blues is over' (Jean Genet). An individual resignation had been superseded by the collective confidence of the 'soul community'.

Black urban riots in Harlem (1964), Watts (Los Angeles) the following year, and Detroit and Newark in 1967, were the 'long, hot summers' when the pressure in the black ghettoes irreversibly spilled over into violent carnivals of the oppressed. By the end of the decade, the universal adoption of the more abrupt adjective 'black' in place of 'coloured' signalled the principled dramaticity of accelerated change.[5] Under the distrustful eyes of white America, the repressed formation of black popular culture created newly charged modes of expression. In the early 1970s, the lengthy funk work-outs of Isaac Hayes, Curtis Mayfield and Bobby Womack set the threatening chatter of wah-wah guitar rhythms and angry brass riffs to accompany assertive black male heroes across the violent screens of a new black American cinema: *Shaft, Superfly, Across 110th Street*.[6] 'Ultra Skin Tone Cream', and its promise to lighten dark skin complexions suffered falling sales in the USA; processed straightened hair began to disappear, to be replaced by the natural or 'Afro' look. James Brown sang '(Say It Loud) I'm Black And I'm Proud' (1968).

It was from the mid-1960s onwards, while soul music began to enter into British pop in its own right, that this sense of black cultural innovation emerged. For 'soul' refers to both a developing set of black Afro-American musical languages and a powerful cultural metalanguage. To white, particularly certain white British, ears, simply the word 'soul' conjures up a powerful 'black mystique', a potential cultural 'Other' compounded of physical and metaphysical associations. 'Soul' hints at the inner depths, at the concentrated and sublimative energies of an autonomous black culture proudly making its way in the racist currents of white America. It simultaneously encompasses black gastronomy ('soul food') and the anguished scream of Albert Ayler's saxophone, the hip dancing of the Jackson 5 and the articulate programme of the Black Panthers. 'Soul' oozes with the indefinable but stylised sense of black urban ghetto life and survival.[7] Concentrated into black music, the idea of 'soul' literally 'seized the time' (Bobby Seale) of a large slice of US black experience in the 1960s.

In Britain, soul music obviously had a different, far more mediated, presence. James Brown trying to mouth the inarticulate, the brooding atmosphere of Otis Redding's pain, the breathy sentiments of Diana Ross: it was these immediate dimensions that were noted and followed. The deep black American undertow that frequently shaped these sounds was widely removed from white British experience. Or, at least that is how it seemed. For, returning to the centrality of dance in this unforseen cultural exchange, there were also – rarely perceived, but subconsciously received – a deeper series of connections activated.

Distilled into the metalanguage of soul and into the clandestine cultural liberation of soul music, is the regular employment of the polyvalent possibilities of a sexual discourse. James Brown, Wilson Pickett, Joe Tex, and other 'soul brothers' were black, proud and... sexist. On the other hand, singers Aretha Franklin, Tina Turner, Betty Wright, Laura Lee and Millie Jackson asserted a female presence and voice in a manner that was strikingly absent elsewhere in pop. The cultural echoes in these women's voices were deeply ambiguous – sexual in a traditional and submissive manner, as well as aggressively independent – but contradictions were also exposed rather than repressed behind the song.[8]

For many, such explicitness in sexual matters only confirmed what they had long believed. Soul music (and Afro-American popular music in general) simply contributed a missing, physical, sexual 'funk' to disembodied European-inspired popular music. The usual reduction of soul music at this point to a musical version of phallocentricity misses an important internal complexity. Soul music replaces the concentrated, driving thrust of rock music by a physical spread into its vertical depths, and by stretching the 'body' out over cross-rhythms and shifting timbres. Richard Dyer has noted of the sinuous rhythmic subtlety of soul and disco that the music works to restore 'eroticism to the whole of the body for both sexes, not just confining it to the penis' (Dyer 1979b, p. 22).[9]

The Afro-American tendency to extend the body in musical terms signifies in the case of soul and disco, Dyer continues, an important marriage of pop's romanticism to the contradictory material possibilities of daily life in the contemporary world. 'Its [disco's] eroticism allows us to rediscover our bodies as part of this experience of materiality and the possibilities of change' (ibid, p. 23). Dyer is intent on explaining disco's centrality to gay culture in the 1970s. But his acute observations also point to the wider powers of soul and disco music within the field of white pop music as a whole: to a previously unsuspected 'openness' of cultural possibilities orbiting around soul's persistent centrality on British dance floors.

Soul music did not magically liberate white, largely working-class, dancers at Bristol's Corn Exchange or the Lacey Lady in Ilford from earlier prejudices, from sexual chauvinism, or, for that matter, racism. But its ambiguous resonance, and its seeming ability to absorb an endless series of precise cultural investments – the mod subculture, 'Northern Soul' fanaticism, gay culture – while all the time remaining Britain's main dance music, is striking. What gay culture explicitly drew out of the music – inscribing a particular male sexuality across its sonorial surfaces – may also help to explain soul's popularity elsewhere. For while soul music revels in the sensual and sexual, in confiding tones and ecstatic sounds, its bodily connotations are rarely exclusive – girls can usually appropriate them as well as boys. Enveloped in sensuality, sexuality does not disappear, but is for the moment diffused. It is everywhere, in a temporary celebration of the senses: in the studied concentration of dance patterns, in the choice of dress, posture and the next record – all suitably reflected and amplified in the mirrored environs of the discothèque.

Parallel to disco music's association with American and British gay cultures, glam rock had also offered another form of stylised male entrance into sexual ambiguities and often, through David Bowie, through Roxy Music, into a personalised embrace of soul music in a second moment. The male sexual hustling manner that British pop had adopted from black R & B in the early 1960s was now challenged by a richer, more ambiguous discourse centred on the sense of the 'body' in music. Across dance, and through the uninterrupted continuity of soul music, it suggests an important, if rarely acknowledged, connection between white Britons and the black American 'Other' that continually haunts so much of British pop.

It is time to turn to an altogether less accessible black music, to reggae; to its history and to its oblique, yet incisive, presence in British popular culture.

An island in Babylon

'And the righteous black man must stand.'
(Big Youth, 'Marcus Garvey Dread')

Reggae, the music of black Jamaica, was not destined to encounter an easy passage into the world of British pop and the domain of white rock music. There was an intuitive suspicion in many quarters that it involved a diversity that was too 'different', too separate from British ways and customs. 'There are two main ways of dancing: separately, several feet apart, cool, casual; or together, thighs between thighs, rocking gently, sometimes almost motionless, openly sexual. Both horrify some whites, particularly the second: "It's disgusting" cried a woman teacher at a school dance, "they're masturbating in there"' (McGlashan, 1973, p. 20). Such overt dancing was only the distant hint of faraway Caribbean events. Or so it seemed initially. It was little suspected that such exotic forms might soon be found to have taken up permanent residence much nearer home, just a few streets away, over the back of an English garden wall. In Britain, reggae remained a slow fuse, persistently burning through the 1970s, here and there spluttering and crackling into life on a wider stage, but fundamentally tied to providing the musical anatomy for Britain's black communities.

A string of chart successes, fronted by Desmond Dekker's 'The Israelites', gave reggae a brief season of widespread hearing at the end of the 1960s. But general reaction at the time, partly stimulated by reggae's then association as the music of white skinhead 'bovver boys', was distinctly cool. The rhythmic insistency and sparse structures of this 'zero degree music' were obviously of little interest to those deep into progressive music's sophistry.[10] John Gee, manager of the Marquee Club, that shrine to the British pop world of the 1960s, had no time for reggae. He concluded that it was 'not helpful to the business, and it's insulting to people who should know better' (*Melody Maker*, 10 January 1970).

In earlier, less sophisticated times, reggae's direct musical predecessor – 'ska' or 'blue beat' – had played to Marquee audiences.[11] Melodisc Records had set up the Blue Beat label in Britain in 1961 to release Jamaican music, no doubt with an eye to homesick islanders. It was soon joined by B & C Records operating out of South London under the supervision of Lee Goptal. In 1968, the most important reggae label of them all, Trojan Records, was formed by Goptal and the white West Indian owner of Island Records, Chris Blackwell. 'Ska' had in the meantime evolved into 'rock steady', which, in turn, was shortly to be transformed into 'reggae'. But the public vicissitudes that reggae faced in Britain confronts us with a largely hidden story. To grasp its powerful subterranean effect we need to consider the volatile historical inheritance, the loaded memory of popular experience, deposited in its Caribbean sonorities.

Shantytown

'You can find the roots if you penetrate the inners.'
(A Rasta drummer in the documentary film *Reggae Sunsplash*, 1979)

However we choose to approach reggae, whether as the condensed musical outcome of the experience of slavery, plantation life, racism and imperialism, or as the involuntary mixture of the Mandingo, Spanish, Yoruba, English, Hausa, Scottish and Akan peoples, there is no avoiding the rich West Indian/West European cultural mix involved. All Caribbean musics intone the accents of this forced marriage.

In Jamaica, the only vestige of its aborigines – the Arawak Indians – that remains today is the name they bestowed on the island: 'Xaymaca', Land of Springs. The vast majority of the island's population are the direct descendants of those West Africans cast into slavery to work the giant plantations on which the lucrative sugar trade was built. There were also the professional auxiliaries (engineers, doctors, lawyers) coming from the colony's home country, along with more or less forced migration (Scottish crofters cleared from their Highland homes), and the adventurers and filibusters that hang out in such colonial situations. It was a complex cultural inheritance, and one which has undoubtedly contributed to the contemporary Jamaican reality that continually appears to elide the national motto: 'Out of Many One People'. The traces of this eventful past are also to be found deep within present day Jamaican popular culture: in its language, music, religion and everyday life.

In the Crown Colony of Jamaica, the joining of Africa and Europe was overseen and supervised by a white ruling caste, later joined by the 'civilising mission' of Christianity. But Christianity, like the English language and European melody, proved to be remarkably pliant to an internal, virtually imperceptible, reconstruction by the slaves and their descendants. The hidden and forbidden shades of West Africa passed by subterranean osmosis into Jamaican popular culture. A fiery fundamentalism, 'predicted on the identification of evil' (Cashmore, 1979, p. 13), mixed beliefs drawn from West African folklore and ritualism with daily Jamaican experiences, common sense and a millenarian Christian mythology.

Christianity was fused with African-derived elements, Methodist hymns with African rhythm. The forbidden 'myal' and 'obeah' cults (the 'obeah' controlled the 'duppies – the spirits of the dead) reappeared in thin disguise. The doctrinal flexibility of the Baptist and Wesleyan missions, and particularly the Pentecost Church with its insistence on supernatural interventions ('possession', 'talking in tongues'), encouraged the volatile adaption of official religion, language and music to the former slaves' culture. Following the ending of slavery in 1834, the cultural identity of black Jamaicans and the sense of 'Jamaica' were deeply fused with these black populist currents.

On 6 August 1962 Jamaica became independent. The search for a 'national identity' in a multiple race society caught between the 'melody of Europe' and the 'rhythm of Africa' (Nettleford, 1972, p. 173), acquired a further urgency and encouraged renewed attention to Jamaica's 'roots'. It inevitably unearthed a damaging schizophrenia. For, despite the fact that over 90 per cent of the population is wholly, or partly, of African blood, 'in Jamaica the blacks are not regarded as the desirable symbol for national identity' (Nettleford ibid, p. 36).[12] This, in the context of an independent black popular culture stamped with the rigid boundaries of poverty and race, explains the ready translation of Jamaica's oral traditions into a fierce religiosity and millenarianism.

In the 1920s, the black Jamaican Marcus Garvey and his 'Back to Africa' movement had profoundly stirred the sentiments of the black excluded, both in the USA and Jamaica. His vision of Africa as the symbol of mental and spiritual emancipation for black people – forced to carry white European structures and traditions on their shoulders and in their heads – was subsequently transformed into a more concrete message by later followers, among whom was the Ras Tafari movement. The Rastas preached a concrete realism, unwilling to defer black salvation to another world they came to public notice following inevitable conflict with the authorities in the late 1940s. The Rastas bore their subsequent social exclusion willingly as they set about upsetting the symbolic world of white society. Ethiopia was declared the true home of the exiled black person, and the way of 'Jah' ('Jehovah') was indicated as the rightful path that reversed the previously enforced exodus into physical, spiritual and cultural slavery.[13] The clash between the 'Babylonian' forces of order and the Rastas that flared up in the late 1940s and 1950s symbolically fused refusal, subversion and crime. It was an explosive combination and one destined to find a deep resonance in Kingston's rapidly sprouting ghettoes.

The historical interweaving of popular religion and worldly suffering that constituted the fertile subsoil of Jamaican popular memory found its most vivid expression in the patois and music of Jamaica's oral culture. The thick accents of the patois and the deep bass drum of Africa pulled together religion, language and music into an indivisible black Jamaican unity. The legendary Rastafarian drummer Count Ossie had provided rhythms for the Rasta community in the Wareika Hills, the ska trombonist Don Drummond named his compositions after Rasta themes: 'Marcus Garvey Junior', 'Addis Ababa'. With the Rastafarian movement 'providing the initial and creative drive for these developments in Jamaican popular music and dance' (Nettleford, 1972, p. 97), the resulting music became an integral part of the complex cultural screen that communicated only obliquely with the outside world of 'Babylon'.[14] Certainly, in the early 1960s, the then government minister and future prime minister, Edward Seaga, tried to advertise a 'soft' version of 'ska', using the smooth tourist combo Byron Lee and the Dragonaires, as Jamaica's 'national' music; but the rhythms were too deep, the accents too elusive, to be so obviously promoted.

'Ska' represented a musical cross-breed between a fiery, indigenous culture and black US music. Coming out of the occasional radio in the shacks and 'dungles' of West Kingston's Trench Town, Back O'Wall and Greenwich Farm – the 'shantytowns' whose populations were annually swelled by new migration from the country – were the sounds of North American R & B and soul music beaming in from nearby Florida. But more than the radio, or the expensive record, it was the travelling discothèque, known as the 'sound system', that carried the latest American sounds from one shantytown to another and up country into the rural parishes.

As the owners of these travelling sound systems, DJs like Duke Reid, Sir Coxsone/Clement Dodd (also known as 'Downbeat'), King Tubbys, V Rocket and Prince Buster, competed in musical warfare for audiences and reputations. Idiosyncratic variations and recognisable trademarks were liberally enlisted in the struggle to achieve the 'boss sound' on

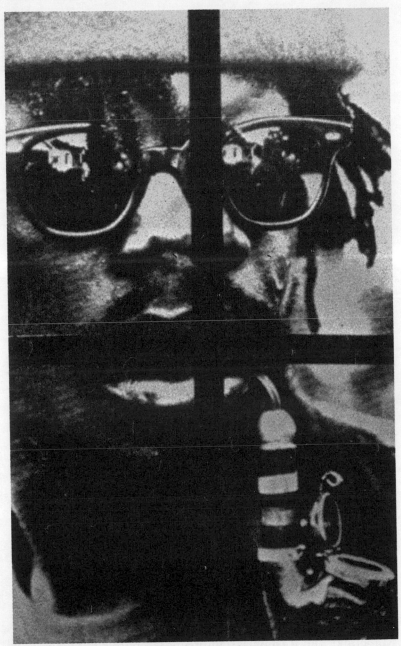

Figure 16. Black Jamaica

the island. Limited imports of American releases and the restricted airplay of such music on Jamaican radio had already made the DJ more than just the relayer of such music. To move one step back up the process, often simply by scratching the credits off the record label, and claim the sound as 'his', seemed commercially and artistically opportune. Initially, this involved only modest alterations: the DJ's style being a combination of his record selection, his booming sound system, his vocal invocations to the dancers, and his titled attributes and extravagant wardrobe. Soon, no doubt prompted by the emphasis that the sound system – frequently playing out of doors under the open sky – had to give to the rhythm and the beat to arrive at the dancers, it became a short step to a DJ format forged upon local bass rhythms and his vocal injections.

The immediate model was the American R & B style of 'scat' singing, of stringing together rhyming words and melodic verbalisation and stretching them out over the rhythms. The Jamaican DJ style, generally known as 'toasting', tended to be a rougher development. Half sung, half shouted vocal patterns that were instrumentally rather than verbally explicit, wove in and out of the loud rhythms. Denis Alcapone talks, shouts and screams his way through the organ riffs and sweet chorus of 'Ripe Cherry', reminding us that he is 'greater than Cassius Clay' and 'sweeter than Sugar Ray'. Augmenting the imported American records, rhythm tracks were soon being recorded in the newly opened Studio One and Federal Recording Studios in Kingston. These provided the essential base for the DJ's act. At this point, the DJs moved directly into record production and, pulling the whole process into their hands, the key power spot in the Jamaican record industry. Producers like Leslie Kong, Lee 'Scratch' Perry and Clement 'Coxsone' Dodd, took singers and players off the streets, gave them a lump sum for their music and, while the musicians often returned to their poverty, launched what was now their 'sound' towards the Jamaican charts.[15]

The practice of DJs 'skanking' or 'toasting' over local 'ridims' (rhythms) now gave the music an inevitable Jamaican edge. The jive talk of Prince Buster and Count Machouki, the Rastafarian impregnated patois of U Roy and

Big Youth, not only unleashed new vocal rhythms but also served to underline local inflections and concerns. The music became immediately more susceptible to the impact of what was happening elsewhere in the patois-speaking communities in Kingston and the country areas. This was openly confirmed with the rise of the Jamaican 'rude boy' in the late 1960s. The rudies, with their urban, male rebellious styles, became the central protagonists of Jamaican ska and rock steady. Ransacking Hollywood's iconography of 'bad guys', black youths in the Kingston ghettoes adopted such sobriquets as Bogart, Widmark, Eastwood and Alan Ladd. These young men lived off a street economy of hustling, petty thieving and ganja dealing, while all the time seeking to transmute American cinema into live street drama, white evil into black heroics. The musical vindication of these 'Johnny Too Bads' (the Slickers) was Prince Buster's 'Judge Dread' sentencing the rudies to 400 years imprisonment, while the cinematic one, *The Harder They Come* (1972), traced the rise of Ivan (Jimmy Cliff) from country obscurity to big city glory in a career saturated in reggae, ganja and retribution.

According to Prince Buster, the Jamaican musicians who laid down the backing tracks for the local DJs took their rhythms from 'Pocomania' (literally, 'a little madness'). Pocomania, although the more appropriate term according to Howard Johnson and Jim Pines is 'Pukkumina', is a Jamaican Afro-Christian cult involving trances and possession by spirits. Its dances, instrumental styles and rhythms have undoubtedly entered Jamaican popular music. The 'myal' religion of the Maroons – communities of escaped slaves who had preserved a long tradition of black independence – was translated into the widespread 'Kumina' and became the spiritual core of Jamaican popular culture: analogous to the role of 'voodoo' in Haiti. Again, its musical instrumentation (which apart from the ubiquitous drums used scrapers, gongs and rattles for percussion), its polyrhythms and vocal patterns, and the subjection of all these elments to the movement of dance and communal participation, seeped into the sounds that musicians, only a step away from the streets, were recording. Also of great importance were the more secular rhythms and music associated with the 'Jokkon-

Figure 17. Saturated in reggae and retribution... *The Harder They Come*

nu' street festivals and the 'buru ridims'. Buru was particularly central for Rasta music where in fact the arrangement of
drums employed is known as the 'buru set'. Buru music gives
much attention to songs supported by percussive rhythms. It
appears that these were once produced by portable percussive
instruments before the drums came to dominate the music:
over bass drum rhythms complex drum leads are played. All
these sounds and patterns, both 'religious' and 'secular', fed
into the broad current of Jamaican popular music.[16]

In Jamaica, popular religious and musical languages continually intersect, bringing the sacred and the secular into a
profound symbiosis. We can hear Clancy Eccles exhorting
God, against a chunky rock steady rhythm, to 'burn dem in
Sodom and Gomorrah', and 'beat dem with the rod of
correction' ('The Rod Of Correction'). When Ras Tafari
sentiments started to be sung by reggae singers in the late
1960s, this secular–religious, Afro-Caribbean continuum was
only further deepened and made more explicit. So, Prince
Buster's explanation, although it may have seemed a bit
fanciful at first, pointed in the appropriate direction. Beyond
the continual attempts to imitate American R & B (still going
on today in Kingston) existed the possibility for the obscured
formation of local musical forces to emerge publicly. Out of
this came ska.

It has been frequently observed that ska, rock steady and
reggae are musics structured 'back to front' with respect to
black American R & B and soul. Putting it very crudely, with
R & B and soul the rhythmic emphasise and shifts in and
around the musical pulse tend to relate to the first and third
beats in a four beat construction, or '4/4 time'. Converting
this into a pulse chart (where the thick line and the arrows
represent the tendency to emphasis the movement of the
pulse), we find something like the following:

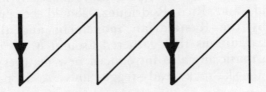

With ska, as will later also be the case with rock steady and reggae, the rhythmic emphasis is 'reversed' or 'overturned'. Falling between the regular beats, the Jamaican ska style produced a stuttering pulse as the drum beats and chattering off-beat accents of the guitar crossed each other's paths.[17] Transformed into a pulse chart, the difference with the more undulating R & B 'boogie' rhythm should be clear:

The sense of the Jamaican pulse is a stammering roll, a sort of chuck-a/chuck-a/ effect. Over this polyrhythmic musical skeleton further layers – the voice, horns, guitar riffs, additional percussion – are added.

The reason for such musical transformations is difficult to trace with any precision. Causal explanations frequently turn out to be illusory. There is evidence of a rich fabric of musical threads. Apart from the popular symbiosis of the mentioned religious and secular currents, the shuffling step of 'mento' (a musical cousin of Trinidad's calypso) also played a part. It can be heard in the music of Toots and the Maytals, in such songs as 'It's You' and 'Monkey Man'. Other connections were more unexpected. The tenor saxophonist Tommy McCook started out playing jazz, then at some time in the late 1940s he used to 'jam' with the great 'buru' drummer Count Ossie at Rasta conventions ('Nyabingi' or 'grounations'); by the early 1960s he was recording for 'Coxsone' Dodd before entering the legendary ska group the Skatalites. It was symptomatic of the fluidity of the Jamaican situation that trained musicians like McCook, the almost mythical Don Drummond, and Rico Rodriquez, should be profoundly affected by the Rastafarian movement and the Afro-Caribbean traditions that gathered around it. At the same time, such musicians also introduced new textures into the making of the ska-rock steady-reggae universe. In particular, their brass playing and its use of the 'open' major sixth and seventh chords achieved a floating, very spacey, sound quite dissimilar from the R & B 'honkers' of the period.

This sense of spaciousness, tugging away at the edges of the musical structure and evoking a presence that hangs in the gaps between the notes, was further exploited once ska's rather frantic pace was slowed down and the music permitted to stretch out in rock steady. 'Where the brass riffs had dominated the ska rhythms, in "Rock Steady" brass only appeared in the instrumentals, the tempo of the record slowed down, and the bass line became the most important feature of the rhythm' (Gayle, 1973, p. 678). As the music slowed down some of the more relaxed and smoother vocal styles of US soul found an echo in Jamaica. This can be heard in the singing of Alton Ellis, Ken Boothe, Delroy Wilson, and early recordings by the Wailers: their 'Soul Almighty' refers directly to 'Wicked Pickett'.

But rock steady also introduced a crucial home grown twist: the full emergence of the bass line as the anchor and diviner of what would later become reggae. Rock steady, and then reggae, brought the booming electric bass into the front line to act as a leading voice and so turned the previous musical frame 'inside out'. Reggae in particular, with the judicious use of rests and unusual phrasings, fully explored the sense of the bass lead. A notable example is the Wailers' 'Concrete Jungle' (it can be heard on the *Catch A Fire* LP, 1973). The centrality of the bass 'voice', with its pauses often filled in by improvised percussion, means that the 'melody and rhythm of a tune is continued, but in a highly masked and abbreviated form' (Clarke, 1980, p. 133). The musical centre of gravity has now shifted deeper down into the 'roots' of the music, removed from the more apparent features of simple melody and obvious rhythm.[18] As Linton Kwesi Johnson reminds us: 'bass history is a moving/is a hurting black story'.

Ethnic dialogues: skinhead

Meanwhile, in Britain Lee Goptal had set up B & C Records to distribute Jamaican music. That was in 1964, the year that

Millie Small had a British ska hit with 'My Boy Lollipop'. B
& C quickly established a series of shop outlets in the major
West Indian community areas of London. Clubs like the
Roaring Twenties club in Carnaby Street, the Four Aces in
North London, the 007 in the East End, and the Ram Jam
Club in Brixton, became important venues for black youth
intent on absorbing the latest sounds from 'JA'. Local sound
systems, with their massive bass speaker cabinets and home-
soldered amplification systems, began to appear. In 1967,
Brixton's Ram Jam Club hosted the Soul Vendors, the rock
steady 'supergroup' of the year.

It was at this point that the Jamaican 'rude boy' and his
black British compatriot encountered in the frenzied rhythms
of ska another sector of dissatisfied youth. These were young,
white and working class. The surly refusal of the utopian
embrace of progressive music by the skinheads was an
uncomfortable reminder of some of the immediate limits of the
counter-culture's ambitions. This is how George Melly vividly
captures the clash towards the end of the 1960s:

> At the open-air concerts groups of C-stream fifteen year old
> drop outs stalked aggressively around the fringes of the
> enormous hairy crowd. They were surgically clean, wore
> their hair cropped, brown boots, and jeans at half-mast
> with braces. They were looking for 'bother' and seemed to
> sense that pop music, once a music cutting across class
> barriers, was now the property of an intelligentsia (however
> embryonic), a potential 'them'.
>
>   (Melly, 1972, p. 122)

A few years previously the mods had looked to black R & B,
soul music and the urban American negro for style and
inspiration. Now, around 1967–8, while Derrick Morgan was
singing 'Tougher Than Tough' and Dandy Livingstone warning the black miscreants in 'Rudy A Message To You', the
skinheads signed a brief contract with Jamaican reggae and
the rude boy style.

The cool and argot of black youth was avidly observed. The
'handed down' appearance of clothing (those half-mast trousers) and the cropped hair known as the 'skiffle' were keenly

imitated. Then, attached to such disturbingly archaic props as proletarian boots and braces, it was all rolled into a distinctive 'skin' style. But it was above all the music, as Carl Gayle notes, that initially held this turbulent alliance together:

> ...by the latter half of 1968, when 'Neville the Musical Enchanter' could claim to be the boss system, he was playing almost anywhere around London regardless of travelling distances, and his supporters grew in numbers and they were most keen and awesome. Most areas he played were white, and not surprisingly many whites came along to hear the sounds.
>
> (Gayle, 1973, p. 678)

Out of this period came such skinhead anthems as the Pioneers' 'Long Shot (Kick De Bucket)', Desmond Dekker's 'The Israelites' and 'It Mek', and the Upsetters', 'Return Of Django'. Such was the support for reggae at the time that it has never since touched the level of British chart success achieved in 1969.

The stylised 'deviancy' that reggae embodied for certain members of black and white British youth (predominantly male) found a focus in the apparently common language of Jamaican rhythms and the Kingston rude boy. The hopeless machismo of the skins then frequently proceeded to beat out its meaning on any unfortunate Pakistani, hippy or gay who happened to stumble across its iron path. The skinhead gangs were known as 'crews', and were widespread in London's East End and the Midlands. They patrolled a restricted area and vision, tightly bound not simply by the chains of class and urban life in a landscape of declining jobs and possibilities, but also through a more precise symbolic attachment to parochial localism and racial chauvinism: 'white roots'. The skinhead culture although doomed in its extremism was by no means outcast in its sentiments. It proudly displayed a rigid crystallisation of views that elsewhere were quietly endorsed and 'common-sensically' applied in the daily business of being 'British'.[19]

It was hardly surprising that the honeymoon between 'rudy' and 'skin' proved to be brief (1969–71). After all, the

skinhead subculture represented a desperate assertion, drawing upon the most marginal prospects for its own future: the
opposed symmetry of defiant black youth and a rigid image of
a 'traditional' white working class that had in the meantime
been extensively remade. It was inevitable that this harsh
fusion of impossible extremes would quickly fracture, and the
skinheads withdraw into their final bastion of 'white ethnicity'
(Hebdige, 1982). The snapping of the links between skinhead
and reggae was precipitated by the effects of Jamaican
cultural change. These injected into the particular conditions
of black British youth, and the sense of reggae within their
culture, a new edge and sensibility. The brief dialogue was
now over. The white 'rudies' were out in the cold, reduced to
clutching grimly onto the ultimate tokens of an imagined
'authenticity': the depressing streets of their own 'white'
territory.

Scuffling in Ladbroke Grove

'de bredrin dem stan-up
outside a HIP CITY
as usual, a look pretty;
dem a laaf big laaf
dem a talk dread talk
dem a shuv and shuffle dem feet
soakin in de sweet MUSICAL BEAT.'
                    (Linton Kwesi Johnson, 'Yout Scene', 1975)

While in Jamaica the ghost of Marcus Garvey, ganja smoke,
and the Ras Tafari movement hung heavy in the air over
reggae right from its early ska days, in Britain all this was less
apparent, more distant. The passage in the 1950s and 1960s of
West Indians to yet another country, this time the colonial
'Mother Country', also threatened to widen the gap between
the experience of Afro-Caribbean popular culture and the
optimistic hopes these black immigrants invested in British
possibilities. By the 1970s many of these hopes had faded. If
older generation Jamaicans had adopted a defensive stoicism,
young blacks were increasingly embittered. Forced back upon

internal resources, Britain's West Indian communities rediscovered the tough sinews of their Caribbean past. The once
secluded power of Ras Tafari began to be translated into a
wider politico-cultural populism.

Second generation West Indian youths – many British born
and bred – began to turn away from their parents' attempted,
but largely foiled, efforts to enter the tepid mainstream of
British society. This reaction was based on a realism produced
in the hardening temper of the late 1960s and 1970s. It had
become clear by then that racism and racial discrimination
was neither personal nor accidental, it was a structural
problem. Black youth became increasingly aware of its profound dilemma: caught between a fragmented colonial inheritance and a present that was daily denied.

A new response had to be found; one more effective than a
low profile resignation. At the outset, the tendency was most
obviously to drift, and to drift into the spaces where meaningful action, rather than the self-obliteration daily demanded at
school and work, might still be possible (Pryce, 1979). To
evacuate the family and the home, meant to move out on the
streets by day and the all-night cafés and 'crash pads' by
night. The twilight zone of the hustlers and petty crime
afforded one possibility. The covert economy of the street –
marihuana, stolen goods, prostitution – became even more
enticing after receiving a stylish youth revamping borrowed
from the flash Jamaican 'rudies'. (A style quite distinct from
the older, sharply dressed, US black urban hustler or 'pimp'
style.) As events turned out, this ostentatious street option
was to prove just as officially unwelcomed in Britain, where
the whole phenomenon was conveniently daubed with the
explosive label of 'mugging', as it had been in Jamaica.

Meanwhile, as early as 1968, in his notorious 'rivers of
blood' speech, Mr Enoch Powell had laid his hands on the
'highly inflammable' theme of race. His argument, that in the
racial tensions created by black immigration lay the seeds of
Britain's crisis and potential downfall, was to become one of
the most strident and dramatic of public themes in the next
decade. It was one to which many white Britishers instinctively responded.

While *The Harder They Come* was playing to packed cinemas

in Brixton, Britain's persistent economic crisis deepened. Slowly, but irreversibly, the whole post-1945 political settlement of public welfare and full employment began to fall apart. Black youth found itself doubly hit. As the first to be unemployed or never employed, he or she quickly discovered the racist edge of the growing crisis. As a symbolic figure, marshalled to explain the causes of that situation, black youth found itself slithering on a tilting social and political terrain where the tributaries of British 'common sense' ran into the common sump of a full blown racism. The public presence of young unemployed black males lounging about on the streets of Britain's decaying inner city zones was obviously too opportune a sign for the crisis watchers to let slip by.

In such a climate, the step to closer surveillance was quickly taken. The 'law and order' question had already experienced a long and neurotic history in Conservative Party Conferences in the 1950s and 1960s (Gamble, 1974). But now, as diverse forms of social unrest were unceremoniously rushed through an escalating set of definitions and the full majesty of the law brought to bear on them, it became inter-party property. Within this staged resurrection of governmental authority the seeds that Enoch Powell and others had scattered in their missionary zeal in the 1960s were now reaped. Race and law and order soon dovetailed into a rich political reservoir for both Conservative and Labour governments, now confronted by a deepening crisis in authority and forced to seek a popular consensus that would legitimate their rule.

Those who were deemed to fall outside the increasingly required deference for this narrowed authority – strikers, squatters, black militants, marihuana smokers, 'bolshie' students – found their 'antisocial' behaviour tackled with different methods and in different moments. Being both structurally, publicly and racially exposed, black youth was amongst the first to feel the full brunt of these adverse social winds. Whereas in more private domains, in the exploration of alternative life-styles, the reactions were initially more sporadic and distanced, out in the exposed sectors of the economy and the grim streets of urban unemployment they were immediate and almost inevitably brutal.[20] The inward march of social reaction left those at the periphery as the first to absorb the discipline of these changing times. Black youth saw before it the nets of the police, the judiciary and the press, and the construction, through the 'mugging' panic of 1972–3, of the insidious formula of black youth = unemployment = street crime.[21]

Through mounting confrontation with the arm of the law, as the 'symptoms' of Britain's crisis came to be monitored and checked, young black Britons were reminded that each of them had 'better think of your future, else you'll wind up in jail' (Dandy Livingstone, 'Rudy A Message To You'). In fact, many 'rude boy' songs were anti-rude, full of dire warnings for those who pursued their evil ways. Both Prince Buster and Dandy Livingstone expressed dismay in their songs for the turmoil caused in the black communities by the violence of the rude boys against other inhabitants in shantytown. An alternative strategy for living in the urban jungle, one that was both more subtle and more complete, would have to be found. Once again, a besieged black culture turned to the secret codes and subterrranean forces of its music. It was in Rastafarianism, its music, symbology and cultural promise , that black British culture rediscovered a 'reality' diverse from the paltry offers of an illusory integration or the localised victories of a vainglorious rude boy defiance.

'Rastaman vibration'

'From the first day on which an African was captured then blessed by some swaggering fifteenth century Portuguese cleric and consigned to a terrible Atlantic crossing, there have been two Africas. There is the geographical entity, with its millions of social realities, and there is the Africa of the exiled Negro's mind, an Africa compounded of centuries of waning memories and vanquished hopes translated into myth.'

(David Jenkins, 1975)

The Jamaican rude boy had briefly provided sections of British black youth with a rebellious model that was subsequently reinforced by the 'pressure' of jobless inner city life in streets increasingly subject to policing. The Rasta, whose life-style had also affected the Jamaican rudies, proposed to overcome the limits of that situation with a global strategy whose own internal 'logic' would be the measure of the world. Where the rudies had convinced themselves to be 'too bad' and 'wicked' in their relations with society, the Rastas refused the prevailing terms of reference and replaced them with a set they had coined themselves. The rude boy had attempted to twist commonsense definitions in the hope of finding a localised negotiation within the spaces of ghetto life, the Rastas decided on a point blank refusal of that reality.

The acute poverty and abject colonial and 'post-colonial' exploitation of a Third World country are among the deeply embedded sources of Ras Tafari and the highly charged symbolism of Garveyism. Garvey's shipping company, Black Star Line – founded in the 1920s and celebrated fifty years later in Fred Locks' 'Black Star Liner' – was to carry the black dispossessed back to their African homeland. At the more enduring, metaphorical level, it was Marcus Garvey who was accredited with having identified Ethiopia as the promised land of the black diaspora. But beyond these public traces, in the hidden cultural undergrowth of popular Jamaica, were further Afro-Caribbean traces – the Maroon traditions, Kumina, the buru rituals – that entwined around the new articulate focus of Ras Tafari. Ras Tafari transformed the inheritance of this ubiquitous 'black spirituality' into a material case against racial, cultural and social oppression. At this point the distinction between 'religious' and secular programmes comes to be obliterated and replaced by a movement towards a pan-African political populism.

A strategic study of the Bible as the key to unlocking the 'reason' for 'suffering' has made the Rasta a new authority on this central text in Jamaican popular culture. It, together with the use of the patois and the medium of music, has formed a black 'community' capable of twisting crucial white cultural forms 'inside out'. The one-time slave now speaks rebellion through what were once his master's texts and cultural property: his language, his religion, his music. The Rastas look to Africa and Ethiopia as their Zion. It provides the symbolic means to trace out the cultural map of black

Jamaica's past, present and future. It represents the moment when the Rastas, and potentially all black people who choose to follow Ras Tafari 'reasoning', become 'liberated from the obscurity of themselves' (Nettleford, 1972, p. 47). The displayed tokens of the Rastas' devoutness or 'dread' – the long plaited 'locks' (an imagined tribute to the style of East African tribesmen, or more simply the 'natural' growth of hair), the woolly hats or 'tams' in the red, green and gold of Ethiopia, the strict dietary laws ('I-tal' food), and the centrality accorded the smoking of marihuana, 'ganja' or the 'Wise Weed' – were gradually transferred from a small group of apparently religious eccentrics into an influential popular current.

This dramatic scenario of black people as dispossessed Africans – robbed of their culture and themselves – was also to give an important eschatological edge to how many young West Indians in Britain perceived their own 'exile' in 'Babylon'. For some, the increasing threat of structural unemployment was symbolically transformed into the holy stigmata of those who had decided to withdraw their labour from supporting the Babylonian system. More extensively, with 'Jah' in everyone – 'I is I' – and through the holy weed ganja being one in 'I', an enforced exile was confidently experienced as a passage towards black redemption. By the mid-1970s, when the 'pressure' on black British youth was increasingly combined with the 'dread' style (if not always the full Rastafarian commitment), it was as though a black 'righteousness' was being paraded among the mounting debris of Britain's decay.

On the racial front, while the 'reserve army of labour' (largely composed of blacks, women and youth) were being shunted into irreversible unemployment, a popular groundswell was being mobilised through a series of despatches from politicians and the popular press. These ranged from competition for a diminishing number of jobs to that engendered species the 'British way of life'. The drastic simplification of complex issues and a twisted imperial inheritance slipped easily into the facile rhetoric of racism, 'precisely because the discourses of the British Nation and the British people are *racially exclusive*' (Gilroy, 1982, p. 278). It was 'tidy racist slogans' that provided the 'neat' explanations for unemployment, city decay, falling social services and a loss in British status; such slogans connected the immediate and the experiential to the great comforting themes of 'nation and race' (Green, 1979). This febrile mythology must have seemed to have been grotesquely confirmed when Rastas ventured out onto the streets of British cities with their strange hair, weird tongue and incomprehensible rhythms.[22] Such a direct affront to British common sense was destined to be the object of disbelief; a form of 'madness' for those, both black and white, who refuse its logic, but which for many black Jamaicans now exists as the unique key to an internal sanity.[23]

It is in this overall context that the secret languages of reggae reappear in deepened form. The response of black British youth to the frosty face of white Britain, and the connection of that response to the arguments of the Ras Tafari movement, were ultimately most effectively sealed together across the common rhythm and space of reggae. It has remained the most effective cultural force in a climate of surveillance, policing and outright reaction. The change in aim amongst black British youth from the limited prospects of the street to a millenarian promise was largely conducted under the banner of reggae and across the catalystic figure of Bob Marley. It was in and around the cultural triumph of Marley that the 'sounds' and the 'pressure' were increasingly fused.

In 1973, the ambitiously produced *Catch A Fire* LP, balancing the more direct 'roots' music on *Burning* (also 1973), was released in Britain. Two years later and Bob Marley emerged from a British tour as 'the archetypal Rastafarian menace, solidly entrenched in the mainstream of English–Jamaican mythology' (Cashmore, 1979, p. 119). Pulling together in a reggae pulse Jamaica's slave past ('Catch A Fire'), her present ('400 Years', written by Peter Tosh, then of the Wailers), and her future ('Rasta Man Chant'), the music tended towards the relentless suspension of immediate temporalities, 'thereby taking the participants into a "timeless" state – and perhaps an apprehension of the divine' (Middleton, 1972, p. 41). Marley encountered not simply commercial success with Island Records but also a cultural triumph. This is well caught in Ernest Cashmore's description of the Marley personae. 'It would not be exaggerating to suggest that Bob Marley was to the seventies wave of English Rastas what Marcus Garvey was to the first Jamaican cultists of the 1930s. He attracted attention, mobilised immense interest and disseminated ideas which were in all probability, unheard of by many young West Indians before his rise to fame' (Cashmore, 1979, p. 108).

But despite Marley's undeniable success and the signings to British record labels of numerous reggae acts (the Maytals, Burning Spear, the Heptones, Peter Tosh, Keith Hudson, Third World, U Roy, the Mighty Diamonds – nearly all on Island or Virgin), the Rastafarian aura now surrounding reggae probably increased the distance between it and the rest of British pop. The explicit and proud negritude of the Ras Tafari movement effectively locked out aspiring white 'rastas'. The outcome was that while some white musicians dabbled a bit in reggae – Eric Clapton illustrating the prevailing distribution of cultural powers by outselling Bob Marley in Jamaica with Marley's own 'I Shot The Sheriff', the Stones recording Clancy Eccles' 'Ripe Cherry' – the contact remained sporadic. The significant exception was to be the more genial inspiration that reggae's musical culture gave to those future white 'exiles', the punks. It is only after punk, in the closing years of the decade, that reggae begins to register in a more insistent manner in other areas of pop.

So, in the mid-1970s, the vast majority of reggae sounds, not occupying the 'superstar' bracket of a Bob Marley or a Peter Tosh, continued to be locked away inside black British youth culture. The majority of British record shops were unwillingly to entertain the idea that they should serve as listening posts for the black dispossessed on wet afternoons. High Street record shops rarely stocked reggae and black youth went elsewhere in search of their sounds. In the middle of the decade they went to the Estate Club in Tottenham hosted by DJ Sir Biggs, or 'stepped ' to the sounds of Sir Nyah at the Cobweb Club in Hornsey, DJ Jah Suffera at the Metro Club in Ladbroke Grove, or Mr Bees in Peckenham. The outlet for reggae records were shops exclusively devoted to the genre situated in the West Indian communities. These, with their sound systems directed outwards onto the street, released the latest sounds of Big Youth, Dillenger, Denis Brown, Fred Locks and Sugar Minott, on the ears of the black 'sufferers' in 'Inglan's' Babylon.

Beneath the flurry of interest surrounding Bob Marley the more underground channels of a British reggae scene developed, largely unobserved by white audiences, and in complete isolation from the major record companies.[24] It is a strong reminder that the cultural power and resilience of reggae has been formed and sustained through the interlocking themes of race and racism. Certainly, in the formation of a British school of reggae, the progressive hardening of racial lines that characterises the 1970s played a significant part. The dramatisation of the spectre of black crime around the mugging scare organised by the police and the press in the early 1970s aided the rise in racist fever as well as supplying further fuel to Mr Enoch Powell's bloody prohecies of race war in Britain. The explicitly racist platform of the fascist National Front party, and a growing acquiescence in accepting the drift, if not the more excessive rhetoric, of its arguments, both inside and outside Parliament, was a grim warning for the future of the black community.

Accompanying this, on the doorstep in the black inner city areas, more traditional police procedures were being replaced by the brusque commando antics of the Special Patrol Group (SPG) and a harsher, inevitably confrontational, style of policing. The 'Suspected Persons Act' ('SUS') was liberally applied to arrest black youths and, implicitly, to clear the increasingly unemployed black poor, the potential 'muggers', off their only stake to 'the life', that is, off the streets. The acrimonious battle between black youth and the police that concluded the 1976 Notting Hill Carnival and the major urban race riot that seized the St Paul's district in Bristol four years later, were the forseeable consequences of such 'endless pressure'.

It was in this highly charged context that a long tradition of black clubs, Saturday night parties or 'shebeens', local sound systems, small independent record labels, and the subterranean success of imported Jamaican records, took on an increasingly distinctive shape as the 1970s progressed. Operating out of London, Birmingham, and other urban centres, labels such as Pam, Daddy Kool, Ethnic Flight and Black Wax built on the earlier success of the Trojan label (declared bankrupt in 1975), and accounted for something in the region of 25 per cent of British reggae sales. British reggae bands like Misty, Aswad and Steel Pulse began to supplement the longer established sounds of the Cimarons and Matumbi. No doubt encouraged by the public success of Bob Marley, and the sharpened cultural focus that external racism and internal Rastafarianism had brought to reggae, British reggae began to emerge from clubs like the Bouncing Ball in Peckenham, blighted inner city zones such as Birmingham's Handsworth, and unknown recording studios like the Gooseberry Studios in Gerrard Street, Soho, and later Easy End studios in the East End.

While generally shunned by a wider audience, reggae continued to expand its musical layers over the persistent 'roots' bass line. The apparent division by the mid-1970s between the hedonism of 'lovers rock' and a serious, committed, ethnic style was actually belied by the ever present bass pulse and the marriage of both 'sweet' and 'roots' reggae in the musical interplay of 'dub' (Gilroy, 1982). 'Dub' comes out of the highly inventive approach to modern recording facilities that had been pioneered by the early reggae DJs, many of whom had later become producers. From 'toasting' over bare instrumental tracks to 'touching' the sound at every level, leaving your fingerprints all over the tape, was the next logical move. Beginning as the instrumental B sides of the song on the A side, the record producer, often drawing on a knowledge of how the DJs were using the music at dances, began to step in and 'cut up' the sound. The vocal was removed or else heavily 'treated', while the instrumental 'voices' were played with, brought forward or set back, dramatically underlined by a ringing echo, or made to drift in and out of phase. The original song had been taken apart and then reformed as a fresh sonorial experience: an effective vindication of reggae's continual 'deconstruction' of inherited musical forms and manners of music-making.

Exploiting multiple track recording studios, plus a whole artillery of electronic effects (echo, reverberation, phasers, etc.), producers Joe Gibbs, King Tubbys, Herman Chin-Loy,

Clement Dodd, and Augustus Pablo, began turning out a series of rich dub tapestries (see the Discography). Bass, drums, guitars and horns were mixed down into swirling sound patterns, the 'voices' phased in and out, rhythms chopped, intensified, suspended and elongated. This highly inventive recording style, later influential on New York 'rap' and soul music in the early 1980s, once again demonstrated that a particular set of cultural relations could successfully bend and discipline the seemingly indifferent technology of commodity production into a precise musical instrument. The inevitable tension that arises between Jamaican reggae, the 'roots', and its gradual immersion in international commercial structures after Marley's success, is neatly complemented by the mixture of 'natural' and 'artificial' sounds that echo one another in the dub process.

If dub and the productions of Prince Far I, Dr Alimantado and Augustus Pablo initially found no favour with white pop music or a space on the radio (a rare exception was Rupie Edwards' 'Ire Feelings' at the end of 1974), this was not the case in British black clubs. Here, in an atmosphere charged with 'Africa', with the Rastafarian reversal of white time, order and history, where the layers of reggae, race and impending retribution were laid on so thickly as to become indistinguishable, dub's multi-textured sound had its home (Hebdige, 1979, pp. 37–9).

Out beyond the immediate reaches of dub and black British youth culture we can travel on a trajectory that with hindsight will deposit us in the post-punk landscape of the late 1970s. The white 'dub' of Public Image Ltd, the Birmingham 'toasting' of the Beat and UB 40, the 2-Tone 'ska' revival of the Specials and the Selecter, the 'bleached' reggae of the Police, and the music of those white 'rudies', the Clash, finally acknowledge the deep reverberations of Jamaican reggae in the hinterlands of white British pop.

Chapter 7

Urban Soundscapes, 1976–

Between the autumn of 1976 and the summer of 1977, a particular music, a highly visible subcultural style, and an increasingly public crisis, momentarily appeared to fuse together. Punk burst upon an unsuspecting London and quickly acquired the dark propensity to serve as a new 'folk devil': a dramatic illustration of the alarming advancement of Britain's diseased state. Marshalled by the popular press, television, radio and public comment, punks were set on a luridly lit stage with a scenario that unequivocally proclaimed social collapse: 'the savage pop music of rebellious youth' (*Sunday Mirror*), 'dole queue rock' (*New Society*), 'a commercial exploitation of sex and depravity' (Marcus Lipton, MP), 'the negation of culture' (Mr Brooks-Patridge, Chairperson of Greater London Council's Art Committee).

For many, then, punk was an all too obvious phenomenon. Others attempted to locate behind the nebulous symbolisation of violence and outrage that surrounded the subculture a deeper political meaning: was it fascist or anarchist? This query undoubtedly bent pop music to a greater deal of political attention and commentary than previously. (A glance at any issue of *New Musical Express* in this period will confirm this.) But finally the signals were confusing, the signs strangely flat and reluctant to respond to received interpretations. The swastika peeping out from under the Karl Marx T-shirts; a punk's pallid body perforated by safety pins, draped in pvc and locked in a dog collar; those glassy, amphetamine-blocked eyes staring out from beneath spiky shocks of garishly dyed hair: these were the disturbing signs that briefly captured the horrified fascination of the outside

175

world. But they were signs that refused to speak in a recognisable language. Punk's infuriating 'dumbness', those 'blank' faces frozen in the press shot, removed it from available referents. Punk could only be defined negatively, as an absence, a perverse void; its internal semantics remained unknown.

This is only one, and the most obvious, event in the fabric of pop's recent history. Many effects, overlaps and intentions were bound together under the volatile indications of punk and its aftermath. Its refusal to respond to available definitions, its deliberate opting out of surrounding realities, can be considered a founding link in a chain that subsequently connects the most disparate musics and protagonists. Punks and 'new romantics', electro-dandies and musical 'deconstructionists' (dub, rap, post-punk 'noise'), are all part of a differentiated reworking of the inheritance of British pop culture that gestured through a mixture of languages – musical, sartorial, sexual, aesthetic – towards sharply changed perspectives. Ideas about 'street credibility', musical populism and the 'avant-garde', indiscriminately rubbed shoulders in the envelopment of the 'city'. Experiences and realities that were once securely considered separate found themselves absorbed in an accelerated expansion of urban images and codes.[1]

Releasing the unnameable

'At this point there comes into play the intonations, the particular way of pronouncing a word. Here, besides the acoustic language of sounds, there also enters the visual language of objects, of movements, of postures, of gestures, such as to prolong the significance, the physiognomy and the combinations until they become signs, and to make of these signs a type of alphabet.'

(Antonin Artaud, 'First manifesto of the theatre of cruelty')

The 'offensive' punk sound of the Sex Pistols appropriately titled 'Anarchy In the UK' was released by EMI on 26 November 1976. Almost exactly a year later, the same group's

LP, *Never Mind The Bollocks. Here's The Sex Pistols*, came out on
Virgin Records. Between these two events the musical manifesto of punk had become public knowledge. At first both the
BBC and London's Capital Radio banned all the Sex Pistols'
singles with the exception of 'Pretty Vacant'. 'Anarchy In The
UK', 'God Save The Queen' and 'Holidays In The Sun' were
all hits, however. The police, meanwhile, unsuccessfully pro-
secuted for the use of the word 'bollocks' on the LP cover.

Beneath all this official flurry a new musical circuit had
sprung up in inner London. At the 100 Club, Oxford Street;
the Roxy, Covent Garden; and the Nashville, Kensington;
young white audiences, sealed together in the sweat and noise,
underwent cultural initiation to the sounds of the Pistols, the
Clash, the Damned, the Buzzcocks, Siouxsie and the Banshees, the Slits, and X-Ray Spex.

Across a musical minimalism of frantic guitar rhythms,
resolutely untutored vocals, often 'political' lyrics, and a
robotic beat (matched by the zombied dancing of the 'pogo'),
these groups proposed the jagged cacophony of shock city in
its terminal stage. The possibility of discussing 'artistic'
qualities and 'musicianship' was brutally mauled. In punk's
almost anonymous simplicity a previous musical sense was
rudely transformed into 'nonsense'. The disbelief of the pop
music establishment was further intensified by punk's repe-
ated invocations of a populist musical technique: 'This is a
chord. This is another. This is a third. *Now form a band*' (Mark
Perry, *Sniffin' Glue*, n. 7, February 1977).

Like rock 'n' roll and skiffle in the 1950s, and beat and R &
B in the early 1960s, punk rapidly produced a major upsurge
in music-making. And from week to week, and gig to gig, the
instructive exchange between the music and its audience was
nurtured and broadcast by the 'fanzines'. These – *Sniffin' Glue*,
Ripped & Torn, *Live Wire*, *Chainsaw*, *Gun Rubber* – were home-
produced, photocopied sheets, put together with a stapler in
the bedroom, that carried gig and record reviews, lyrics and
interviews. After London, on housing estates, and in schools
and clubs in cities as diverse as Belfast and Birmingham,
Edinburgh and Bristol, there began to emerge a local punk
music and journalism.

Punk's musical genealogy – the London timbres of the early

Stones, Who and Kinks, together with the later dark America
of the Velvet Underground, Iggy Pop, the New York Dolls
and the Ramones – spoke in the sharp tones of a direct,
aggressive sound: simple in execution and intentionally polar-
ising in its effects. But punk's home-grown accents and themes
were not the latest replay of an earlier British moment or a
subsequent Americana.[2] Deliberately celebrating their location in the English metropolis, punk sought a novel intensity.
The black-tinged singing of a Mick Jagger, Rod Stewart or
Stevie Winwood was replaced by the bleached larynx of what
is best described as Johnny Rotten's or Joe Strummer's
'anti-singing'.

Punk was a strikingly 'ethnic' music. Its crude, 'home-
made' sound produced a white 'noise' that was as offensive to
more normal pop as the indecipherable 'monotony' of reggae's
rumbling bass and choppy rhythms was mysterious. An
eventual dialogue between these two margins was, as Dick
Hebdige demonstrates, by no means accidental (Hebdige,
1979). Looking to the edges of society for cultural provocation and social stigma, punks inevitably rekindled the perennial intercourse between black culture and white youth styles:
punks were 'niggers' (Richard Hell), their music 'white
reggae' (Johnny Rotten). Reggae's proud insistence on black
ethnicity and its concrete syntax of 'suffering' was a particularly attractive prospect for punks desperate to avoid the
sentimental embrace of much pop, or, the other trap, a
nebulous 'artiness'.

During the extreme summer of 1976, the wan body of punk
– clothed in tatters held together by chains, safety pins and
sticky tape – became the temporary stage of crisis, its sartorial
breakdown the apparent mirror of a moral one. But punk's
attention to the human frame, singularly concentrated in its
abrasive vocal and instrumental encounter with musical
forms, significantly turned a section of white pop back towards the ambiguities of the body: the 'forbidden' zone that
tends to be linked with black music. Apart from reggae, disco
was the other major interlocutor here. But where disco's
appeal was direct, punk's was characteristically oblique. The
body was not so much embraced as perpetually displaced – a
clothes hanger for styles, an object of deliberate abuse and

neglect, an absent source of sex and sentimentality. Simply the song titles – 'Career Opportunities', 'Oh Bondage! Up Yours!', 'Pretty Vacant', 'Rip Off', 'High Rise Living' – tell the story. While exaggerating the persistent investment of stylised identity in sexuality, all that rubber, chains and sado-masochistic imagery, punk temporarily suspended pop's regular romanticism for its own, strangely asexual, 'street' one, and provoked a certain confusion of sexual roles.

Sexism did not magically disappear. Punk continued to present itself in masculine outlines. Still, its reactive style, working on an unlikely amalgam of glam rock ambiguities, stylised differences, and not unaffected by distant echoes of Women's Liberation, also shocked into life a new conflictual female image within white pop. Emerging out of a collection of dirty macs, old school uniforms, dustbin liner skirts, stiletto heels, cosmetic masks and defiant vocals, a space for women as active protagonists within the production of the music appeared. The disturbance of the 'unnatural' voices of Siouxsie Sue, Poly Styrene, and the Slits, shattered the existing mould of female singing in pop. The slightly earlier, largely isolated, example of the American Patti Smith was now replaced by a more collective reconstruction of the white female voice.[3] This new figure did not fit easily into the traditional iconography reserved for women in pop. It was a shift, as Laura Mulvey once put it, towards the possibility of women becoming public 'makers of meaning' (Mulvey, 1975).

The musical press in the meantime could hardly choose to ignore punk's provocative presence on the London circuit, or a growing national interest in the phenomenon. The cultural shock that was sometimes generated, anticipating some of the fractures that punk was to produce elsewhere in pop, was revealingly captured in an article in *Melody Maker* at the time:

> It is this irresponsible emphasis on violence and mundane nihilism – perfectly expressed through the Sex Pistols' 'Anarchy In The UK' – that is so objectionable. An artist like Kevin Coyne, say, has, with songs like 'Turpentine' (a fierce comment on repressed violence in suburbia) and 'House on The Hill' (about a mental institution), explored

themes no less challenging or pertinent, but his work has been graced with a fine eloquence and sensibility.[4]

The initial reaction among the three major musical papers, however, was uneven. The violent directness of punk also recalled the divisive effect of rock 'n' roll. When this was noted, critical approval often followed. It inevitably produced its own partisan code of journalism:

Glen Matlock and Steve Jones plug in and Paul Cook sits behind his kit as Rotten just hangs from the mike stand, rips open a can of beer, and burns the crowd with glassy, taunting, cynical eyes. Spiky dyed red hair, death white visage, metal hanging from lobes, skinny leg strides, red waistcoat, black tie and safety pins – he looks an amphetamine corpse from a Sunday gutter press wet dream. Something thrown from the audience hits him full in the face. Rotten glares at the person who did it, lips drawn back over decaying teeth. 'Don't give me your shit', he snarls, 'because we don't mess... This first number's dedicated to a Leeds councillor, Bill Grundy and the Queen – fuck ya.[5]

This writing, with its sharp eye for detail, its dead-pan reportage of punk's provocative manner and its deliberate oversight of where the performance ends and the 'public' begins, betrays a fresh set of cultural cues.

England's dreaming

'Actually we're not into music.
Wot then?
We're into chaos.'

(A Sex Pistol)

At the outset, it was less internal musical effects and more punk's dramatic public style that aroused so much attention. The crossing of a male working-class style with art school bohemia, something which had also been centrally present in the coolly nuanced postures of the mods (but not, significantly

enough, in the proletarian skinheads or the gaudy idiosyncra-
cies of the teds), was central to punk. Only now the earlier,
subtle exchange was replaced by a wild overlap. When punk
brandished class credentials it studiously avoided the flat cues
of the respectable white working class. With its tattered
clothing, public swearing and spit, it chose the marginalised
vestments of the urban damned: the lumpen-proletariat. Such
constructs, and the gestures towards analogies in Rastafarianism and reggae music, did not obliterate the presence of class
in punk's make-up. But the symbolic labour involved alerts
the external eye to a novel complexity, a 'shocking' reworking
of 'culture' and 'class'. Proud of its 'dumbness', punk was yet
the most articulate of subcultures: anti-art in intention it
adopted a politics of ruptural aesthetics; denying the prevailing sense of 'class' and 'politics', it offered a most explicit
social radicalism.

But if punk did not directly represent the sonorial rebound
of class, neither was it merely a glib commercial ruse, a vulgar
con dreamed up by the Sex Pistols's manager Malcolm
McLaren. McLaren's inspired management of punk's leading
group has often been linked to the Dada-inspired logic of the
International Situationists. It was an image later reinforced
by McLaren himself in the Pistols' cinematic obituary, *The
Great Rock 'n' Roll Swindle* (1980).[6] But Malcolm McLaren
('cash from chaos') was only one of the 'authors' of punk.
Between the subculture and the Situationists there existed less
personalised links, brought together in a common programme
to subvert the passive society of 'boredom'. Within existing
social bondage there may well be 'no future', but there always
remained the possibility of the perverse gesture; the moment
when the imagination takes over to reveal 'an oasis of horror
in a desert of boredom' (Baudelaire).[7]

Punk's pronounced Dada streak was to be discovered,
beyond the self-conscious statements of Malcolm McLaren
and Bernie Rhodes, then manager of the Clash, in the rich
chaos of punk's everyday style. Here were the slogans daubed
on the cultural fatigues of punk's battle dress: DESTROY.
ANARCHY. Here, a passive public was displaced by those
who had constructed a 'situation'. Here were the 'livers'
seeking to break the invisible fetters of a complacent environ-

Figure 18. Recycled histories and sartorial cut-up: Johnny Rotten

ment. The Dadaist logic of sucking in the trivia, the rubbish and the cast-offs of the world and then stamping a new meaning on the chaotic assemblage was there in both punk's music and sartorial regime. Earlier subcultural styles, like earlier musics, were 'cut-up', mixed and re-signiffied. Drawing on elements taken from the diverse wardrobes of the teds, the mods and the skinheads, the previous rigidity of these styles was transformed into new, flexible options: greased quiffs alongside closely cropped heads, mini skirts with suspendered stockings, Dr Marten boots besides winkle-pickers (Hebdige, 1979, p. 26). It was precisely the unnatural synthesis, the 'inauthentic' collage, that was paraded.

Meanwhile, the media's expectations of punk's outrage were soon gratified. The case of the Sex Pistols swearing on Thames Television's Bill Grundy Show – 'Uproar as viewers jam phones', *Daily Mirror* – was only the first in a series of well-publicised incidents. Packers at EMI's Hayes record pressing plant refused to handle the Pistols' first record, 'Anarchy In The UK'. Then the press attempted to stage a punks versus teds battle as a revival of the mods and rockers clashes of thirteen years previously. A girl was blinded in one eye by broken glass at a punk concert. Johnny Rotten was physically assaulted in an attempt to slash the 'face' of punk. With all this negative reaction around punk even the record companies began to get cold feet. First EMI, and then A & M, cancelled their contracts with the Sex Pistols, paying out thousands of pounds in compensation for their broken agreements.[8]

The outcome was that punk found itself drenched in violence and surrounded by public outrage. Like all previous subcultures, punk was inevitably the object of public stares and reproach, but this time the invectives did not move only in one direction. Breaking the cycle of insult and condemnation, punk not only adopted this public curse – 'punks like to be hated' (a punk) – but proceeded to play it back at the media in clothing and musical 'insults', and in the sexual aberrations suggested by its fetishistic closet of pvc, rubber and bondage clothing. The punk universe perversely echoed the official cries of 'crisis', while emphasising a sinister off-beat of wasted urban styles that locked together the highly disruptive themes

of sex and violence: the provocative explicitness of the name
Sex Pistols really summed it up.

The passage from punk to the national headlines only makes
sense when some of the wider rhythms and currents of the late
1970s are also acknowledged. Then the sensationalism and
shock surrounding the subculture and its music acquires a
further layer of sense, an unsuspected texture of indications.
But at this point we have to tread carefully in order to avoid a
self-defeating clarity where the sense of punk is 'flattened' out,
or simply evaporates altogether. After all, punk was not
directly a response to anything; its own rhetoric and practice
was largely built around an absence, a refusal to be defined.
This 'refusal', however, whether consciously or involuntarily,
was a gesture that existed on the obverse side of the public
representations of 'crisis' and political emergency.

A 'punk future' is how a *Daily Mirror* editorial referred to
the mass exodus of school leavers into unemployment in June
1977, a generation 'turning sour before our very eyes'; punk as
the symbol of crisis. With the seams apparently coming
undone there was the danger of anarchy, or worse. For a brief
moment, the blanched, staccato features of London's punks
were transformed into the shock troops of an advancing wave
of chaos. While elsewhere Britons were being exhorted to steel
themselves for a long, hard haul through the crisis, it was clear
that this new threat could not be permitted to pass uncon-
tested. When, in the midst of the Royal Jubilee celebrations,
the Anarchy Tour of the Sex Pistols and the Clash was
discovered to be on tour, many town councils and university
authorities duly denied this alien host access to their premises.
Official language was acquiring a shriller tone, and the public
consensus, increasingly sensitised to unwelcome change, was
easily shocked into rigidity.

The dismantling of the 'Welfare State', record levels of
unemployment, the rumbling of Scottish and Welsh nationalism, the drawn out war in Northern Ireland, growing racial
friction, and then urban rioting in Brixton, Toxteth, and other
hot spots in the summer of 1981, is a growing list of dramatic
reminders of a crisis that seems destined to be prolonged.[9]
Despite this mounting succession of shock waves, the perverse

insularity of a popular conservatism – a particular 'common sense', or 'Englishness' – tenaciously clings to institutions and perspectives that seemed fit for embalming a century ago. Encouraged, rejuvenated and extended over the last two decades around such mobilising points as 'race' and 'law and order', this popular humus has recently been radically re-tilled under Mrs Thatcher's direction. A right-wing ascendancy with a rich idealism and global grasp, rooted in the institutions and experiences of everyday life, has swept away the narrow pragmatism of previous Conservative *and* Labour governments, replacing it with the prospect of 'Englishness'. It appears both 'modern' and attractively invigorating in its drastic boldness, and yet successfully draws upon the deepest of sentiments and 'traditions'.[10] A renewed inheritance of the 'island race' (Winston Churchill), it has been further stamped with historical warranty by the public revival of the British Crown around the Royal Jubilee (1977), the Royal Wedding (1981), and the triumph of 'principled nationalism' – the staged military epic cruelly enacted in the war over the Falklands in the spring of 1982.

In this rigid scenario, while the ship of state lets down anchor into the traditional sentiments that have sturdied its frame in the past, the moment of punk and its smouldering after-effects may seem only a peripheral and transitory side-show. But, back in 1976, punks did in their own way begin a sharp interrogation of existing contexts. Through their music and stylistic commitment, they suggested and enlarged the spaces for subversive cultural 'play' within the seemingly banalised heartlands of daily life. The poverty of the present was not so much rejected as regenerated. Punk proclaimed the necessity of violating the quiet, everyday script of common sense. It proposed a macabre parody of the underlying idealism of 'Englishness' – that dour pragmatism that sees no future beyond the present, and no present except that inherited, apparently unmodified, from the past. By exaggerating and playing on such links until they snapped – punk's style was the amalgam of all previous subcultures, its music the summation of all rebellious youth 'noise', its social manners the perverse opposite ('I try so hard to be nice', Johnny Rotten) of 'normal' conduct – punk momentarily rubbed their inner lifelessness into local movement. More than that punk did not, and could not, achieve. But it remained a defiant manifesto whose energy has frequently illuminated much of subsequent white pop. Turning surrounding orthodoxies inside out, as it were, punk crudely, but effectively, revealed that an arbitrary, but widely accepted, order was susceptible to criticism and change.

The pulse of Africa in the body electric

In an interview with the magazine *Black Music & Jazz Review*, Harvey Fuqua, one-time singer in the 1950's black doo-wop group the Moonglows, and now a noted record producer as well as manager of the black gay disco star Sylvester, recalled those earlier days.

> We started off recording about 12 songs for Chess – on one track mind you. It wasn't like they've got 32 and 64 tracks to play with like today. They'd put the microphone right in the middle of the room and everybody stood around it, the band, the singers, everybody. If you wanted more of an instrument or singer you'd have to either move back or forward. And you didn't necessarily use drums then; you could use a telephone book and slap it. It was wild.[11]

A quarter of century has passed from the simple recording of 'doo-wop' to the technological sophistications involved in disco music and reggae dub. In that arc of time, black sounds and rhythms, which once 'seemed cabalistic, incomprehensible to the experience of Western Europe' (Joseph Conrad), have continually shadowed, intervened upon, and broken new ground for white British pop music. We have repeatedly seen how dance music is in permanent debt to Afro-American and Afro-Caribbean cultures. This was reaffirmed in the late 1970s with disco, with reggae, and with rap; but these influences also extended beyond dance, beyond white soul and funk and the rediscovery of ska, to experiments in avant-garde pop music.

In 1975, Bobby Womack released the LP *Safety Zone*. It is a record that serves as well as any other issued in the middle of the decade to follow the emergence of black disco. (Other significant examples were George McRae's 'Rock Your Baby', 1974; and Van McCoy's 'The Hustle, 1975.) Womack's vocal style, a mixture of gospel preaching, velvet soul, talk-over raps and falsetto shrieks, was accompanied by a chorus and imaginative arrangements that drew upon sparse but effective injections of brass over a basic drum/bass/wah-wah guitar section. In particular, it is with the concluding song on the LP, 'I Feel A Groove Coming On', that a disco future for soul music is exposed. After a talk-over introduction the eight-minute song settles into a looping regular tempo which is interrupted by Womack's voice and a jagged piano solo in the middle from pianist Herbie Hancock. Here is the innovative ploy of disco: the musical pulse is freed from the claustrophobic interiors of the blues and the tight scaffolding of R & B and early soul music. A looser, explicitly polyrhythmic attack, pushes the blues, gospel and soul heritage into an apparently endless cycle where there is no beginning or end, just an ever-present 'now'. Disco music does not come to a halt. It just fades out of hearing... Restricted to a three-minute single, the music would be rendered senseless. The power of disco – soon to be technologically matched with the introduction of lengthy disco-mix singles – lay in saturating dancers and the dance floor in the continual explosion of its presence.

By the mid-1970s, the New York disco scene was an overground success. At Studio 54, the Xenon, Infinity, Les Mouches, and thousands of venues outside fashionable Manhattan, the disco boom was sanctified. Among the laser beams and mirrored dancing, everyone was a 'star', a 'Saturday night hero'. But while disco offered the possibility of a democraticised spectacle, gave the night back to dancing, and reproposed the body as cultural protagonist, the disco sound went on to affect deeply the subsequent sonorial economy of the rest of pop.

Disco's apparently hypnotic aural simplicity – a looping pulse over a regular beat – was in fact the outcome of a lengthy distillation, a complex junction of several musical routes. With its 'fractured bass lines, choked rhythms and choppy brass' (Ian Hoare), the profane gospel of James

Brown in records like 'Cold Sweat' (1967), 'Mother Popcorn' (1969), and 'Superbad' (1970) had been a central force. This, and the stretching out of soul in popular black film scores, led to a greater extension in timbres and a relaxation in structure. The eclecticism of Sly Stone, the influential guitar inheritance of Jimi Hendrix, the polyrhythmic wall of sound developed by jazz trumpeter Miles Davis, and Africa/America cross-fertilisation in the Hispanic rhythms of Cuba and Puerto Rico, were all further contributions.[12] Finally, before the New York studios set the whole synthesis moving to a cosmopolitan dance beat, the 'Philly Sound' of Philadelphia's Sigma studios had already taken some important steps in fusing many of these elements together.

The condemnation of 'commercialism' which tended to greet disco music, for which the most popular sound of the decade (the 'People's music', Peter York), went by largely unremarked in significant parts of the British musical press until the end of the 1970s, does not explain the importance of its success. Disco's immediate proximity to a large dance floor public certainly encouraged a lot of commercial attention. The film *Saturday Night Fever* (1978), in particular, appeared to confirm the cynics in their judgement of the disco boom. Here was a familiar story: a white, Italo-American (shades of Fabian, Frankie Avalon *et al.*), parading as the social protagonist of a music that was unmistakably black in formation, transforms disco into a palatable white spectacle.[13]

But disco also had its 'roots'. It, too, had begun as a music from 'below': a cheap, all-night entertainment involving soul records being overlapped, phased in and out, to form an uninterrupted soundtrack for dancing urgencies and the desires of stylised romance and leisure. It was particularly among New York's minority black and gay cultures that disco had its early home – at gay clubs like the Haven, the Sanctuary, and Harlem spots such as Betterdays and This And That Gallery. According to Tony Cummings, it was around 1972 that these two cultures began to intermingle in shared dancing venues, and a year later *Billboard* introduced the term 'disco hit'.[14] The meeting between gay and black cultures around the erotic centrality of the dancing body was an important contemporary parallel, at the time largely ignored, to glam rock's more coldly intellectual confusion of male sexual stereotypings.[15]

In Britain, it has always been dancing, not the radio or other media, that has permitted the principal access to black musics and cultures. In the 1970s, it was once again in Britain's clubs and dance halls that the music of BT Express, Disco Tex, the Fatback Band, Carol Douglas and Gloria Gaynor was taken over by both gay culture and wider crowds of dancers.

> Discos have been fundamentally very important on the growth of black music acceptance in Britain. Maybe the radio would have picked up on soul again without discos. But certainly discos *extended* the '70s soul boom. For one thing, there are a lot of black music records which are made first and foremost FOR discos and just don't get radio play even if they become huge in the British clubs.[16]

The fact that disco became an extremely successful commercial sound does not demonstrate that commerce was able to direct and determine the reception and use of the music. Nor could the rebound have been foreseen as disco seeped into other areas of pop, into reggae, into a black British school of funk (Linx, Junior Giscombe), into varying shades of pale funk (Haircut 100, Funkapolitan, Rip Rag and Panic), and into the white electro-dance music of the 1980s.[17] As we have repeatedly seen elsewhere, even the most tightly controlled commercial recording is finally unable to prescribe its eventual response. Disco, with its flood of weekly record releases, its domination of dance, its sartorial fashions and films, was virtually an industry in itself; but it was no exception to the uncertain rules of cultural consumption.

And then the other side of disco still remains: in the dance frenzy, different black musics – disco, reggae and rap – continue to appropriate modern sound reproduction and in the process successfully reassert oral street cultures within an electronic medium. Whether it is the disco DJ building up layers of sounds on the turntables, the reggae dub masters at the console, or the smart microphone chatter of the rappers, all three illustrate the potential of modern technology to re-present, to simulate specific 'roots' in the making of contemporary urban music.

'Rap' stands at the other extreme from the sophisticated use of studio gadgetry employed in disco and reggae. In New York, towards the close of the 1970s, young black males in the same culture that spawned spray-can graffiti artists and the acrobatics of 'break' dancing, took the simplest and most widely available devices in the recording chain – turntables and microphones – and transformed them into musical instruments in their own right. Rap is New York's 'sound system'; the black youth culture of Harlem and the Bronx successfully twisting technology into new cultural shape. Rap is sonorial graffiti, a musical spray that marries black rhythms and the verbal gymnastics of hip street talk to a hot DJ patter over an ingenious manipulation of the turntable. First introduced to British ears by the Sugar Hill Gang's 'Rapper's Delight' (1979) and club hits such as Kurtis Blow's 'The Breaks', it is probably now most widely associated with the success of Grandmaster Flash and the Furious Five ('The Message, 1982). On a pair of turntables, previous recordings (including classical music) are phased in and out, speeded up, cross-cut and counterpointed to create an idiosyncratic soundtrack of imperative dancing rhythms over which Grandmaster Flash, J. Walter Negro, Trouble Funk, Treacherous Three, and the Zulu Nation 'check out' the English language, resetting it to ghetto-sensical rhymes, rhythms and reason.[18]

Back in Britain, apart from Bob Marley and the earlier skinhead interlude, reggae had meanwhile remained a distanced sound. Its dancing steps and off-beat emphasis never settled down into a wide acceptance. But, once again, punk was an important catalyst. Punks saw in the 'exile' of Rastafarianism, in the millennium tones of reggae, and in the concrete refusal of black British youth to recognise Authority, a composite rejection close to their own stylistic aspirations. The connection, divided by race, experiences and prospects, was largely symbolic, but it had pertinent effects upon the subsequent course of white pop music.

Johnny Rotten's publicised knowledge of reggae, revealed in interviews on London's Capital Radio and with the Rock

Against Racism paper *Temporary Hoarding*, and the Clash regularly including reggae material in their repertoire, was further extended by the playing of reggae between live acts at punk venues. The Rastafarian Don Letts was resident DJ at the Roxy during its punk heyday, making the 8mm film *The Original Punk Movie* there, and as one of the organisers of Rock Against Racism described this type of interchange: 'Reggae is so laid back and sort of calculated whereas punk is wild and energetic. It works fantastically well at gigs in terms of getting a sort of breather and then getting into really moving around.'[19]

Such exposure did help to give reggae and native black musicians a wider, that is, white, audience. Groups such as Matumbi managed to move from the small Rama label to EMI; Birmingham's Steel Pulse was signed to Island and released the important *Handsworth Revolution* album (1978). But even with these changes, British reggae, and reggae in general, has not found a substantial following outside the black West Indian communities. Reggae groups still struggle hard and generally unsuccessfully for recognition beyond their black constituencies. The music is respected more than before, it is even highly influential elsewhere in pop, but its strong cultural overtones, its black 'roots', and particularly, the fundamentalist ring of the Ras Tarafi credo, tend to keep it apart. The only partial exception has been the black poet Linton Kwesi Johnson. Johnson writes in a black English patois that fuses dark political scenarios with the startling effects of dub. Under the guide of Matumbi's Denis 'Black-beard' Bovell (a pioneer of English dub), Johnson has produced some of the most important British reggae recordings in the late 1970s (see Discography).

Despite the slow advance of reggae, contemporary black music now publicly dominates white pop more than ever before.[20] Initially sampled in a search for additional 'colour' – the Rolling Stones, Rod Stewart, Blondie, for example – it also led into the full-blown proposal of 'white reggae' in the case of the Police. But the most significant convergence of white and black, suggested in the cultural proximities of reggae and punk (Bob Marley released 'Punky Reggae Party' in 1977), emerged in an avant-gardist post-punk sound (PIL, Gang of

Four, the Pop Group), and in the guise of a revival. It was mixed ethnic ska-playing groups, the Specials, the Selecter, both from Coventry, and Madness from London's Camden Town, that constructed the more accessible bridge between black sounds and white British pop. Shortly afterwards there appeared the inter-racial 'Brum beat' of Birmingham's UB 40 and the Beat. This music, building on ska, reggae, and later more novel musical indications – listen to the Beat's *Wha Happen?* (1981) – has, against a backcloth of mounting racist rhetoric and political reaction, effectively publicised white pop's continual debt to black music.

Another beat, another rock 'n' roll heart

The important realignment of cultural forces along the divide between the musical territories of black Afro-America and white pop was also accompanied by some important subsidiary shifts. Surviving among the side effects and soured memories of the 'Woodstock nation', London pub rock remained as an important trace of an earlier 'underground' philosophy. From its beginnings in the early 1970s, pub rock represented an explicit refusal of the bombastic appearances progressive rock had by then adopted. Stressing musical honesty and directness, often achieved by crossing rock with country music and dusting off R & B classics, the London pub rock scene developed largely apart from the town centre. It was to be found in Camden Town, in the Greyhound in the Fulham Road, the Hope and Anchor, Islington, and the Nashville Rooms in West Kensington, nearly all, incidentally, future sites of punk. From out of town, from Canvey Island and Southend, came the frenetic R & B of Dr Feelgood, the Kursaal Flyers, and the proto-punk Eddie and the Hot Rods. R & B was also offered by Kokomo, Dogs and the 101ers (who included Joe Strummer of the future Clash), while a more personal variant came from Kilburn and the High Roads. By 1975, the R & B wave had largely swamped the earlier country–rock sounds of Bees Make Honey, Ducks Deluxe and Brinsley Schwarz. The small pub venues served as the stamping ground for much of what later came to be known as the 'new wave'. Nick Lowe and Brinsley Schwarz, both of the latter named group, came from here. Lowe went on to join Dave Edmunds in Rockpile and producing Elvis Costello. Schwarz joined the Rumour, Graham Parker's group. In the meantime, Ian Dury left Kilburn and the High Roads to propose his own inventive brand of musical quirks.

This R & B derived music, although rarely finding wide public success, was to represent an important impetus in British pop in the mid-1970s, both before and after punk. Echoing many of the timbres and sentiments of the contemporaneous 'street wise' music of the American East Coast (Patti Smith, Bruce Springsteen), its musical shadows offered a murky contrast to the white intensity of punk. Although not embracing the latter's wider reach, it rarely fell back into a simple revivalism of the spirit of rock 'n' roll. While taking several lessons from punk's attack on rock music's complacency, its own referents tended to be more strictly musical and revolve around the sticky contact of intimate 'authenticities': direct music, harsh streets and stark emotionalism.

Spitting out lyrics to the accompaniment of an updated R & B tempo (i.e. Graham Parker's 'Heat Treatment', 1976; 'Discovering Japan', 1979), much of the music reiterated a classic rebellious stance that was now imbued with a bruised male romanticism. The self-confident tones of the white R & B of a previous decade was tempered by a certain world-weary wisdom. The American singer Bruce Springsteen, 'the future of rock 'n' roll' (Jon Landau), was considered the Messiah of this new awakening. His 'street poetics' offered the bleak vision of a scarred America, viewed from motor-bikes and cars that cruised beneath darkened skylines towards destitute highways, 'chasin' something in the night'.

British variants either tended not to arrive at the scale of this existential angst or else maintained an ironic veil. While Ian Dury humorously played, and the Jam offered a very British tempered beat music, Elvis Costello went on to produce an ironic catalogue of pop music's history. Moving from an off-centred revisit of rock 'n' roll minus the sexual bravado (*My Aim Is True*), through a cynically detached beat music (*This Year's Model*) to eclectic raidings of Stax soul music, ska and country, his work achieved an impressive bringing together of many of the pluralities and tensions of British pop music in the course of half a dozen LPs between 1977 and 1981 (see Discography).

Such a marked degree of self-consciousness also found an echo in musical journalism. Both *Melody Maker* and *New Musical Express* began turning over column inches to forgotten aspects of pop's past, and in particular to recuperating details from the musical crucible of the 1950s. The combination of these tendencies – pub rock, revitalised white R & B, a self-conscious 'new wave', journalistic retrospectives – also prepared the spaces soon to be occupied by more precise revivalist currents: rock 'n' roll (the Straycats, Matchbox, the Polecats), the pop of the 1950s (Darts), 'mod music' (the Chords, Secret Affair, and a new mod magazine: *Maximum Speed*), soul of the mid-1960s (Dexy's Midnight Runners), and ska. Obvious differences in audiences and execution the second time round prevented these musics from being a transparent replay of their illustrious predecessors. Sometimes they verged on the grotesque and promised only the reactionary stasis of stale nostalgia; more frequently they provided important incentives for new beginnings.[21]

The co-presence in the late 1970s of virtually all the most important musical styles that have gone into the making of British pop – from rockabilly to ska, from soul to beat music, from funk to country – is worth reflecting upon. It marks the practical end of any attempt to view pop as the linear movement of new, more complex, musical forms replacing and obliterating older, simpler, ones. This idea, once central to progressive music, is now lost among the multiple directions of a heterogeneous present.

Pale figures in an electronic funk

Alongside the attempts to recapture the heat and passion associated with earlier moments in pop – mod London, *circa* 1964, in the case of the Jam; the R & B/soul tradition and the example of a singer like Van Morrison in the case of Graham Parker and Kevin Rowlands of Dexy's Midnight Runners – another, decidedly cooler musical proposal was also constructed. This juxtaposed funk/disco rhythms, synthesisers and electronics with a concern for the formal devices of musical syntax.

Experiments in the 1970s with Afro-American rhythms and the sonorities of soul and disco owed much to David Bowie's precocious interest in this area. After the futuristic soul music of *Young Americans* (1975), Bowie had gone on, sometimes working with Brian Eno and Robert Fripp, to develop the possibilities of a white funk music on *Station To Station* (1976), *Low* (1977), *Heroes* (1977). He was equally interested in parts of the avant-garde (i.e. Philip Glass), and, coming from a slightly different direction, the German electronic rock music of the early 1970s. The latter, which had a major effect on the post-punk music of Public Image Ltd (PIL), for instance, had also made a suggestive contribution to the formation of disco's insistent rhythms. This complex genealogy – funk/disco/avant-gardism/Teutonic rock/Bowie – was again to play a part, with Brian Eno again on hand, in the production of the white neurotic funk of New York's Talking Heads.

It was not long before punk's refusal to crystallise led to its extremely volatile elements bursting their momentary form. After 1977 a gap opened up between its avant-gardist and populist wings. Groups such as PIL (formed by Johnny Rotten née John Lydon after the disbandment of the Sex Pistols), the Gang of Four, the Pop Group, and others, sought, with a mixture of previously separated musical languages – crossing punk's searing attack with reggae dub timbres and disco-funk rhythms – to continue punk's musical shock experiments with noise, minimalism and repetition in a new mode.

The alternative appeared to be to press on with the more accessible radical populist strain that remained closer to punk's original interventory style. This was a path chosen by the Clash, although they frequently added reggae and strains of rock 'n' roll to this musical base.[22] In fact, the populist musical rhetoric sown by punk has continued right into the 1980s, becoming, if anything, commercially far more successful than it was back in 1976. The Epping anarchist band Crass, along with the Anti-Nowhere League, Vice Squad, Discharge, and The Exploited (*Punks Not Dead*, 1981) have continued punk's uncompromising manner.[23]

PIL, the Pop Group and the Gang of Four, on the other hand, took a step away from populist immediacy, abandoned the shock of 'raw expression' and substituted it with the disruption of a musical montage that alienated as much as it explored existing musical languages. If we listen to PIL's early music, the provocatively entitled 'Death Disco' (1978), for example, or the subsequent sounds on their second LP, *Metal Box* (1979), the adoption of diverse musical languages and their novel relocation in a series of dissimilar connections is clear. In 'Albatross' and 'Poptones' on the latter record, the pulse is built around dark bass figures and an insistent percussion. Over this 'funky/reggae' base, ringing, repetitive guitar riffs are laid and joined by the 'unnatural' textures of Lyndon's voice. The whole mix is then subjected to punctuation by synthesisers, phasing and echo.

This rearrangement of common musical elements involved a conscious attempt to reconstruct, to resignify, pop music. Analogous experiments were also occurring in New York. Theoretical Girls, DNA, and the 'No wave', were exploring a post-punk soundscape which involved laying sound over sound to produce 'noise' music and to abolish those barriers ('music'/'noise') that punk had initially put so much in crisis.[24] In this novel context, the 'repetition' of the Afro-American pulse crosses – whether inadvertently or self-consciously is hardly the point – the researched repetitivity of the classical avant-garde (Eric Satie, Terry Riley, Steve Reich and Philip Glass).[25] While Joe Bowie's Defunkt, James Chance, and the Raybeats mixed up funk with R & B, jazz and shock aesthetics.

Abandoning the global refusal that punk had espoused, these groups turned to a tactics of attrition. By interrupting, disrupting and estranging existing pop music conventions, the music itself became a moment of 'politics', an intentional subversion of prevalent expectancies. Moving away from the ambitious idea of producing the wider conditions for the music's reception, this development has turned to the task of revealing the internal conditions of musical labour. Employing sets of frequently jagged syntheses – guitar and bass riffs, electronic noises, obsessive percussive rhythms, the incongruous 'word salads' of many of the lyrics – the scaffolding of the music is put on show. The overlay and unusual proximity of such diverse musical ideas offers no easy resolution; the music that emerges is not directed towards reconciliation but remains open, finally unresolved. The listener is either drawn into following the productive play of the construction or else repelled by the naked joins and clashes of the collage.

Whatever the verdict on the resulting sounds, this 'deconstructed' music insists on a 'shocking' revelation. It becomes no longer possible to visualise pop as the simple outcome of certain musical inspirations, fortuitous styles and influences, all requiring protection from the mummifying hand of technology and commerce. The languages of pop, its sensorial textures, are now clearly demonstrated to be a particular type of construction, a specific form of production. In moving out of the impotent limbo in which spent punk energies threatened to come to rest, the 'deconstructionists' worked for the suspension of meaning in the present all the better to be 'vibrated by the reflexes of the future' (André Breton). Interrupting and interrogating the 'normal' mode of pop's reception, they have sought to capture the 'subterranean connections of dissimilars' that hit the audience 'like a bullet' (Walter Benjamin). By putting together apparently incongruous musical forms, vocal styles and lyrics, the generally assumed semantic fixity of pop as 'entertainment' is abruptly jolted. It is temporarily replaced by a paradoxical expression which, through its mere presence, challenges existing musical and cultural expectations.

It has been towards that threshold that an important splinter of post-punk music has constructed a path. Although turning away from obvious solutions, this 'avant-gardist' pop music continues to occupy a space within the commercial structures of the pop music industry. It has remained firmly tied to pop music's internal formation and has not sought the 'legitimised' art exit that progressive rock so avidly pursued in the early 1970s.

Remaining an integral part of the popular cultural field, this music has also effected less severe proposals. The most immediate consequence, apart from an unsuspected disco popularity (i.e. Kraftewerk's 'Trans-Europe Express'), has been that a whole wave of electronically synthesised dance music – Gary Numan, the Human League, Heaven 17, Depeche Mode – has taken up these immediate and more distant experiments to produce what Paul Tickell in *New Musical Express* calls 'electro-pop' – an integration of the modern and the traditional (electronics and dance), of the avant-garde and pop. It exists as a complex tribute to the ambiguous but potent cultural powers invested: 'is it sound (microcomputers, synths, tapes, and humans minding machines) or a sensibility (precision flashiness, discos and clubs, and leisure as dream-time)? '(Paul Tickell, *New Musical Express*, 19 December, 1981).

The paradoxes of crisis

Crises have many sides, some positive, some negative, and many quite simply ambiguous. The late 1970s was a period of crisis for British pop, both in its musical languages and institutions. It was also a period in which wider social conflict and an escalating political unrest seemed to press in upon pop's internal economy in an often very direct fashion. From the defiant slogans of punk and the apocalyptic Rastafarian 'solution' of reggae, through ideological shifts in music journalism and the successful establishment of the Rock Against Racism campaign, to the extreme white ethnicity around 'Oi' music, British pop was regularly criss-crossed by the symbols of political ferment. Swastikas and CND, race and youth, commerce and anti-capitalism, sexism and a growth in women's music, were all sucked into the contradictory continuum of its styles.

In all this, punk was, of course, the notorious instigator: held responsible both for an internal revolt within pop and for translating social crisis into musical and subcultural rhetoric. Yet an important aspect of punk, caught between narcissism and nihilism, had been its disdain for the 'obvious', for 'sense'. Its incipient populism remained in tension with its reluctance to communicate with the external world. This second tendency, accompanied by an increasing recourse to technical means for reproducing the imaginary, was succeeded by a series of proposals that appeared to disregard the existence of an exterior altogether. Face masks and fashion costumes, surrounded by drum machines and programmed synthesisers, replaced links to the 'street' and its associated 'authenticity' with a refusal to consider that there need necessarily exist a moment of 'authenticity' at all. The logic of 'origins', the subsequent explanations and romantic attachment that flow from them, is ignored. Musical and cultural styles ripped out of other contexts, stripped of their initial referents, circulate in such a manner that they represent nothing other than their own transitory presence.

Adam and the Ants taking a drum beat from the central African state of Burundi and then a rap format from New York's North Harlem, the languid mixtures of Culture Club, or the musical duck soup of the master mind himself, Malcolm McLaren, results in a constant collage of unexpected proximities. The pedantic rationality of 'good taste' is replaced by a pluralism of pleasure.

We might say that previous perspectives and expectancies, tied to the particular knowledge of a single, monumental history, have been abandoned for the recognition of horizontal histories circulating in the body of social experiences and everyday life. Here feminism has been the crucial, if often unacknowledged, protagonist. The once presumed 'homogeneity' of the present, the 'meta-narrative' (Jean-Francois Lyotard) of history, is sliced up into diverse frames, shifting perspectives and possibilities. In this apparently dispersive, but actually more specific, detailed, 'post-modern', world, the 'artificial', the 'imitation', the 'plastic', are no longer an embarrassment. They, too, have their particular stories; they, too, are 'real'.[26]

Ever since punk's minimalist rage apparently turned the musical clock back, pop's brief but rich history has increasingly reverted to its earlier status as a 'passport to the country of the "Now"' (George Melly). Pop's past stops being a mausoleum of picturesque relics and turns back into a contemporary reservoir of musical possibilities. The so-called 'revivals' of ska, rockabilly, white R & B and soul (for many never went away, merely disappeared from the wider public ear and eye), the major growth in cross-over musics that mix

Figure 19. Soul 'revival'

past and present, and often several presents, are the unmistakable imprints of this change. Several years on from the punk onslaught, and well into the 1980s, there exists a notable carnival of musical styles, from the presence of white funk and black rap, to the bubbling edges of 'juju' (Nigeria), 'soca' (Trinidad), and the rediscovery of 'salsa' (Cuba/Puerto Rico/New York), together with all the mixtures that can be established in between. Traceable to the breach initially made by punk, this situation promises a 'proliferation of margins' (Rosetta Brooks) rather than a predictable return to a renewed 'mainstream' and a subordinated 'alternative'.

A sequential version of pop's history has been transgressed, violated. Causal explanations have been circumvented by a confusion of cultural margins, by 'revivals', by the cyclical 'return' of musics and styles from the 'past'. A disregard for teleology has also aided a distinctive movement sideways, an overflow across previous musical and aesthetic boundaries.

The gesture of Dada towards the mundane objects of the everyday and an aleatory mode of expression, and of Pop Art in the 1960s towards the shapes, textures and pleasures of popular culture, have more recently been consummated in a contemporary *bricolage*. In a series of overlapping histories – of urban popular culture, of the avant-garde, of popular song – we rediscover objects and relations we thought we knew only too well. We find ourselves in an unsuspected cultural 'mix', or 'dub', a nomadic journey amongst 'objets trouvés'.

Meanwhile, distinctions between the 'private' and the 'public' become increasingly blurred. Public spaces are invaded by a growing number of private music apparatuses. The lo-fi transistor radio (introduced by Sony in 1955) has been replaced by the hi-fi portable cassette player, reggae shops turn their sound systems towards the street, car stereos and the Sony Walkman introduce a further mobility. The urban soundscape undergoes an extensive reshaping, while the public, caught in a 'wraparound sound' (Murray Schafer), is 'an examiner, but an absent-minded one' (Walter Benjamin).

In this situation, where a state of maximum reproducibility provides the 'standard', the *common ground*, for cultural encounters, for a new, expanded heterogeneity, the 'sense' of music changes. Past and present statements – from an original Sun recording of Roy Orbison to a Human League promotional video – become part of a pregnant 'now', only the flick of a switch away, part of a 'transversal knowledge' (Alberto Abruzzese).

The negation of the institutional authority of the past and the transformation of its traces into a living storehouse of contemporary choices has not been limited solely to music. A whole gallery of rapidly changing sartorial obsessions have travelled across the dance floors, night clubbing zones, and recently resurrected cocktail bar habits in Britain's major cities in recent years. Punk had ruthlessly ransacked the 'junk yard' of history and parodied revered subcultural memories by blasphemously confusing their once distinctive wardrobes. Later styles swapped that ironic eye for the seduction of the masquerade. Punk's insistence on the artifice of the spectacle

Figure 20. Risk clothing

is taken one step further. The 'new romantic' season of
1980–1, modelled on the catwalk of *Top of the Pops* by Adam
Ant: Red Indian/Pirate/Highway Man, offered an uninterrupted theatre of exchangeable mannequins. Zoot-suited hips-
ters, space cadets, gauchos, Miladys and Turks, drifted back
and forth in time and across cultures...

The male dandy or 'fop', the female 'sex symbol', become
new, self-consciously inhabited icons. Imitating Bryan Ferry,
Debbie Harry or Siouxsie Sue, the 'narcissistic self-
knowledge' (Krystina Kitsis) involved in the self-possession of
the image leads to a potentially critical play with both the
spectacle and the 'normal': the 'performance' becomes full
time; its distance from conventionality no longer a mere
gesture, but a parallel reality set in the context of the latter.
Emerging from its marginal past, the seclusion of 'camp' is
translated into the repertoire of the profane. Johnny Rotten of

Figure 21. *The Face.* **Boy George**

the Sex Pistols or Boy George O'Dowd of Culture Club, like many others on the London night life circuit, were 'dressing up' in public long before they became 'stars'.

Behind these spectacular horizons exist the nameless contributions of the young metropolitan stylists, those 'hiding in the light' (Dick Hebdige). For the new 'masters of disguise' (Peter York) who populate an apparently referent-less land-scape – 'It [fashion] gives you security' (Sandy, *New Musical Express*, 19 December, 1981) – there was a complete stylist's kit on hand. At the Smile salon there are hairdressers Keith and Ollie; while for fashion design, Melissa Caplan, Vivienne Westwood, Willie Brown and Antony Price; clothes from Kensington Market and the Great Gear Market off the Kings Road. Clubs such as the Cabaret Futura (Wardour Street), Le Beat Route (Greek Street), the Ultratheque (Glasgow), and the Rum Runner (Birmingham), offered some of *the* places for being seen. While for those wishing to check their fashion silhouette and life-styles against verbal judgement, there are the magazines *i-D* and *The Face*.

It is punk and its aftermath that hangs like a pall of smoke over the tail end of the 1970s and the opening of the 1980s. Nowhere is this more apparent than in the public fashions, styles and faces of pop in these years. It extends from punk's shock assemblage through the mobile disguises of different waves of urban stylists to the angrily screwed up face of a skinhead, 'Made In London' tattooed across his forehead, thrusting a two-finger salute at the camera. Yet it is the major revival in the skinhead subculture in the early 1980s that diverts us from this internal history, propelling us back towards the wider semantics of public unrest.

Gathering in the vicinity of Petticoat Lane in East London, and around the aptly named shop, The Last Resort, the skins represented a hard extension out of the extremes of punk. But, unlike many punks, they had decidely not gone 'soft'. Frozen back into a harsh, brutally rigorous, masculine style, this refound subculture maintained itself, in its boots, rolled up jeans, shorn scalps, tattooes and vitriolic nationalism, out beyond the threshold of 'acceptability'. Its music, the Cock-ney Rejects, Angelic Upstarts, Cocksparrer, the 4 Skins, and other Oi bands, carried on the frustrated proletarian street sounds earlier associated with Sham 69 and the 'Sham Army': angry slogans and football terrace chants, the music of the 'unrespectables', of the 'working class gone bad' (Hebdige, 1982). The once flexible inner-city economy of casual labour and seasonal employment that could support the skinhead option has been increasingly rationalised away, removed from the possibilities of unskilled youth. Unprepared for such a fate, the skin remains a desperate actor, reduced to white marginality and playing out his days in a series of reports on urban decay, unemployment, racism, hooliganism and street violence.

But despite such evidence, the interchange between the particular threads of British pop and the wider drama of an overall social crisis remains deeply ambivalent even when it promises to be most clear. The apparent fit betwen punk and left-wing populism in the period 1976–8, upon which Rock Against Racism successfully constructed its campaign, or racism, the National Front and the skinhead revival, temporarily culminating in the burnt out Hambrough Tavern after an Oi concert and racial riot in Southall in July 1981, seem obvious cases. Also many punk songs, the Jamaican inspired rhythms of UB 40, the Beat and Fun Boy Three, the 'committed' lyrics of the Clash and the Jam, and, coming from another direction, the cry of white ethnicity in Oi, have all signalled 'politics'. This frequently genuine radicalism can, however, ultimately prove to be a misleading signal. That parts of pop have become susceptible to explicit political inflections is a measure of the present situation. But the sentiments invested in the music, born of a realism produced in the materiality of a specific moment, practice and place, at best sit uneasily with existing political scenarios, at worst, in open antagonism with them. The significance of declared political signs cannot substitute for the wider sense of British pop and its own internal realities. It is to this final aspect that I now wish to turn to in the following Conclusion.

Conclusion: In the Realm of the Possible

'A luxurious object is still of this earth, it still recalls, albeit in a precious mode, its mineral or animal origin, the natural theme of which it is but one actualization. Plastic is wholly swallowed up in the fact of being used: ultimately, objects will be invented for the sole pleasure of using them.'

(Roland Barthes, 1973)

In a profound sense, contemporary popular culture is 'plastic'. Like Barthes' definition, it is mass produced, resilient and pliable, expendable and adaptable. Although regularly criticised for these attributes, the 'false' and 'plastic' connotations of popular culture are its most significant quality: 'the very idea of its infinite transformation' of 'ubiquity made visible' (Barthes, 1973). And like plastic, popular culture has spread like a flexible film across the surfaces and actions of our daily lives, binding them into apparently prosaic patterns.

In certain moments and particular situations, British pop music has appeared as the carefully chosen score for a spectacular subcultural performance; here stitched into the exaggerated 'neatness' of the mods, there as the noisy chorus in the outlandish disintegration of the punks. In the black West Indian communities, in the case of reggae, it has become a central element in a notable cultural resistance. Elsewhere, pop has persistently provided a pervasive warranty for dancing, bedroom fantasies, romance, and, more simply, for those innumerable points of individual affirmation that prick the routines we inherit.

But while the obvious commercial structure and urban organisation of British popular culture may stamp a recognisable shape upon these diverse possibilities, it can also easily divert our attention from their imaginative scope. Today, however, habits, tastes and pleasures that were once masked from history are increasingly emerging. They have forced an irreversible change in our understanding of what is 'culture'. The continual polemic around the terms 'popular' or 'mass culture', invariably a thinly disguised struggle for the arbitration and custody of culture as a whole, can now be peeled back to reveal what Raymond Williams once called a 'long revolution' under the skin. The culture that emerges from that process is the outcome of a struggle through the contradictory production and uses of the present for a culture that, despite its obvious commercial organisation, is more dynamic, and potentially more democratic, than the tired conservative prospects it encroaches upon and supplants.[1]

Romance, the body, and the city

'Hey, does my silhouette look okay?'
(From Amos Poe's film *Subway Riders*, 1981)

Pop music is generally used, responded to, and each day appropriated through romance. In romance pop acquires its most extensive imaginative resonance. When romanticism is discussed, typically the reference is to teenage girls constructing fantasies around the pin-ups and records of male stars. But this is only one example. In fact, romance permeates every pore of pop.[2] The dark outlines of an altogether harsher, predominantly masculine influenced, romanticism of night streets and rear-view mirror scenes, of motor-bikes and cars, of being with the boys and staring at the girls, runs right down the middle of pop's symbolic universe, from Elvis to the Clash. Because its universality lends it a 'natural' air of invisibility it is all the more insidious; suggesting that it is only in the 'irrational' projections of the female psyche that romance is to be found in pop. In the meantime, male romanticism loses its gender and passes unobserved into the measure of 'reality':

Figure 22. Dancing in the 1980s

'Being a man is an entitlement not to *masculine* attributes but to non-gendered subjectivity' (Black and Coward, 1981).[3]

Abandoning received notions of romance and tracing its presence within pop music, we quickly discover the necessity to travel beyond the limits of 'common sense'. The forms of contemporary leisure and its pleasures are more detailed and intricate than we initially assumed. It becomes necessary to extend the reportage: it being on the social surfaces of daily events – where the ordinary and the exceptional are unified – that we discover the prose of the world (Lefebvre, 1978). The original presentation of rock 'n' roll as an insult to 'good taste', or of disco as an invitation to lobotomy, were subverted in daily use and habits, and in time officially put aside. In the same fashion, the shifting display of juvenile girls' 'private lives', of black urban youth culture, white male subcultures, and an overarching web of urban romanticism, involves cultural investments whose charged extensions regularly pass unobserved. Although sometimes noisy and provocative, as in

Figure 23. 'Private' bodies, public encounters

the case of punk, but usually far less obstrusive, it is the loaded relation between music and these particular spaces that continually connect and undo the 'public/private' divisions of everyday life in a series of imaginative reworkings.

Music can be considered an important 'counter-space' (Henri Lefebvre) in our daily lives. Its power lies in a temporary suspension of the division between the 'private' and the 'public', between the imagination and the routines, roles and social relations in which we regularly find ourselves locked. As such, music is not an 'escape' from 'reality', but an interrogative exploration of its organising categories. Imagination and 'reality' are brought together in a significant friction and exchange. And the major site of this encounter is the frequently repressed zone of the body.

The corporeal intensity of electronic sonorities, along with the wrenched sentiments of soul, the screeched angst of punk, the shouts of white R & B, reggae's patois and the rap's verbal contortions, propel the body into the centre of pop. Concen-

trated in dancing and the visceral immediacy of a musical
performance (on record or 'live'), it is this physical sense of
the musical 'now' that is crucial to pop culture. It is the body
that ultimately makes, receives and responds to music; and it
is the body that connects sounds, dance, fashion and style to
the subconscious anchorage of sexuality and eroticism. Here,
where romance and 'reality' are fused together, common sense
is often taunted, teased and twisted apart.

If romance is the central medium of pop, and the body its
privileged sounding board, it is the city that provides its
fundamental stage. The city is the urban 'body', the place of
the contemporary imagination; and through the technological
reproduction of the imaginary, metropolitan textures – their
copies and local reworkings – enter every corner of our lives.
In the city, at night, after the office blocks, shopping centres
and streets are deserted by the work-force, the centre is turned
over to a night society; the other side of sombre, daytime
labour. Nocturnal groups stop off at dance halls and clubs,
entertainment centres and bars. The 'technological destruc-
tion of distance' (Oscar Handlin) achieved with rapid and
(until recently) cheap transport, encourages the city to change
its face every twelve hours. For the night shift even the
chronometrical limits of leisure can be stretched by imbibing
the appropriate stimulants, particularly the aptly named
'speed'.

The epicentre of commercial popular culture has been the
urban metropolis, which, with rare exceptions, means London. Yet it would be a mistake to overlook the effects of local
inflections that have often played back to the capital a revised
and sometimes novel idiom. The clamorous case of the
'Mersey Sound' remains indelibly stamped upon the mythology of British pop. In reality, the 'Northern Soul' circuit, and
the continual bubbling under the surface of Jamaican and
British reggae throughout the 1970s, have proved even more
persistent. None – formed at the cross-roads of urban popular
culture and under the shadows of a London-based music
industry – have escaped the metropolitan mould. But some
have forced its intersections wider apart. Especially after punk
burst upon pop we have been encouraged to look outside

London to other urban centres, to Coventry, to Birmingham, to Glasgow, Manchester and Liverpool, for new sounds.

While overlain by London fashion, tangible evidence of regional forms and variations do emerge. And somehow music on a Friday night at Rock City in Nottingham is marked in a different way from that of London's Le Beat Route. The same music, the same record, can be crossed by different cultural pressures and requests, diverse pleasures. The culture struggle over the use and sense of pop music is also one over its democratic potential and cultural devolution. To put it another way, over its potential to resonate with 'the "dense and concrete" life... a life whose main stress is on the intimate, the sensory, the detailed and the personal' (Hoggart, 1958, p. 81).

Contemporary popular culture is experienced directly on the immediate surfaces of everyday life: coming out of the radio, the record grooves, the headphones; off the adverts, the television screen... Daily immersed in its presence, its prevalent mode of reception is 'distracted reception' (Benjamin, 1973). Mistakenly dismissed by many observers for passivity, it is this distracted mode, spread through the empire of electronic reproduction to our confrontation with all existing visual and sonorial languages, that augurs a change in the 'rules of the game', a 'reinforcement in 'our capacity to tolerate the incommensurable' (Lyotard, 1979), and a state in which we all become 'experts' (Benjamin).

In pop music, in its romance, its tastes, its styles, and its pleasures, there exists a detailed use and flexible dialogue with the languages of contemporary urban culture: languages that apparently pose us as their 'subjects'/objects. It is these practical, often 'private', interrogations of surrounding public circumstances – whether in the gymnastic display of break dancing or the choice of lipstick colour – that transform the seeming 'obviousness' of popular culture into an imaginative conquest of everyday life. Here, we are now inside another 'knowledge'; one quite distinct from the narrow perspectives of 'High Culture', its rational concentration and formal aesthetics. This transfiguration of official realities, of *their* explanation of social experiences, represents both a victory over the inevitable and demonstrates the unsuspected promise of popular culture: the possibility of change in a changeable reality through the continual fusion of the imagination and the lived.

Discography

The records indicated below are largely restricted to recordings, singers and groups mentioned in the course of the book. They represent the immediate sonorial context for the descriptions and arguments made in the preceding chapters. I have presented them following that logic. The rapid turnover in record releases and reissues means that records are constantly changing their catalogue numbers, consequently only the label is indicated.

1 Living in a modern world

It is clearly important at the outset to have a preliminary idea of Tin Pan Alley and the nature of popular music before rock 'n' roll and 'pop' make their appearance. As always, earlier historical moments invariably turn out to be a lot more complex and varied than a rapid dismissal suggests. To realise just what American influences on commercial popular music after the 1920s meant in sound terms, the double album *Kings Of Swing* (RCA) and *Million Sellers Of The Fifties* (Embassy) permit a dip into a wide spectrum of US popular music – ranging from Benny Goodman to Frankie Laine. This listening can be set alongside the earlier examples of British urban folk music found on *The Iron Muse* (Topic) and the tail end of the music hall and its transformation into 'variety': *On The Halls* (EMI).

The distinction between all these different popular styles and the sounds of the Afro-American tradition can be dramatically tested by sampling the eerie intensity of the pre-war rural blues of Robert Johnson (*King Of The Delta Blues Singers*, CBS), and then the dark power of the post-war urban blues. In the second case, Muddy Waters is best heard on *Chess Blues Masters* (Chess), Howlin' Wolf on *Howlin' Wolf* (Chess), Elmore James, if only for the perennial blues motif 'Dust My Broom', on *The Best Of Elmore James* (Sue), B.B. King, *Live At The Regal* (ABC), John Lee Hooker's idiosyncratic tone and brooding voice on *Dimples* (DJM), and Bobby Bland on the magnificent *Two Steps From The Blues* (Duke).

Returning to British popular music in the inter-war years and the immediate post-war period when dance bands rules the air waves and popular dance, the Decca series *The Bands That Matter* devotes individual records to the bands of Roy Fox, Lew Stone and Ambrose. A selection from the pre-war BBC broadcasts is to be found on the two volumed *Dance Bands On The Air* (BBC Records). For an idea of the American 'crooner' style almost any record by Bing Crosby or Frank Sinatra would do, for example Sinatra's *The Very Best Of Frank Sinatra* (EMI). A large debt to Afro-American music, particularly jazz, lies among his notes and phrasing.

'Tape was introduced at the back end of 1948 and editing tape just scared people to death' (American record producer Tom Dowd, BBC Radio One, 3 January 1982). The relation of tape possibilities to the newly discovered immediacy of black music by white popular taste, and the importance of all this for subsequent pop music, can be appreciated when listening to Little Richard's studio constructed 'Keep A-Knockin'', and other such classics as 'Tutti Frutti', along with Lloyd Price's 'Lawdy Miss Clawdy'. These, and others, will be found on *This Is How It All Began*, volume 2 (Speciality).

2 A formative moment, 1956–63

Apart from the already mentioned *Million Sellers Of The Fifties* (Embassy), other examples of popular US recordings of the period are contained on *Juke-Box Hits Of The '50s* (RCA). The latter record offers a selection that runs from Johnny Ray's 'Just Walking In The Rain' to the Orioles's 'Crying In The Chapel' and the Platters with 'The Great Pretender'. For British performers who occupied the Hit Parade of the period – Winifred Atwell, Dickie Valentine, etc., – you will have to look out for budget-priced records cashing in on nostalgia, or else second-hand record shops.

'Heartbreak Hotel' and 'Blue Suede Shoes' can be found on the Presley compilation two record set, *40 Greatest* (RCA). It contains many of Presley's most noted hits between 1956 and the end of the 1960s. But to reach into the texture of the Presley epic, and into the mythical beginnings of rock 'n' roll and what, especially for white Britishers, was a new musical 'America', it is essential to hear Elvis on *The Sun Collection* (RCA). This has nearly all the songs he recorded in Memphis under Sam Phillips' supervision between 1954 and 1956, prior to his move to RCA and global acclaim. The shifting currents of blues, country music, gospel and Tin Pan Alley (Dean Martin was a favourite with Elvis) are well caught in the experimental excitement that hangs in the air over these sessions. Each song provides a particular angle on the productive tension involved in this critical moment of musical transition. In 'Milkcow Blues Boogie' Elvis actually demonstrates to us the rockabilly manner of seizing upon previous black and white popular musical forms and shaking them up. The piece begins slowly with Elvis stretching a blues holler over a slow, tripping, old style, country blues rhythm; then he interrupts the song, and, in a phrase that resonates with epic intentions, shouts: 'Hold it fellas! That don't mo-ove me! Let's get real... re-eal gone for a change!'. The tempo is immediately cranked up, and the song shoots off. Elvis jumps into the music, takes it apart, and then sets it down in a crazed rockabilly pulse. (For a fine description of Elvis's recording of this song, see Marcus (1977), pp. 172–6.)

Along with Presley's early recordings it is necessary to add other material coming out of the Sun studios in the period 1955–7. Some of the more obscure rockabilly sounds, including Roy Orbison's memorable 'Domino', can be found on *That Rockabilly Craze* (Charly). Then there is Jerry Lee Lewis with *The Original Jerry Lee Lewis* and Carl Perkins with *Rocking Guitarman* (both on Charly). Carl Perkin's version of 'Blue Suede Shoes' – he wrote the song – will be found on the second record. All these recordings display unmistakable white country music overtones. So it might be worthwhile at this point listening to Jimmie Rodgers's *A Legendary Performer* (RCA), Hank Williams's *40 Greatest Hits* (MGM) and Bob Willis and his Texas Playboys with *The Bob Willis Anthology* (CBS), to get some sense of the country sounds which, along with white southern gospel music, were crossed with the blues in the making of southern rockabilly.

Country music also lay directly behind the historically important, though musically thinner, sound of Bill Haley and the Comets. Their pioneering hits in the mid-1950s can be heard on *Golden Hits* (MCA). Coming from another direction was the extremely influential Chuck Berry. Just think what the early Rolling Stones owed to him, or of all those performances of 'Johnny B. Goode' by white groups in the 1960s. Surprisingly, one might think for a black performer, country music was also to be found here: 'By adding blues tones to some fast country runs and yoking them to a rhythm-and-blues beat, he created an instrumental style with bi-racial appeal' (Christgau, 1973, p. 144). All the classic Berry songs – 'Carol', 'Bye Bye Johnny', 'Back In The USA', 'Brown Eyed Handsome Man' – will be found on *Motivatin'* (Chess).

Those wishing to dig back deeper into the early makings of pop music will find Louis Jordan's *The Best of Louis Jordan* (MCA), featuring the 'jump' R & B of the 1940s, essential listening. So too, is *Doowop Doowop* (DJM) which illustrates the street corner black vocal groups of the 1950s. The relaxed R & B style of New Orleans on Fats Domino's *20 Greatest Hits* (United Artists) and the mumbling guitar of Bo Diddley's *Golden Decade* (Chess) are also important contributions not to be missed.

The importance of the electric guitar for pop's characteristic sound in the 1950s and 1960s is well in evidence on the above records, particularly the Chuck Berry collection. But it was initially developed in the fields of jazz, urban blues and country music. *The Origins Of Modern Jazz* (Quadrifoglio) features the electric guitar of Charlie Christian, along with Theolonius Monk, Dizzy Gillespie and Kenny Clarke, from live recordings at Minton's and the Uptown House in Harlem in May 1941. The light, sophisticated Texas guitar style of T-Bone Walker was influential on a whole school of black electric guitar players (B.B. King, Amos Milburn, Albert King) in the 1950s who subsequently became the models for innumerable white guitarists in the 1960s. Walker's guitar style can be appreciated on *T-Bone Blues* (Atlantic). In country music, the key figure was Merle Travis. In 1957 he recorded 'Merle's Boogie', employing the 'trick of slowing down the recording machine while taping the guitar part' (David Toop, 'Finger Picking' and 'Double Talking', *Collusion*, n.4, London 1982). Travis was important for the guitar styles of Chet Atkins, a regular player on Elvis's early RCA sessions, and through him on the overall 'Nashville sound' of the following decades. He can be heard on *The Best of Merle Travis* (Capitol).

The use of the electric guitar sound in the light, foot-tapping rhythms of the Shadows can be followed on *20 Golden Greats* (EMI), while Duane Eddy ('the twang's the thang') is on *Legend Of Rock* (London). The extension of black R & B through the extension of tonal colours, permitted by adding strings, can be observed on the Drifter's *24 Original Hits* (Atlantic). The pushing of such tendencies into the almost manic orchestration of Phil Spector's 'wall of sound', widely associated with such black girl groups as The Ronnettes and The Crystals, and culminating in 'River Deep–Mountain High' by Ike and Tina Turner, is to be found on *Phil Spector: 20 Greatest Hits* (Phil Spector International).

Teenage sentimentalism dominates much pop after the initial wave of rock 'n' roll had passed. It is best sampled on *From Bobby-Sox To Stockings* (MGM). But for a compilation album that covers most of the angles of British pop in the late 1950s and early 1960s, *The Roots Of British Rock* (Sire) is highly recommended. Here you will find the yodel of Frank Ifield ('I Remember You'), skiffle (Lonnie Donegan's 'Rock Island Line'), the commercial success of Trad jazz and the Tornadoes with 'Telstar'. British forms of teen ballads can be found on Cliff Richard's *40 Golden Greats* (EMI), Billy Fury's *The Billy Fury Story* (Decca) and Adam Faith's *The Best of Adam Faith* (Starline). For those who believe that the native stabs at rock 'n' roll might be worth searching out, there is *Focus On Tommy Steele* (Decca), but, late as it was, *Best Of Johnny Kidd And The Pirates* (EMI) is more successful.

American music of the late 1950s, apart from the cloying vacuity of Fabian and Tommy Sands, also boasted Buddy Holly and the Crickets, the Everly Brothers and Eddie Cochran. Holly, hailing from Lubbock, Texas, sang rockers and ballads, mixed country and blues, usually performed with a group line-up of two guitars, bass and drums, and although dead before he was twenty-three produced a musical heritage that subsequent pop has continually returned to (i.e. the Stones with 'Not Fade Away', or Elvis Costello's first album, *My Aim Is True*, Stiff). A major selection of his work is to be found on *Legend* (MCA). The Everly Brothers came from a country music family: after hearing their father's guitar style on the radio Merle Travis abandoned the banjo for the guitar. They were among the pioneers of white harmony singing in pop. Their eventual successors in this sense were the Beatles, but it is important to note that the Everlys were largely unaffected by black music. Their hits in the 1950s are on *Don And Phil's Fabuluous Fifties Treasury* (Janus). Eddie Cochran, the rocking, rebellious white boy with the 'Summertime Blues', was extremely popular in Britain, where he met his untimely death in a car accident. All his significant records, except 'Three Steps To Heaven', are on *Legendary Masters* (United Artists).

The black pop sounds of this period can be found on the already mentioned records of the Drifters, the Phil Spector collection and the Coasters's *20 Great Originals* (Atlantic). American dance records, again tapping a black music genre, received a major fillip with the success of Chubby Checker and 'The Twist' (Columbia), later followed by Little Eva's 'The Locomotion' (London).

British skiffle, apart from the tracks included on *The Roots Of British Rock* (Sire), can be found in a more concentrated form on Lonnie Donegan's *The Donegan File* (Pye). The folk–blues styles that skiffle both drew upon and later stimulated in Britain can be heard on *Leadbelly's Last Sessions* (Folkways). An important sign for the future was a little known EP released in 1961 on Topic Records. Featuring acoustic guitar instrumentals by Davey Graham and the father of British R & B, Alexis Korner, it indicated a growing appropriation of the blues: later to be translated into sounds as varied as the Rolling Stones and Fairport Convention.

3 Britain's 'Inner Voices', 1963–6

To the pop albums mentioned towards the close of the last chapter, especially *The Roots Of British Rock* (Sire), the addition of such US sounds as *The Golden Age Of Sam Cooke* (RCA), the voice of 'Little Miss Dynamite', *The Brenda Lee Story* (MCA), Del Shannon's *The Best Of Del Shannon* (Contempo), Roy Orbison's *All Time Greatest Hits* (Monument), the macabre teenage operas of The Shangri-Las on *Golden Hits Of The Shangri-Las* (Philips), and not forgetting Elvis with *Blue Hawaii* (RCA), to have some idea of Presley as the smoochy, Hollywood ballader, gives the wider context of the British charts around 1962–4.

Mersey Beat '62–'64 (United Artists) is a useful collection that exudes some of the raw excitement of Johnny Sandon and the Remo Four, The Escorts, The Undertakers, and countless other Liverpool groups who were never to enjoy the success of the Beatles or Gerry and the Pacemakers. Another collection, *The Beat Merchants* (United Artists), supplies the varied musical, and geographical, spread of home-cured British sounds, particularly those of white R & B. Alexis Korner can be heard playing 'I Got My Mojo Working' with the legendary London R & B harmonic player Cyril Davies on the Decca compilation, *Hard Up Heroes*.

All the recordings of the Beatles, including such rarities as when Pete Best, not Ringo, played drums and Stu Sutcliffe bass in their Hamburg days in the early 1960s, are readily available. After the release of 'Love Me Do' in 1962, their LPs in chronological order were: *Please Please Me, With The Beatles, A Hard Day's Night, Beatles For Sale, Help!, Rubber Soul* and *Revolver* – all on Parlophone. That takes their recording career up to the end of 1966.

Britain's Helen Shapiro ('Don't Treat Me Like A Child', 'Walkin' Back To Happiness') and Dusty Springfield – *A Girl Called Dusty* and *Golden Hits*, both released by Philips – represented two distinctive voices in the early and mid-1960s, later joined by Cilla Black, *Cilla* (Parlophone), and Sandy Shaw: *Sandy Shaw* (Pye).

The British R & B scene had its first public success with the Rolling Stones, and the music on *The Rolling Stones* (Decca) offers a sharp sense of one of the main tendencies in the British R & B world: Chicago electric blues, white bohemia and arrogant male sexuality. Their music is subsequently extended, particularly through borrowings from black soul, on the next two LPs – *Rolling Stones 2* (Decca) and *Out Of Our Heads* (Decca) –

before blossoming into their own self-penned, worldly Londonesque blues style on *Aftermath* (Decca).

Another tendency in the British R & B club scene at the time is caught on Georgie Fame and the Blues Flames's *Rhythm And Blues At The Flamingo* (Columbia). To this should be added *Five Live Yardbirds* (Columbia) and *The Animals* (EMI). The legend of Eric Clapton, together with the blues crusade of John Mayall, is to be found on *Blues Breakers* (Decca).

In London by this time, the three major forms of black music that had taken hold can be crudely divided between Chicago electric blues, early soul and Tamla music, and Jamaican ska. The Chicago style, pioneered in the 1950s by Muddy Waters and Howlin' Wolf, was continued and extended by the likes of Otis Rush, Buddy Guy, Albert King, and from Texas, Freddie King – all favourites with white British guitarists; check the above Mayall LP for Clapton showcases featuring the music of Freddie King. A cross-section of Chicago blues can be heard on *Modern Chicago Blues* (Testament), and the three-volumed *Chicago/The Blues/Today!* (Fontana).

The first record of the James Brown double album *Solid Gold* (Polydor) gives many of the influential sounds of 'Soul Brother Number 1' from the club favourite 'Night Train' (also found on the Georgie Fame LP), through the controlled frenzy of 'Out Of Sight' to the exclamatory 'Papa's Got A Brand New Bag'. The early soul music of Marvin Gaye – his 'Can I Get A Witness' and 'Hitch Hike' appeared on early Stones's LP – can be found on *Anthology* (Tamla Motown). Behind these singers stands Ray Charles, a force acknowledged by nearly all the 'white soul' singers of the 1960s. Listen to his *A 25th Anniversary In Show Business Salute* (Atlantic) collection.

When Georgie Fame recorded his LP in 1963, one of the songs he included was The Miracles's 'Shop Around'. 'Shop Around' had been a hit for Tamla Motown in 1960. Written by Motown's owner Berry Gordy and Smokey Robinson of The Miracles, this song launched the success of the Motown label. The Miracles's triple album *Anthology*, Diana Ross and the Supremes with *20 Golden Hits* and Stevie Wonder's *Greatest Hits* (all, naturally, on Tamla Motown), capture the most salient features of the early and middle part of the Motown epic. This can be further filled in – Mary Wells, The Contours, The Marvelettes, Martha and the Vandellas: sounds and inspirations that later appeared in the music of both the Beatles, Stones (the Stones's 'Street Fighting Man', 1968, was a cynically chic remake of Martha and the Vandellas's 'Dancing In The Streets') and the Who – by listening to the five record set, *The Motown Story* (Motown).

The darker, rougher, soul music coming from the South, especially represented on the Memphis labels Stax and Volt, had an enormous reception in British clubs and the mod subculture. The key records here are *The Best Of Otis Redding* (Atlantic), Wilson Pickett's *Greatest Hits* (Atlantic), *Best Of Sam And Dave* (Atlantic), and not forgetting Booker T and the MGs – the swelling organ chords of Booker T and the knife-like guitar lines of Steve Cropper in 'Green Onions' mesmerised British dance floors around 1963–4. It can be found on *Best Of Booker T And The MGs* (Atlantic).

The 1979 LP, *Intensified! Original Ska 1962–66* (Island) reissued many of the sounds that were popular in the clubs at the time. It can be supplemented by Prince Buster's *Fabulous Greatest Hits* (Fab).

A very different sort of experiment, involving the blues, folk music and the acoustic guitar was then taking place in Soho. It is best represented on the following three records. Davey Graham's *Folk, Blues And Beyond* (Decca) is an impressive synthesis of blues, funky jazz (Charlie Mingus and Bobby Timmons), British folk tunes and Arabic inspired modal tunings. Another important record, destined to influence the singer–guitarist style, was *Bert Jansch* (Transatlantic), while the high point of the 'folk-baroque' style is found in the collaboration between Jansch and John Renbourn on *Bert And John* (Transatlantic). These recordings stand as one of the important bridges between the seeds sown by skiffle and later electric folk and progressive music.

The second wave of groups after the Beatles and the Stones, often closely associated with the mods, are best represented by the Who with *Meaty, Beaty, Big And Bouncy* (Track) or *The Story Of The Who* (Polydor), and the Kinks with *Kink File* (Pye). Other sounds of 'swinging London' – the Small Faces, the Zombies – can be found on *Hard Up Heroes* (Decca), while coming from out of town were two prodigious voices: Stevie Winwood with the Spencer Davis Group, *Best Of Spencer Davis* (Island), and Van Morrison with Them, *The World Of Them* (Decca).

4 The dream that exploded, 1966–71

I have said little about the Californian surfing sound of the early 1960s. A cross-over of white doo-wop inspired vocals and Chuck Berry rhythms, surf music was at first largely instrumental – The Ventures, The Safaris ('Wipe Out') – until Jan and Dean, and then the Beach Boys, added lyrics that focused on white California's two major teen cults: surfing and 'wheels'. The first is extensively covered on *Golden Summer* (United Artists), the second on the Beach Boys' *20 Golden Greats* (Capitol) and any Jan and Dean record circa 1964.

Dylan's LPs were all important in different ways. His 'folk' period is probably best displayed on *The Times They Are A-Changin'* (CBS), while *Bringing It All Back* home (CBS), recorded after the 'British invasion', firmly points towards a folk–rock perspective. The Byrds took 'Mr Tambourine Man' from this album. The next two records, *Highway 61 Revisited* and *Blonde On Blonde* (both on CBS), mark the passage of Dylan's voice into a growing word mosaic ('Like A Rolling Stone', 'Desolation Row'), and the swirling envelopment in electric sounds provided by The Band ('Visions Of Johanna', 'Just Like A Woman', etc).

The American folk revival and its immediate antecedents can be heard on *Leadbelly's Last Sessions* (Folkways), Woody Guthrie's *Dust Bowl Ballads* (Folkways), and Pete Seeger's *Broadside Ballads* (Folkways). Among the important contemporaries of Dylan was Joan Baez. *The First Ten Years* (Vanguard) offers a useful panorama of her pure vocal style and its application to both traditional and contemporary material. Phil Och's politically committed songs are to be found on the retrospective double album (he committed suicide in 1977), *Chords Of Fame* (A & M). The sophisticated musical suggestion of Judy Collins is to be listened to on an important transitional LP, both for her and much of the folk movement, *In My Life* (Elektra).

Apart from the London folk club scene gyrating around Les Cousins in Greek Street indicated in the above mentioned records of Graham, Jansch and Renbourn, the compilation four record set, *The Electric Muse* (Island), tracing much of the story of English folk music in the 1960s, is well worth searching out. It covers from A.L. Lloyd, Shirley Collins and the Young Tradition to Pentangle, Fairport Convention and Steeleye Span. Pentangle in their own right are best on *Sweet Child* (Transatlantic), while Fairport Convention's *Leige And Lief* (Island) is an important electro-folk album. Donovan is to be heard on his third LP, *Sunshine Superman* (Pye). Far less folksy than his previous two LPs, it suggests a lot of the acid-influenced, folk-rock, counter-culture sounds of the mid-1960s, particularly in the freakish 'Hampstead Incident'.

Meanwhile, in the USA folk–rock pushed ahead. The Byrds were undoubtedly the major group. But this music, which also drew upon country strains as the 1960s advanced, can be found all over the place: the Byrds's *Mr Tambourine Man* (CBS), The Band's *The Band* (Capitol), The Lovin' Spoonful's *The Lovin' Spoonful File* (Pye), the Grateful Dead's *Workingman's Dead* (Warner Brothers), Buffalo Springfield's *Retrospective* (Atlantic), and so on.

The harder 'acid rock' of the West Coast is heard to good effect on the Dead's *Live Dead* (Warner Brothers), this features such 'head' classics as 'Dark Star' and 'St Stephen'. The second album by the Jefferson Airplane, *Surrealistic Pillow* (RCA) showcases Grace Slick's voice, particularly on the LSD rewrite of Alice in Wonderland, 'White Rabbit', and the powerful 'Somebody To Love'. Their musical manifesto against 'Amerika' is *Volunteers* (RCA). Country Joe and the Fish in their most pertinent period – Berkeley, the movement against the war in Vietnam, LSD, the counter-culture – are on *I Feel Like I'm Fixing To Die* (Vanguard). Janis Joplin is best captured on *Cheap Thrills* (CBS), while Quicksilver Messenger Service's *Happy Trails* (Capitol) gives another idea of the musical feel of the San Francisco sound around 1966–7. From Los Angeles, there were the 'politicians of the erotic', *The Doors* (Elektra), and Love with *Forever Changes* (Elektra). The monumental coming together of many of these diverse musical styles took place at the public celebration of the counter-culture in upper New York State in 1969 at Woodstock. The triple album *Woodstock* (Atlantic) offers a selection of some of the performances: Jimi Hendrix, Sly and the Family Stone, Joe Cocker, The Who, Ten Years After, Ritchie Havens.

Eric Burdon's abandonment of Newcastle Brown for San Francisco's version of Nirvana is chronicled on *Winds Of Change* (MCA), while the less forced experimental sides of the period are brilliantly explored by another expatriate Briton, Van Morrison, on *Astral Weeks* and *Moondance* (both on Warner Brothers), together with Tim Buckley's *Goodbye And Hello* (Elektra).

The Zappa records mentioned in this chapter were released on either Verve or Bizarre, and a retrospective of the early Mothers's material, *Mothermania*, covering the period 1965–7, can be found on Polydor. At this point it would also be appropriate to mention the unusual, often outright weird, recordings of Captain Beefheart and his Magic Band: *The Captain Beefheart File* (Pye), and for those who want more, *Trout Mask Replica* (Straight) and *Clear Spot* (Reprise).

The Beatles's *Sergeant Pepper's Lonely Hearts Club Band* (Parlophone) was, of course, a major catalyst in pop music in general and in indicating its more sophisticated potential. Behind it lay the varied British 'underground'. Coming out of the folk clubs, the Incredible String Band used sitars, tin whistles, guitars and finger cymbals to produce an esoteric musical web on *5000 Spirits Or The Layers Of The Onion* (Elektra) and *The Hangman's Beautiful Daughter* (Elektra). The first two Pink Floyd LPs – *The Piper At The Gates Of Dawn* and *A Saucerful Of Secrets* – have been reissued as an offensively packaged double album, *A Nice Pair* (Harvest). Other major sounds of the period are *Family Entertainment* (Reprise) from Family and the reissue of the first two albums of Soft Machine, *Volumes One and Two* (Probe). Between the London 'underground' and public success, Jimi Hendrix's electrifying presence is probably best appreciated by comparing the explosive shock of his first LP, *Are You Experienced?* (Track) with the multilayered electronic textures of the double record *Electric Ladyland* (Polydor). Electric blues groups of the period are clearly led by Cream and *Disraeli Gears* (RSO), followed by Fleetwood Mac's *Fleetwood Mac* (CBS) and later Free, *The Free Story* (Island). Traffic offered a more soul-oriented trajectory, listen to *Best Of Traffic* (Island). The Rolling Stones, after their slightly uncomfortable encounter with 'flower power' – *Their Satanic Majesties Request* (Decca) – found their urban blues feet again with *Beggars Banquet* (Decca). The opening song 'Sympathy For The Devil' was subsequently woven into a fascinating sequence of the Stones in the recording studio building up the song in Jean-Luc Godard's film *One Plus One* (1969).

The beginnings of British progressive rock after the underground gestation period had definitively closed, can be sampled on Jethro Tull's *Living In The Past* (Chrysalis), King Crimson's *In The Court Of The Crimson King* (Island) and the Genesis album *Tresspass* (Charisma), on which 'The Knife' appears.

While several of the progressive rock groups looked to classical motifs and harmonic structures others looked to jazz. In the USA the first group to come to public notice playing jazz-rock was Blood Sweat & Tears. Their first LP, *Child Is Father To Man* (CBS), was released in 1968. A year later Chicago released *Chicago Transit Authority* (CBS), while Sanatana introduced Latin rhythms into West Coast rock, *Abraxas* (CBS). There were also jazz–rock groups in Britain such as If and Nucleus, but it was British guitarist John McLaughlin who, after playing with Miles Davis, pushed this music to a new fervent intensity on *Birds Of Fire* (CBS), along with Weather Report's *I Sing The Body Electric* (CBS), also released in the same year (1973).

5 Among the fragments, 1971–6

Further developments in British progressive music towards the hallowed reaches of 'art' can be found on Emerson Lake and Palmer's *Pictures At An Exhibition* (Manticore), The Moody Blues's *In Search Of The Lost Chord* (Deram), the Yes LP, *Close To The Edge* (Atlantic), Van Der Graaf Generator's *Pawn Hearts* (Charisma) and Genesis with *Foxtrot* (Charisma). Included here is also the 'progressive' exception on the Tamla Motown label, Stevie Wonder with *Innervisions*. Pink Floyd's *The Dark Side Of The Moon* (Harvest) was among the more interesting statements of this period. But, as I have tried to indicate, the full coming together of progressive themes in an independently produced artistic expression was Mike Oldfield's instrumental opus, *Tubular Bells* (Virgin). Tucked behind some of this music was Terry Riley's *A Rainbow In Curved Air* (CBS). Released back in 1969 it was a musical approach – a regular electronic pulse accompanied by cyclical structures and repetitive rhythmic figures – which, flanked by similar proposals from La Monte and Philip Glass, found a place in the later experiments of David Bowie and pointed to another relevance in an electro-funk context a decade later.

In the meantime, British electric blues rolled on. Headed by the Rolling Stones and the menacing breakdown of *Exiles On Main Street* (Rolling Stones Records), Rod Stewart's *Every Picture Tells A Story* (Mercury) marked out a more sensitive reworking of the tradition. Elsewhere, there was the revivalist sound of Creedence Clearwater Revival, *Chronicle: The 20 Greatest Hits* (Fantasy), the crafted tunes of Elton John, *Elton John* and *Tumbleweed Connection* (both on DJM), and heavy metal, to which I shall return a little further on. These last mentioned records, making up a rock 'mainstream', are to be contrasted with teenybopper pop and the world of show business and pop ballads. For some idea of the latter at the time, in one of its most flamboyant forms, listen to *Tom Jones Live At Caesar's Palace* (EMI).

The 'authenticity' of country music guaranteed it an entrance into the progressive fold. This movement was largely blazed by Dylan with *John Wesley Harding* (CBS) and *Nashville Skyline* (CBS). His contemporaries in the field of country music are best represented by Kris Kristofferson with *Me And Bobby McGhee* (Monument), Willie Nelson's *Shotgun Willie* (Atlantic) and Waylon Jennings with *Dreaming My Dreams* (RCA). Another important voice was Merle Haggard, a particular favourite in the area of country–rock. He is best listened to on *Songs I'll Always Sing* (Capitol).

Country–rock itself was heavily encouraged by the LP the Byrds released in 1968, *Sweetheart Of The Rodeo* (CBS). But it was probably the Flying Burrito Brothers who offered the most successful fusion of country and rock on *The Gilded Palace Of Sin* (A & M), while Gram Parsons's pained voice, underscored by Emmylou Harris's harmony, can be heard on *Grievous Angel* (Reprise). The group that went on to bask in international success with this musical mixture was the Eagles. Their best work is probably contained on *Desperado* (Asylum): desert sunsets, Tequila, cowboys and broken hearts. Equally maudlin, but less directly indebted to country music, were Crosby,

Stills, Nash and Young – the final sounds of the Californian experiment. The group's *4 Way Street* (Atlantic) offers a comprehensive picture of their mixed acoustic-electric styles.

A more robust version of country–rock was developed by a series of groups in the southern states of the USA. Often known as 'southern boogie', its most well-known practitioners were probably the tragically marked Allman Brothers, listen to *Brothers And Sisters* (Capricorn), and the equally unfortunate Lynard Skynyard, *First And Last* (MCA). Both groups lost keys members in road accidents and a plane crash. Mentioning the Allman Brothers there is also a connection here through Duane Allman to Eric Clapton's American metamorphosis as Derek and the Dominoes with *Layla* (Polydor).

Out of these crossings between the blues and beat, country and rock, guitar virtuosity and commercial success, emerged much of the impetus for the mainstream US rock music of the 1970s: impeccably executed, smoothly produced and easy on the ears. There were exceptions, Alice Cooper (*Greatest Hits*, Warner Brothers), leanings towards heavy metal with Boston (*Boston*, Epic), but the more usual sonorities are represented by the string of LPs Chicago recorded for CBS, Fleetwood Mac's *Rumours* (Warner Brothers), the Doobie Brothers's *Captain and Me* (Warner Brothers), Steely Dan's *Greatest Hits* (ABC), Peter Frampton's *Frampton Comes Alive* (A & M), etc.

The singer–songwriters meanwhile existed at the meeting of several musical routes: country and folk 'authenticity', artistic sincerity, and the still glowing embers of the counter-culture. This can be sensed on Neil Young's *After The Goldrush* (Reprise), but is even more in evidence on James Taylor's *Sweet Baby James* (Warner Brothers) and in a diverse key in Leonard Cohen's doom-dripping songs of isolated alienation on *Songs From A Room* (CBS). Britain offered the rhythmically more lively Cat Stevens, *Tea For The Tillerman* (Island), while a little later a distinct Californian style appeared with Jackson Browne's *For Everyman* (Asylum). There was also the hugely successful Paul Simon, *Still Crazy After All These Years* (CBS), and the later, very different song writing introspection of the late 1970s in the urban vignettes of Tom Waitts, *Small Change* (Elektra).

Carole King's *Tapestry* was released on A & M, while Laura Nyro's *New York Tendaberry* is on CBS. The earlier recordings of Joni Mitchell – *Ladies Of The Canyon, Blue* – are on Reprise, while her later recordings are on Asylum.

Heavy metal publicly got under way with the success of Led Zeppelin, although a listen to Cream's *Wheels Of Fire* (Polydor), recorded in 1968, or the Jeff Beck Group (including Rod Stewart on vocals) with *Truth*, also recorded in the same year, betrays many of the 'roots' of subsequent heavy metal. *Led Zeppelin I* and *Led Zeppelin II* (both on Atlantic) were released on public ears as the 1960s dissolved into the 1970s. Their example of high-volumed guitar riffing was quickly followed by Deep Purple, *In Rock*, *Machine Head* (both on EMI), Black Sabbath, the selection on *Greatest Hits* (NEMS) gives a clear idea of their repertoire, and a myriad of other groups. In the United States there was Grand Funk Railroad and Blue Oyster Cult, *Blue Oyster Cult* (Columbia). British heavy metal from the mid-1970s into the

1980s can be sampled on Motorhead's aptly titled *Overkill* (Bronze), Judas Priest's *Killing Machine* (CBS), Saxon's *Wheels Of Steel* (Carrere). There also exists a compilation that covers the 1979 and 1980 Reading Festival – a high point in the heavy metal calendar – which has contributions from Whitesnake, Michael Schenker, Budgie, *et al.* on *Reading Rock* (Mean).

For a selection of teenybopper music there is David Cassidy's *Greatest Hits* (Bell), The Osmonds's *Greatest Hits* (Polydor) and the Bay City Rollers with *Once Upon A Time* (Bell). In the area of teenybopper/glitter rock – where white beat is crossed with Tamla costume – there is Gary Glitter's *Greatest Hits* (Bell), the Slade's *Sladest* (Polydor) and T. Rex's *Electric Warrior* (Fly). For the story of Marc Bolan and his transition from 'underground' hero of the 1960s to a glitter prince of the 1970s, there is *The Words And Music Of M. Bolan 1944–77* (Cube). The Jackson 5 who only belong in part here – they are also among the important new black sounds of the 1970s – can be heard on *Greatest Hits* (Motown). Another peripheral case is that of Mott the Hoople ('All The Young Dudes'); they can be found on *Greatest Hits* (CBS).

The harsh urban American music that passed virtually unnoticed in the 1960s but was later destined to take on such importance is to be heard on *The Velvet Underground & Nico* (MGM) – the record supposedly produced by Andy Warhol – and *Loaded* (MGM), together with the MC 5's *Kick Out The Jams* (Elektra), and Iggy Pop and the Stooges's *Fun House* (Elektra). The New York Dolls can be found on *New York Dolls, Volumes 1 and 2* (Mercury).

Roxy Music's *For Your Pleasure* (Polydor) was probably their most stylish statement – from the night scene cover to the empty hedonism of 'In Every Dream Home A Heartache'. Subsequent music can be sampled on *Greatest Hits* (Polydor), and their continuing contribution to the electro-pop dandyism of the 1980s on *Avalon* (Polydor). The Bowie records mentioned were all released on RCA, as were Lou Reed's *Transformer* and *Berlin*. After leaving Roxy Music, Brian Eno made a series of increasingly more audacious LPs – *Another Green World* (Island), *Taking Tiger Mountain By Strategy* (Island) – that carry us into the environmental sounds/'noise' music and pop avant-gardism examined in the last chapter of this book.

6 The release from obscurity: black musics, 1966–76

James Brown's *Solid Gold* (Polydor) and Marvin Gaye's *Anthology* (Motown) provide two significant starting points here. Also the Gene Chandler collection, recorded around 1961 and including the quirky 'Duke Of Earl', gives a useful glimpse on early soul music in the making, *Just Be True* (Charly). The Motown sound of the later 1960s is well to the fore on the Temptations's *Anthology* (Motown), while another crucial influence was that of Sly and the Family Stone; listen to their *Greatest Hits* (Epic). A more self-consciously militant black music is to be found stirring on Curtis Mayfield's *His Early Years With The Impressions* (Probe), although signs of this type were certainly not absent from James Brown ('Say It Loud I'm Black And I'm Proud'), Marvin Gaye ('What's Going On') and Sly Stone. These can all be added to such Curtis Mayfield anthems as 'We're A Winner' and 'People Get Ready'.

The interweaving of blues and gospel in the different accents of soul can be followed on Ray Charles's double LP *A 25th Anniversary In Show Business Salute* (Atlantic), which, despite the unpromising title, features all the elements – blues, gospel, jazz tinges, strings, country music echoes – in a productive flux. 'I've Got A Woman', 'Hallelujah I Love Her So', and many other seminal recordings will be found here. Aretha Franklin, the daughter of a noted Baptist preacher, shows the gospel of soul at work on *Ten Years Of Gold* (Atlantic). The urgent message of The Staple Singers on *Be What You Are* (Stax) well illustrates the successful transformation of the gospel quartet format into a riveting contemporary soul sound. Al Green's smooth falsetto offers an altogether softer gospel tone on *Greatest Hits* (London).

The more extensive musical territory of soul, where musical genres slip away to be replaced by an elusive envelopment in the 'black community', can be dipped into by listening to some of the sounds developed by black jazz musicians in the 1950s and 1960s. In such pieces as 'Wednesday Night Prayer Meeting' and 'Eat That Chicken', both found on *The Best Of Charlie Mingus* (Atlantic), the black bass player reworks the relations between modern jazz and its blues and gospel 'roots'. John Coltrane's music also represents a magisterial extension of a blue universe. It is everywhere in evidence, from *Blue Trane* (Impulse), through his important collaboration with Miles Davis on *Kind of Blue* (CBS), to the 'sheets of sound' he developed on *A Love Supreme* (Impulse) and *Meditations* (Impulse). The duo John Coltrane–Rashied Ali, *Interstellar Space* is also on Impulse. Ornette Coleman with *Free Jazz* (Atlantic), Archie Shepp's *Mama Too Tight* (Impulse) and Albert Ayler's *Ghosts* (Fontana), all dug deep into the textures of Afro-American music and extended the possibilities of 'soul'. These sounds all form an important part of the black 'soul community' and its growing cultural militancy in the 1960s.

The black dancing sounds that kept British feet busy throughout this period are highly represented on the various *Motown Chartbuster* albums released towards the end of the 1960s. This music was used not only by the regular clientele of the Top Rank suites, but also by skinheads, some soul freaks, and sometimes noted by the more 'hip' white blues fans. In the early 1970s, the Motown sound in Britain was challenged by the Philadelphia production of Gamble, Huff and Bell and the rise of 'street-funk' bands extending the work of James Brown and Sly and the Family Stone. The 'Philly sound', including the O'Jays's 'Back Stabbers' and 'Love Train', along with the deep soul ballad of Harold Melvin and the Blue Notes's 'If You Don't Know Me By Now', will be found on *Phillybusters: The Sound Of Philadelphia* (Philadelphia International).

'Street-funk' brought in a jazzier feel and pointed towards some areas of a disco future. Different versions can be sampled listening to the *Greatest Hits* (Polydor) of Kool and the Gang, Earth Wind and Fire's *Open Our Eyes* (Columbia), War's *The World Is A Ghetto* (United Artists) and the Crusaders's *The Best Of The Crusaders* (Anchor). It is also worthwhile listening in to the tricks of the old master James Brown on the live LP, *Superbad* (Polydor).

Meanwhile, Motown with the Norman Whitfield production of The Temptations ('Papa Was A Rolling Stone') offered equally sophisticated funk: *All Directions* (Tamla Motown). Lengthier exercises were first pioneered by Isaac Hayes and his 1969 LP *Hot Buttered Soul* (Stax), but fundamentally encouraged by writing scores for black films. Hayes's own 'Theme From *Shaft*' is on *Chronicle* (Stax) while Curtis Mayfield's *Superfly* soundtrack is on Curtom.

The exclusive rarity of 'Northern soul' – nearly all imported, restricted to rapidly deleted singles, and firmly tied to particular dancing venues – means that short of attending an 'all-niter' and noting the records played and exchanging hands at fabulous prices (£50 for a rare sound on the Detriot Ric-Tic label in 1982) they are often difficult to hear. After reading Dave Godin in *Blues & Soul* in 1970, where the term 'Northern soul' was apparently coined, and a series of articles by Tony Cummings in *Black Music* around 1974–5, it should be possible to trace some of the records and performers in the soul music racks of the more specialist record shops. A further guide has recently been offered in Neil Rushton's 'Out On The Floor', *The Face*, n. 29, September 1982, where lists of northern dance records on imported US labels and native UK labels are given. Among them is the useful US compilation album *Sold On Soul* (United Artists). Another compilation worth hunting down is *Solid Soul Sensations* (Pye).

Back in Chapter 3 some ska recordings were suggested. To these should be added The Skatalites's *Best Of The Skatalites* (Studio One). Byron Lee and the Dragonaires's polished, tourist sundown, reggae can be heard on *Regay Splash Down* (Trojan), while Delroy Wilson's *Better Must Come* (Trojan) well expresses the rougher, but pressing, sentiments that were simmering down in shantytown. U Roy's *Version Galore* (Virgin) gives one idea of Jamaican DJ 'toasting'. A style that was later taken up by Big Youth, *Dreadlocks Dread* (Virgin) and I Roy, *Presenting I Roy* (Trojan). Unfortunately, many of the early toasters did not record but Denis Alcapone's 'Ripe Cherry' toast can be heard on *Tighten Up. Volume 5* (Trojan). On the same record there is Clancy Eccles's 'Rod Of Correction', also mentioned in this chapter.

Behind all these developments lie the more persistent strands of black Jamaican popular music. Examples of Kumina music can be found on *Bongo, Backra and Coolie* (Folkways). Buru 'ridims' played by the legendary Count Ossie and the Mystic Revelations of Rastafari are displayed on the three-record set *Grounation* (Ashanti).

The eight-volumed *Tighten Up* (Trojan) collection offers nearly all the major sounds that were around during the late rock steady/early reggae transition. Another useful compilation, which includes the classic rock steady song 'Stop That Train' (or 'Draw Your Brakes'), is the soundtrack to *The Harder They Come* (Island). This has major contributions from Jimmy Cliff, Desmond Dekker and the Slickers. The Duke Reid produced collection, *Hottest Hits* (Virgin), along with The Heptones's *On Top* (Studio One), The Pioneers with *Long Shot* (Trojan) and Slim Smith's *Early Days* (Total Sounds) are all essential listening at this point.

Studio One Presents Burning Spear (Studio One) and the Wailers's *African Herbsman* (Trojan) are two important records that reveal the state of

Jamaican reggae in the early 1970s before it started attracting international attention. Subsequent recordings by Bob Marley and the Wailers mentioned in this chapter were all released by Island in Britain.

The passing skinhead interest in reggae in the late 1960s is documented in a discography in Knight (1982), pp. 48–51. Many of the records mentioned there will be found among the above mentioned Trojan LPs along with Prince Buster's *Fabulous Greatest Hits* (Fab) referred to in Chapter 3.

By the mid-1970s reggae had both greatly spread its influence and also its internal soundscape. Burning Spear's *Marcus Garvey* (Island), Culture's *Two Sevens Clash* (Joe Gibbs) and *Harder Than The Rest* (Virgin), The Mighty Diamonds with *Right Time* (Virgin), and Gregory Isaac's *Extra Classic* (Conflict) illustrate the richer timbres entering reggae around this time. The 'roots' line of the bass and drums was extended, with the fussy 'rockers' drumming of Sly Dunbar becoming highly popular, while the use of brass and multiple track recording greatly widened the 'spread' of the sound (i.e. Culture's *Harder Than The Rest*). All this provided an effective counterfoil to the stark vocals which were now regularly strung out across Ras Tafari themes.

While British reggae was slowly emerging, and I will return to that development later, in Jamaica it was 'dub' that marked the most radical new direction in reggae. Joe Gibbs's *African Dub Almighty. Chapter 1 (Lightning)*, issued in 1973, along with the 1970 recording *This Is Augustus Pablo* (Randy) sets out the early steps in a direction that was to become increasingly sophisticated by the late 1970s. *King Tubbys Meets Rockers Uptown* (Yard), *Vital Dub* (Virgin), and *Cry Tuff Dub Encounters, Part 2/Prince Far I in Dub* (Virgin), are all recommended, while Joseph Hoo Kim's *Vital Dub* (Virgin) reworks many of the songs associated with the Jamaican vocal trio The Mighty Diamonds in an examplary display of reconstructed rhythms and timbres.

Later developments in toasting can be heard on Dr Alimantado's *Best Dressed Chicken In Town* (Greensleeves), a punk favourite, Dillenger's *Bionic Dread* (Black Swan) and Tapper Zukie's *MPLA* (Virgin).

A glance through the racks in any specialist reggae shop will reveal an enormous quantity of reggae that is frequently overlooked and lost beneath the militant Ras Tafari aura the music generates. But in the life of the black community 'sweet' reggae clearly has an important place. Some examples here could include Bob Andy's *Lots Of Love* (Sky Note), George Faith's *To Be A Lover* (Island) and Sugar Minott's *Live Loving* (Studio One).

7 Urban soundscapes, 1976–

The two essential punk LPs are the Sex Pistols' *Never Mind the Bollocks* (Virgin) – it contains all their singles – and the Clash's *The Clash* (CBS). For the live fever of a punk venue in the still heady spring of 1977 there is *The Roxy London WC2* (Harvest). This contains live material from the Buzzcocks and X Ray Spex, along with the now dimly remembered Slaughter and the

Dogs, Johnny Moped, *et al*. Another useful compilation, covering second-string punk groups of the 1976–7 season is the double LP *Burning Ambitions* released on the French label Cherry Red. Punk's rough populism, what it would call 'roots' or 'street level' music, was frequently translated into a flood of small, independent record labels. These apparently mushroomed around the subculture's early leitmotif: musical populism + recording independence = cultural autonomy. But as the idea of 'authenticity' (hence the measurement of 'autonomy') was also a rather non-punk concept, the whole formula remained precarious. Both punk and these recording initiatives ended up finding their own contradictory spaces within existing commercial categories. But in the process they produced an important series of fractures across the music, the music industry, and in musical journalism and criticism.

Later recordings by Siouxsie and the Banshees, *The Scream* (Polydor), released in 1978, the Slits, *Cut* (Island), produced by Dennis Bovell and released in 1979, and the Mo-dettes's *The Story So Far* (Deram), issued a year later, represented an important female prospect in punk, even if successive events have failed to live up to that promise. Here it is also necessary to mention the American singer Patti Smith. Her LP *Horses* (Arista), released in 1976, is an important musical statement, setting pop's multi-voiced tradition in a new, assertive, female mould. But the record really worth searching out is the first record she made: 'Hey Joe'/'Piss Factory'. 'Hey Joe' begins as a spoken monologue directed at Patty Hearst and her experience with the Symbionese Liberation Army. It then modulates into a muted guitar and piano accompanied version of the song once made famous by Jimi Hendrix.

Such self-conscious cross-references also illustrate the intentional artistic pose of much American punk. Before the advent of the later 'tasteless' American punk groups at the end of the 1970s (i.e. the Dead Kennedys) the only major exception were the monosyllabic sidewalk anthems of the Ramones: *Rocket To Russia* (Sire).

For an awareness of the state of the British Hit Parade and the 'middle of the road' sounds to which, along with the guardians of progressive rock, punk caused most offence, I suggest a quick listen to Abba's *Greatest Hits* (Epic), *Wings At The Speed Of Sound* (EMI), and The Carpenters's *Horizon* (A & M).

The Bobby Womack LP *Safety Zone* is on United Artists. The complex black heritage of the disco sound can be researched in the already mentioned James Brown LPs, Sly Stone's *Stand* (CBS) and Miles Davis's *Bitches Brew* (CBS). Latin rhythms are already well in evidence in the street funk recordings mentioned in the previous chapter; similarly, the key 'Philly' sounds have also been indicated there.

The soundtrack for *Saturday Night Fever* (RSO), which, apart from the Bee Gees, also features Kool and the Gang and the Trammps among others, is essential for appreciating the explosion of the disco boom in the late 1970s. But to this should be added Gloria Gaynor's *Love Tracks* (Polydor); Chic's *C'est Chic* (Atlantic) – later through the work of Nile Rodgers to be an influential force all over pop, from Blondie to Bowie – Manu Dibango's

Makossa Music (Creole), Grace Jones's *Nightclubing* (Island) and the compilation *Souled Out* (K-Tel). With these records it becomes possible to taste the sonorial spread and diverse musical currents of what is frequently dismissed as the 'monotony' of disco.

The polished, light, British funk music of the early 1980s can be tested on Linx's *Go Ahead* (Chrysalis), while white versions are numerous, i.e. the music of Spandau Ballet. The music of ex-members of the Pop Group, found on Rip Rag & Panic's *I Am Cold* (Virgin), and involving the co-operation of ex-Ornette Coleman partner Don Cherry, is an interesting experiment in cross-cultural music. Pig Bag's *Lend An Ear* (Y Records) offers lighter fare.

The best introduction to rap music is the double album *Rapped Uptight* (Sugarhill). It includes nearly all the sounds that count: from the Sugarhill Gang's 'Rapper's Delight' through contributions from Trouble Funk, the Treacherous Three, Sequence – the all female rappers, to Grandmaster Flash and the Furious Five with 'The Message'.

Steel Pulse's *Handsworth Revolution* was released on Island. Matumbi were playing reggae music (along with the Cimarons) long before Steel Pulse and other new groups began to appear in the late 1970s. *Point Of View* (EMI) offers a good example of their musical style. Matumbi's Dennis Bovell is also the leading dub master in Britain, this can be discovered listening to his *Brain Damage* LP (Fontana). Linton Kwesi Johnson's first LP, *Dread, Beat And Blood* is on Virgin, while *Forces of Victory* and *Bass Culture* were recorded for Island.

The white reggae of the Police is best exposed on their second LP, *Reggatta De Blanc* (A & M). While the ska revival can be heard in action on *The Specials* (Chrysalis), the Selecter's *Too Much Pressure* (Chrysalis), and the Beat's *I Just Can't Stop It* (Arista). Birmingham 'dub' is to be discovered on UB 40's *Signing Off* (Graduate).

The Clash have regularly drawn upon reggae music right from the days when they featured Junior Murvin's 'Police and Thieves' on their first LP. *London Calling* (CBS) is a double album that apart from illustrating their use of reggae rhythms and textures is probably their most successful record and sums up, along with the Pretender's *Pretenders* (Sire) and the Jam collection *Dig The New Breed* (Polydor), a lot of the rejuvenation in British pop at the end of the 1970s.

The earlier pub rock scene can be listened to on Ducks De luxe's *Before The Flood* (RCA). Around the mid-1970s, this circuit received the shock of the R & B powerhouse of Dr Feelgood, *Stupidity* (United Artists) and Eddie and the Hot Rods, *Teenage Depression* (Island). American street angst, apart from Patti Smith, is well to the fore on Bruce Springsteen's *Darkness On The Edge Of Town* and *The River* (both on CBS); it later stretched into the bucolic depression of *Nebraska* (CBS).

The Ian Dury record to hear is *New Boots And Panties* (Stiff). Graham Parker's 'Heat Treatment' is on *Heat Treatment* (Vertigo), while 'Discovering Japan' is on *Squeezing Out Sparks* (Vertigo). Costello's *My Aim Is True* was released by Stiff. *This Year's Model* is on Radar, *Get Happy!*, *Trust*, and the more recent *Imperial Bedroom* are on F Beat, a subsidiary of CBS. Another singer to mention at this point is Joe Jackson and his LP *Look Sharp!* (A & M). In his later work, Jackson harks right back to the jump R & B sound of Louis Jordan.

The Bowie LPs mentioned here – *Young Americans, Station To Station, Low* and *Heroes* – are all on RCA.

Keeping punk alive in the 1980s are groups like Crass, *4 Stations of the Crass* (Crass Records) and Discharge, *Hear Nothing, See Nothing, Say Nothing* (Clay). A selection from this fervent latter-day punk scene, with contributions from The Exploited, UK Subs, Angelic Upstarts, and others, can be found on *Punk and Disorderly III* (Gram). Some of the beginnings of this hard line tradition with its mixture of punk and skinhead following – the last LP in the Oi series, *Oi! Oi! that's yer lot!* (Secret), has a 'drunk' side and a 'punk' side – is well in evidence on Sham '69's *Tell Us The Truth* (Polydor). Here the football terrace choruses of the live audience on the first side of the record intermingle with such populist sentiments as 'George Davis Is Innocent', 'Rip Off' and 'Borstal Breakout'.

The PIL album *Metal Box* was a limited edition. It was reissued as *Second Edition* (Virgin). The Gang of Four's work can be heard on *Solid Gold* (EMI). Theoretical Girls no longer exist, but a recent example of New York 'noise' music is Glenn Branca's *Ascension* (99), while one of the more successful funk experiments has been Defunkt's *Thermonuclear Sweat* (Hannibal).

Some elements of electro-dance music had an early precedent in Kraftwerk's *Trans Europe Express*. It is also worth recalling the insistent electronic pulse of several German groups of the early 1970s at this point: Tangerine Dream, *Phaedra* (Virgin), Amon Duul II, *Dance Of The Lemmings* (United Artists), and Can. These groups influenced both such post-punk avant-gardists as PIL and the more popular electro-dance music. Gary Numan's *The Pleasure Principle* (Beggars Banquet), John Foxx's *Metamatic* (Virgin), The Human League's *Dare* (Virgin), and Duran Duran's *Rio* (EMI), have all plugged the dance floor into synthesisers and drum machines.

Discovering 'juju' music could begin with King Sunny Ade's noted LP *Juji Music* (Island), and could be followed up by listening to Ade's *Juju Music Of The '80s* (SALPS). Island Records are issuing quite a few records of West African music, so there should be no difficulty in exploring further in that territory for whoever is interested. For soca, calypso and Jamaican 'mento', I would suggest a trip to a specialist record shop such as Sonny Roberts's Orbitone Records (2 Station Offices, Station Road, London N.W. 10). For Latin rhythms, again a specialist record shop, and the LP *Latin Roots* (Cariño) is worth searching out.

Brian Eno's *Music For Airports* (Polydor) was the first of a series of records appropriately entitled 'Ambient'. A more recent has been *Ambient #4 On Land* (EG Records). In between, he has released other sound experiments: *Music For Films* (Polydor), *Before And After Science* (Polydor). Glenn Branca has already been mentioned. Laurie Anderson became widely known in 1982, obtaining a hit with 'O Superman'. Her sonorial work from that period is on *Big Science* (Warner Brothers).

At the other bitter extreme of the musical spectrum, 'Oi' music, overseen by *Sounds* journalist Gary Bushell, has been offered to the public in a four-record Oi set on the Secret label. The 4 Skins, who gained public notoriety after playing the Hambrough Tavern, the night it was burnt, have released an LP with a suitably ambiguous title: *The Good, The Bad & The 4 Skins* (Secret).

But, to end on a more optimistic note, one of synthesis rather than disintegration, take Michael Jackson's *Thriller* (CBS) and discover how heavy metal can be crossed with black dance music ('Beat It'), dubious sentiments with beautifully choked vocals ('Billie Jean'), and topped off with sexual ambiguity and physical excitement ('Wanna Be Startin' Somethin').

Notes and References

1 Living in a modern world

1. Dick Hebdige has made a fine analysis of some of the principal cultural motives that brought together English intellectuals as diverse as Evelyn Waugh, George Orwell and Richard Hoggart in a common critical front against the 'spectre of Americanisation' (Hebdige, 1981).
2. After experiments induced by the wartime experience, the BBC 'streamlined' its programming and adopted 'American methods of presentation and continuity, together with a change in policy towards programme scheduling, which imposed a new pattern on popular broadcasting and favoured the development of programmes with a serial or series format' (Cardiff and Scannell, 1981, p. 69).
3. Writing of the music hall, Bernard Waites comments that by 'the late nineteenth century, popular song was habitually absorbing and adopting American influences' (Waites, 1981, p. 45). Colin MacInnes also noted a similar tendency (MacInnes, 1969).
4. Charles Curran in the internal Conservative party magazine *Crossbow* in 1962, quoted in Gamble (1974, p. 78).
5. In the classic discussion of this tradition, Raymond Williams, writing in the mid-1950s, observed how the term 'masses' was a new word for mob, and the traditional characteristics of mob were retained in its significance: gullibility, fickleness, herd-prejudice, lowness of taste and habit. The masses, on this evidence, formed a perpetual threat to culture' (Williams, 1963, p. 288).
6. Recent historical studies all agree that between 1880 and 1920 an important adjustment occurred in British urban culture. The increasing separation of the work place from the home, the rise of city suburbs and cheap public transport, led to a falling away of a work-located culture. Home and pleasure became less directly tied to the routines and politics of work (Stedman-Jones, 1974). The new concentration of labour processes in industrial zones, and the winning of shorter working hours through trade union agitation, encouraged an expanded and novel sense of 'leisure'. It was now increasingly organised in 'private' time and out of private pockets.
7. This position was most forcibly argued against popular music and the 'culture industry' in general by the German philosopher Theodor

232

Adorno. For a critical response to some of Adorno's precise objections, see Chambers (1982).

8. The twelve bar form tends to be the usual structure of the blues. But it is a tendency, not an iron rule. Eight and sixteen bar blues, not to speak of even more unusual measures, as Muddy Waters reminds us, will be encountered: 'See, my blues is not as easy to play as some people think they are. Cause here, this is it, I may have thirteen beats in some song, and an average man he not used to that kind of thing. He got to follow me, not himself, because I make the blues different. Do that change thing when I change, just way I feel, that's the way it went. I mean you take that song 'Just To Be With You'. Now that's a good blues tune, and I made it just the way I felt, sometimes I play thirteen, sometimes I play fourteen beats. And I got just as good time in the blues as anyone' (Guralnick, 1978, p. 72).

9. Note that I use the term 'official' (or 'classical'). European folk music contains many examples of 'blues' type pentatonic scales.

10. A major example is 'bottleneck' guitar playing. Here a knife or bottleneck applied to the strings of the guitar allows the player to bend, slide and slur entire chord shapes up and down the guitar neck. As Trevor Wisehart notes, there is no equivalent of this in European 'functional harmony' (Shepherd *et al.*, 1977, p. 171).

11. 'In the 27 years since B.B. [King] hit with 'Three O'Clock Blues' he must have performed the song, at a conservative estimate, about 5,000 times. Five *thousand* times. Now I can't speak for 4,997 of those performances but I was present at three of them and, if my memory serves me right, on each occasion B.B. has turned out solos whose only resemblance has been the twelve bar structure on which they were built' (Chris May, *Black Music & Jazz Review*, November 1978, p. 43).

12. 'Transatlantic octopus' was a phrase coined by the BBC's Director of Outside Broadcasting in a report he prepared in 1929 on 'the degree to which the BBC may be affected by USA control of world entertainment' (Scannell and Cardiff, 1982, p. 180).

13. It all appeared in a much clearer light later, especially in the epoch of 'progressive rock' music where musicians ran up hundreds of hours of studio time in recording an LP. But pop's beginnings were not that different. Elvis spent many hours in the recording studio working on his sound until Sam Phillips was happy that he had got down something novel on tape. I am not suggesting that Presley was simply 'constructed' in the very simple recording facilities of the Sun recording studio, only pointing out that the studio and the subsequent record was now a point of departure for a musical career of radio coverage, live shows and television appearances, *not*, as it had once been, a point of arrival.

14. This permanent 'now' also made death 'even more absurd that ever' (Morin, 1962). The absurdity of death in a context of mechanical reproduction is counteracted by the idea of death as transcendence. It opens up the possibility for the attainment of iconic immortality in the perpetual circulation of a reproducible image: James Dean, Marilyn Monroe, Jimi Hendrix, Brian Jones, Sid Vicious – 'living out' their

symbolic presence on so many T-shirts, shopping bags, bedroom posters and practised gestures, beyond the immediate reach of history and chronological time.

2 A Formative Moment 1956–63

1. Steve Race in *Melody Maker*, 5 May 1956. The whole article is constructed around the 'monstrous threat' represented by rock 'n' roll.
2. Compare the section 'Popular music' in the preceding chapter.
3. White southern gospel was particularly important in the formation of rock 'n' roll. Most biographies of Elvis Presley, for instance, insist upon it. For further details of this musical genre in the post-war period immediately prior to rock 'n' roll, see Wolfe (1981).
4. This title is borrowed from a *Melody Maker* article of the time criticising rock 'n' roll. It is worthwhile quoting the complete phrase to remind ourselves today just how high the stakes were once felt to be in this cultural clash. 'It is one of the embarrassments of democracy that this is the age of the common man. The achievement of fame in popular music today demands a rabble rousing technique' (Tony Brown, *Melody Maker*, 21 July 1956). Once again, it was the voice of the unruly mob that was nervously identified.
5. In July 1954, the Television Act, setting up commercial television became law. In September 1955, the new regional commercial programme companies began broadcasting. The stiff, patrician cultural policy of the BBC suffered a rather abrasive shock with the introduction of ITV. The latter, dependent on advertising for its revenue, and therefore needing to guarantee large audiences, began to produce a new sense of 'popular entertainment'. Ranging from US action series like *Dragnet* and *Highway Patrol* to the native serial drama of *Emergency Ward 10*, the variety of *Sunday Night at the London Palladium*, and the symbol of uninterrupted television popularity, *Coronation Street* (it began in 1960), a more flexible media construction of what was 'popular' was introduced.
6. *Melody Maker*'s rival, *New Musical Express*, had carried such charts since its first issue in 1952. The difference between the two papers on this point can be explained by the fact that *Melody Maker* considered itself far more a musician's paper (with a strong constituency in the jazz world) than *NME*.
7. In the period 1959–60, a rash of bribery scandals broke out in the USA. More than 200 DJs, including the daddy of rock 'n' roll, Alan Freed, were convicted of accepting payments for playing certain records: 'payola'. With high investments and uncertain futures facing most recordings, the role of the DJ could become a neuralgic point in determining success.
8. Television soon became an important channel. Here the BBC were forced into adopting a more pragmatic approach as it dealt with direct

competition from ITV programmes. The BBC offered *6.5 Special* while ITV had *Oh Boy!*. Later there was ITV's *Thank Your Lucky Stars*, which was matched by the BBC's more sombre *Juke Box Jury*.

9. In one way or another, all comments on Elvis Presley are comments on an epic myth. In a brilliant essay, 'Presliad', the American writer Greil Marcus has exposed the essential 'Americanness' in the heterogeneous components and subsequent shaping of the Presley presona; see Marcus (1977). Richard Middleton, in an interesting examination of Presley's various musical styles, has offered a corrective to the linear 'decline' of Presley's musical–biographical trajectory (from daring innovator to show business immobility) that Marcus, despite himself, tends to suggest (Middleton, 1980). But it is Albert Goldmann (1982) who provides the most exhaustingly morbid account of the Presley epic. He traces the rise of our hero from poor southern white stock to the youthful owner of a fleet of Cadillacs and his establishment of many of the precedents of rock 'n' roll – 'Portrait of the Artist as a Young Punk'. After which, cocooned in a growing diet of pills, shoddy Hollywood films, splended isolationism and Las Vegas shows, Elvis becomes prisoner of the 'American Dream': a junky recluse who rarely ventures outside the walls of his Memphis home, Graceland, has a world at his beck and call, and is swindled by a manager who has the finesse of a fair ground huckster.

10. Probably the only British rock 'n' roll record of any significance was Johnny Kidd and the Pirates's 'Shakin' All Over', and that was released in 1960.

11. These chart positions come from Jasper (1979). No claim is being made here as to their accuracy as a map of popular tastes in Britain at the time. The frequent failure of the national record charts to register significant cultural and commercial movements, for example, the sales of reggae and "Northern Soul' records in the 1970s, is well known. However, in their limited and sluggish way the charts tend to reflect the broad, symptomatic shifts if not all the details. It is in this sense that they are used here and elsewhere in the book.

12. For more on the important mixture of black urban music and studio production in the late 1950s, widely associated with the work of Ahmet Ertegun, Jerry Wexler, the teenage prodigy Phil Spector, the songwriting team of Leiber and Stoller, and the foundation of Tamla Motown, see Millar (1971).

13. Birmingham Feminist History Group (1979). Following this logic, girls went to dances to be 'picked up', courted and then, having found a marriage partner, were expected to abandon the dancing floor. 'Dancing is extremely popular with the girls until marriage, when it is dropped at once. Sometimes when Marian, aged 22, sees her sister getting ready to go to a dance she is envious... Marian used to be very keen on dancing too, but she and her husband never go dancing now they are married' (M. Kerr, in Mungham, 1976, p. 85).

14. For a useful, and amusing, account of the jazz world and life on the road between British dance halls in the first half of the 1950s, see Melly (1970).

3 Britain's 'Inner Voices', 1963–6

1. Adapted from black dancing patterns, the Twist was taught to American youth by Chubby Checker on Philadelphia's *American Bandstand*. Under the avuncular eye of Dick Clark, the master of ceremonies of this nationally networked television show, the dance, despite all the wiggling bottoms and piston-actioned hips, rapidly became strangely asexual in effect – exuberant rather than prurient.

2. *Thank Your Lucky Stars*, hosted by Brian Mathew, also acknowledged the commercial rationale of pop music, but in a less patronising fashion than *Juke Box Jury*. It adopted a more 'open market' policy, preferring to act as a showroom of choices rather than the direct overseer of commercial trends. A brief part of the show was regularly turned over to a record jury, but this time apparently drawn from the teenage audience present in the studio. Records were never simply 'hits' or 'misses', but were awarded a score motivated by phrases like 'I like it', 'It's good for dancing to'. At least here nebulous show business values and attempts at market forecasting were a little less evident. Apart from this more obvious teenage slant, *TYLS* was a music show. Groups and singers played (mimed actually), and the whole song, not just a snatch, was heard.

3. See Andrew Gamble's particularly acute analysis of this theme and its political consequences in Gamble (1981).

4. The 'Scopitone', for example, was an unsuccessful attempt to anticipate the video disc. On this specially constructed juke box each record was accompanied by a colour film of the singer or group performing.

5. A good indication of the state of affairs was that it was only in July 1964 that the very pop oriented *New Musical Express* began carrying an LP chart.

6. The idea of 'double tracking', rather than being viewed as a means to boost and extend sonorial possibilities, was still largely considered a device to 'cloak the flaws' and hide 'inexperience' (*New Musical Express*, 26 February, 1965).

7. And, of course, into the whole discourse of industrial design. See Hebdige (1981), pp. 48–50.

8. *The Observer* and *Sunday Telegraph* launched their colour supplements in the autumn of 1964.

9. Colin Fletcher's observation on the transmutation of Liverpool youth gangs into potential beat groups at the end of the 1950s and the beginning of the following decade is important (Wheen, 1982, p. 20). It underlines how music became a new totem for male youth street culture, with a subsequent shift from fights over local territory to challenging existing leisure provisions by occupying dance halls with their bodies and their music, and encouraging teenage clubs to open.

10. The 'natural' vocalising, 'open' chords and generally 'minor' sound of many of the Beatles's songs, also recalls, apart from the blues, the modal tunings characteristic of folk, medieval and renaissance music. Modal scales being 'derived from the behaviour of the human voice, they

naturally predominate in all musics melodically conceived' (Mellers, 1976, p. 203).

11. See Middleton (1972), pp. 167–70.

12. The permissive spread of 'bohemia' opened up a two-way traffic of unforseen consequence. In one direction, it lent its blessing to resignifying parts of popular culture, particularly the pop music world of dandified attire, drugs and sex. In the opposite direction, it laid open aspects of traditional culture (that is culture with a capital C) to popular infections. Now much of this may simply be an example of what Tom Wolfe likes to refer to as 'radical chic'. But, the long-term effects of such an interchange in the rapidly moving feast of urban life can reveal unsuspected tendencies. For the moment, I will leave you with a recent observation from Jon Savage: 'If Andy Warhol took A-heads, transvestites and hustlers up-town with him, then the Rolling Stones took the Bohemian tradition of non-conformism and self-expression that was nurtured in their jazz club roots to a mass, youth audience of a scale and immediacy hitherto unseen, and unreckoned' (Savage, 1982).

13. The ambiguous shock generated by the music of the Rolling Stones is well caught in a debate that occurred in 1968 between Alan Beckett and Richard Merton. Beckett argues that, while not 'major innovators', the successful adoption of the 'erotic narcissism' of the blues in their music permitted the Stones to break with the 'facile intimacy' of sentimental romanticism (Beckett, 1968). Merton replies by saying that it is precisely that fact that makes the Stones major innovators in pop. The Stones have exposed a central taboo – sexual inequality, and they 'have done so in the most radical and unacceptable way possible: by celebrating it' (Merton, 1968, p. 30).

14. A list of white British pop musicians of this period associated with art school would include Keith Richards, John Lennon, Pete Townshend, Ray Davies and Eric Clapton.

15. Georgie Fame's live LP *Rhythm and Blues At The Flamingo* (1964), gives a good idea of the music played in such a club: James Brown's 'Night Train', 'the Miracles' 'Shop Around', Prince Buster's 'Humpty Dumpy', and such R & B classics as 'Baby Please Don't Go' and 'Let The Good Times Roll'.

16. To what degree the brief period of the pirate radios contributed to this situation is difficult to say. Certainly, the pirates offered a wider and more knowing range of pop, one much closer to London's clubland scene than the BBC.

17. This is reported in Melly (1970), also see Mungham (1976) on the cultural restrictions of the provincial dance hall.

18. The musical entwinings of soul and gospel are further examined in Chapter 6.

19. In one of his songs, 'There Was A Time' (1967), James Brown announces that he is literally doing 'the James Brown'.

20. On 2 April 1965, after the Musicians' Union put an end to miming on television, *RSG!* went live. This presented no hitch, it simply suggested the opportune extension of the programme's own ethos.

21. George Melly makes an interesting observation on the effect of televised pop on teenage fashion at a national level. 'When I was touring in the 50s fashions took an almost incredible time to spread. Even the large provincial centres like Liverpool and Manchester were at least six months behind, while in small Yorkshire mining communities as late as 1960 it was still possible to find teddy boy suits, and not only that. They were tailored in ruby red or billiard-table green cloth. As for the borders of Scotland the girls' dresses had hardly altered since the middle 30s. *RSG* changed all that. It made pop work on a truly national scale' (Melly, 1972, p. 170).

22. In February 1963 in the *Evening Standard*, Maureen Cleave noted the 'Continental connection' in the Beatles' hair style, a 'French style' cut adopted while they were in Germany, after they had dropped their rock 'n' roll quiffs.

23. This description of a mod wardrobe, *circa* 1963–4, comes from Hamblett and Deverson (1964). Also see the Who's film *Quadrophenia* (1979) for an accurate reassembling of the sartorial props of 1964.

24. 'When Jerry Rubin and Abbie Hoffman appeared on *The Dick Cavett Show* in body paint there wasn't much further to go in that direction. But to go in the opposite direction and take formality to an extreme can become outrageous and people are confused by it. They think, yeah, he's got on a coat and a tie, and they can't quite put their finger on what's unsettling about it' (Wolfe, 1982).

25. For an extremely perceptive and fascinating analysis of the attempted appropriation of this black 'reality' by successive white British male subcultures see Dick Hebdige's study (1979), pp. 46–70. In the case of the mods it should be noted that their worldly 'cool' also made more than a passing reference to that other exiled community: the London criminal underworld.

26. An important study of this orchestrated confrontation will be found in Cohen (1973).

27. While amphetamines tend to heighten one's sense of relation to reality, producing a 'hyperreality' as it were, LSD distorts and rearranges the original referent ('reality'), often to the degree of temporarily blotting it out and imposing an alternative order of sensations.

28. The earlier, collective responsibilities of wife, motherhood and the family that had been persistently addressed by magazines like *Woman* and *Woman's Own* in the 1950s, was now supplemented by a publicisation of female individuality and pleasure in newer magazines like *Honey* and *Cosmopolitan*. See Janice Winship's important analysis of this shift (Winship, 1980).

29. Again, Janice Winship has drawn out the potential and contradictory importance of the active female intervention in the world of goods. 'While commodities have "invaded" the personal arena, they have also made that arena public... so that in a limited way, through commodities, the *masculine* construction of femininity can be turned back into men's faces by women themselves: showing that it is indeed a masculine construction' (Winship, 1981, p. 29).

30. As is to be expected, it is the Rolling Stones who provide the paradigm. Listen to 'Play With Fire', '19th Nervous Breakdown', 'Paint It Black', 'Have You Seen Your Mother Baby'. Another striking perspective is that provided by the Italian film director Michelangelo Antonioni. His film *Blow-up* (1966), telling the story of a 'trendy' young photographer who inadvertently stumbles across the evidence of a murder, is finely organised around schizoid shifts between the shiny surfaces of 'swinging London' life and a suggested emptiness in its fashionable pursuits.

4 The Dream That Exploded, 1966–71

1. Again, the Rolling Stones, admittedly amongst the most 'American' of British groups: from *Beggars Banquet* (1968) to their obsessive Stateside culmination in *Exiles On Main Street* (1972).
2. Dylan had been known of in 'hip' British circles before 1965. The Animals had their first major hit electrifying a US folk song – 'The House Of The Rising Sun' – taken from Dylan's first LP. In 1964 he had recorded a lengthy studio concert for BBC 2.
3. The other contemporary folk singing success, apart from Donovan, was Joan Baez. Her 'pure', unobtrusive voice, although completely opposite in style from the rough country evocations of Dylan's singing, was equally directed towards highlighting the verbal sentiments of song.
4. These concepts, and their centrality in the formation of later rock music, have been well explored by Simon Frith (Frith, 1981).
5. See Jeff Nuttall (1972) for a rich map of these radical bohemia-pop culture connections.
6. Among the Merry Pranksters – the travelling Californian 'happening' organised by Ken Kesey and with whom the Grateful Dead played – was Neal Cassady, the mythical 'Dean' of Kerouac's *On The Road*.
7. Here we are at the level of metaphorical options. The choices are imaginative as much as physical, the 'landscapes' fundamentally psychic, the internal geography often hazy and fluid. The 'Indian', the mythical 'outsider', untainted by industrial society and urban life, could just as likely turn out to be a guru from the Asian subcontinent as the native of the plains and deserts and woods of North America. When you live on the Pacific shore to go West involves going to the Orient, going to the 'East'.
8. Confronting the widespread references to the 'Orient' (I-Ching, Buddhism, Transcendental Meditation) in the hippies' mythology – for relatively few actually made the physical translocation – it is worthwhile recalling how Roland Barthes once posed himself in front of the 'East': 'I do not observe an oriental essence with love. I am indifferent to the East, it only provides me with a repertoire of features which organised and playfully arranged permit me to "flatter" the idea of an unheard of symbolic system, one completely separate from our own' (Barthes, 1970).

9. Ken Kesey, the organiser of the Pranksters and author of *One Flew Over The Cuckoo's Nest*, was a latter day beat: rock music and 'acid' replacing be-bop and 'tea'. For more on such cultural cross-currents in American bohemia in the 1960s, see Tom Wolfe's classic account *The Electric Kool-Aid Acid Test* (1969).

10. Suggested listening here would be Country Joe and the Fish's *I Feel Like I'm Fixing To Die* (1968), the Doors' *The Doors* (1967) and Jefferson Airplane's *Volunteers* (1969). There was also the MC 5 from Detroit. Originally managed by White Panther John Sinclair, the MC 5 probably came nearest to a successful projection of a guerrilla rock group on the live *Kick Out The Jams* LP (1968).

11. Reading Richard Neville's somewhat offensive guide to the counter-culture, *Playpower* (1971), the limits of the personal liberation practised, and its complete domination by heterosexual masculine needs requires little pointing out.

12. This attention to the personal and cultural dimension has been repeatedly insisted upon in subsequent political commentary. One of the first observations of this type occurs in Hall (1969). Such a train of thought produced an important modification in the way that the possible transformation of society was conceived. It has posed a central challenge to an older marxist model that argued that only after a substantial and irreversible change in society's essential economic 'base' would daily culture and social relations experience corresponding alterations. The probe made into the tissues of contemporary society by the cadres of the counter-culture pointed to the need for a more articulate *political* understanding of social relations and cultural realities in advanced capitalist countries. If the counter-culture never managed to implement fully its declared aims, it nevertheless opened up crucial questions about such a complex transformation as 'revolution'.

13. While in California Frank Zappa was experimenting with 'decon-structed' musical collages, in a then musically unfashionable New York the Velvet Underground were also beginning to cut up the existing musical spectrum in a radical way. But where Zappa drew on various musical genres, many completely foreign to the pop experience, the New York group remained firmly within the appearance of the pop song. Mobilising the 'shocking' characters and harsh, urban 'noise' of New York street life, the subsequent music was pushed to the edge and out beyond easy definitions. The importance of this demonstration was not lost on important areas of pop in the next decade. It was to be a strategy that came to be amplified in the conscious popular artifice of David Bowie and Roxy Music, and later in the even more significant case of punk. The Velvet Underground are discussed in the next chapter, when, in the 1970s, their delayed affect in pop finally begins to fall into a wider register.

14. *Rolling Stone*, based in San Francisco, appeared for the first time in November 1967. It was intended as a fortnightly paper firmly committed to the sounds and ethos of the counter-culture and its 'revolution'. It went on to become the success story of 'alternative' publishing. A mounting

circulation and ensuing commercial pressures from the music business saw it change shape and policy over the period 1968–73. By the early 1970s it had become established as *the* American rock magazine, but it was now 'hip' to a far vaster and more nondescript white middle-class public than the term 'counter-culture' conveys. Today it averages more than 3 million copies an issue. For further details, see Frith (1978) pp. 144–6.

15. For example, the dingy R & B club sound of Zoot Money's Big Roll Band changed overnight into the blinding strobe-lit Dandelion's Chariot, Eric Burdon became a West Coast evangelist preaching 'acid' and love, and ex-Spencer Davis prodigy, Steve Winwood temporarily retired with his new group Traffic to a country cottage in Berkshire to 'get it together'.

16. Hendrix also sported a black-Red Indian-gypsy wardrobe. It consisted of Afro-hair, amulets, headbands, fringes, flamboyant jewellery, bandana, boots, and much oriental finery. Together with his tortured guitar sound it brought together a series of dark, marginal souls. It seemed almost inevitable that this isolated black superstar should be become a symbolic crucifix in the white counter-culture.

17. For more on the precise politico-cultural importance of '1968', see, among others, H. Lefebvre, *The Explosion* (1969); H. Marcuse, *An Essay On Liberation* (1972); A. Quattrocchi and T. Nairn, *The Beginning Of The End* (1968); and Juliet Mitchell, *Woman's Estate* (1971).

18. See note 12 above.

19. For the traumatic effects of the Manson murders on the US counter-culture see Ewen (1972). Jeff Nuttall noticed a similar sobering affect on the British avant-garde underground – then contemplating such happenings as 'publicly disembowelling a human corpse and hurling the guts at the audience' (Nuttall, 1972, p. 129) – affected by the Moors Murders in 1965. Ian Brady and Moira Hindley were a couple of 'working-class libertines' who translated their private Sadeian fantasies into the murder of two children and a teenager. They tape-recorded the tortures and eventual murder of the young girl victim. Two years later Pamela Hansford Johnson (Lady Snow) published *On Iniquity*, a book that purported to demonstrate that Brady and Hindley were the inevitable products of a 'permissive society'.

20. A year later the film *Performance*, starring Mick Jagger and James Fox, was released. Directed by Donald Cammell and Nicolas Roeg, the film traced the shifting line between the worlds of a pop recluse and a London 'villain' on the run from gangland retaliation. Playing with identities – an effective remedy for the spiritual nadir of the two protagonists – the film was an interesting comment on the stylised amoralism that fundamentally connected the apparently dissimilar, but equally image conscious lives of a pop star and a gangster.

21. See Hall *et al.* (1978) and Gamble (1974).

22. These particular phases of progressive rock are part of a context quite distinct from what might be called the 'clever' pop of the 1960s. The latter category ranges from Phil Spector's famous 'wall of sound', through many recordings by the Beatles, the Who, the Zombies, etc., to

such US groups as Vanilla Fudge. These musics remained firmly committed to an insistent beat and an 'intentional' sound, achieved by building 'inwards', rather than a 'classical' style linear development (see Chester, 1970). I am grateful to Simon Frith for pointing out this distinction to me.

23. Not everybody took these changes lying down. Parts of the Anglo-American rock music critical establishment drew back from the more extravagant 'artistic' claims and vulgarisation of the earlier cultural ideals associated with rock music. But it was usually to little avail. While Van Morrison may well have remained a critic's choice, it was Jethro Tull, ELP, Genesis, etc., who drew the biggest crowds and inflated progressive music's commercial standing. On the Continent, the disillusionment with this development was often fierce. It coalesced in a militant refusal to accept the later disassociation between revolutionary politics and the retreat into 'art' of subsequent progressive music. Many European critics had demanded more of rock, having constructed a fervent political identification with the US West Coast music of the 1965–8 season: '...pop music/rock died around 1968–69. Probably at Chicago (August 1968)!' (Daufouy and Sarton, 1972). Similar sentiments were also expressed in Germany and Italy. For these commentators, the cultural powers and political *intentions* involved in the period 1965–8 were considered sufficient for rock to have reached out beyond commercialism, not to explore the freedoms of 'Art', but to pose itself in the vanguard as a direct alternative to 'capitalist music'. But the contradictions in such a position are finally merciless. How could rock music, with its type of production and distribution, immediately subtract itself from the rest of the institutionalised and capital intensive field of pop? Such an insistence on a politically 'pure' alternative meant that successive rock was simply condemned as being sonorial publicity for fickle consumerisms.

5 Among the Fragments, 1971–6

1. Here I am referring to the record re-released in 1973 at the height of Bowie fever by RCA. The LP was originally issued on the Mercury label in 1969 with the title *Man Of Words, Man of Music*.

2. Although issued in 1973, *Tubular Bells* remained amongst the top selling LPs in Britain for both 1974 and 1975. Composed and performed solely by Oldfield, the record is a fitting summation of many of the 'artistic' and technological ideals of progressive music. It launched the fortunes of the recently founded Virgin Records.

3. Amongst the major black sounds of 1969 were Marvin Gaye's classic 'I Heard It Through The Grapevine', and 'Too Busy Thinking About My Baby'. While from Jamaica there was Desmond Dekker's 'The Israelites' and 'It Mek', the Upsetters with 'Return Of Django', and Harry J and the All Stars with 'The Liquidator'.

4. Royston Eldridge writing in the first issue of *Sounds*, 10 October 1970.

5. The capital of country music is Nashville, Tennessee. Bakersfield, the home of Merle Haggard – a Grateful Dead favourite – and Buck Owens is the centre of California's country music. Here is not the place to go into the variegated territory of US country music except to underline its persistent influence on the course of white American pop: from the birth pangs of rock 'n' roll to the 1980s and Bruce Springsteen's doomed nostalgia and country boy solitude on *Nebraska* (1982). Set in a subordinate, southern white culture, country music proposes to be 'Jeffersonian', that is, to celebrate democratic individualism. However, it frequently turns out to be 'Jacksonian – intensely chauvinistic, racist, majority-oriented, and anti-aristocratic in the worst as well as the best sense. That is to say that it voices both sides of populism: the democratic and the fascistic' (Christgau, 1973, p. 202). It is undoubtedly the oldest and most popular of white popular music genres in the United States. For further details, see B. Malone (1968). In *Lost Highway* (1979), Peter Guralnick appears at times to have defected to a melancholic country version of 'reality'. Plunging back to certain 'roots' and the mirage of an 'organic community' of musicians and audiences – the evidence of resistance to 'homogenisation' thanks to 'artistic integrity', he concludes: 'So – and this is the final step in my simplified syllogism – what is entertaining people on a mass level is no longer genuinely popular culture – in which the audience at whom the entertainment is aimed, out of whom the entertainment has sprung, continues to have a real impact – but a pale evisceration, a pathetic dilution of a rich cultural tradition' (Guralnick, 1979, p. 14). It is worthwhile setting the underlying pathos of this account alongside the very different version presented in effervescent montage of Robert Altman's film *Nashville*.

6. All The Band's material was imbued with the tones of a mythical, rural America, and while not necessarily 'country' in musical form was deeply so in sentiment and expression. This is especially evident on their first two LPs: *Music From Big Pink* (1967) and *The Band* (1968). Californian rock music was particularly prone to adopting country music, listen to the Grateful Dead's *Workingman's Dead*, but also *American Beauty*, both released in 1970.

7. Suggested listenings include Judy Collins, *Wildflowers* (1968), Joni Mitchell's *Ladies of the Canyon* (1970) and *Blue* (1971), Carole King's *Tapestry* (1971), Laura Nyro's *New York Tendaberry* (1969), and, once again, the later work of Joni Mitchell: *For The Roses* (1973), *Court and Spark* (1974), *The Hissing of Summer Lawns* (1975), and *Hejira* (1976).

8. See McRobbie and Frith (1978) and the reply by Taylor and Laing (1979). Among the earliest commentators on this dimension in rock music is Christgau (1973), pp. 113–8.

9. Writing in the US publication *Rolling Stone* in 1971, Jon Landau noted: 'Zeppelin forced a revival of the distinction between popularity and quality. As long as the bands most admired aesthetically were also the bands most successful commercially (Cream, for instance) the distinc-

tion was irrevelant. But Zeppelin's enormous commercial success, in spite of critical opposition, revealed the deep division in what was once thought to be a homogeneous audience. That division has now evolved into a clearly defined mass taste and a clearly defined elitist taste' (quoted in Shepherd *et al.*, 1977, p. 189). Restricting, in the best progressive rock tradition, their recorded output to LPs, the first six albums of Led Zeppelin each sold more than 2 million copies. In 1972, a year in which the group released no new material, they accounted for 18 per cent of the business of Atlantic Records (figures from Palmer, 1977, p. 275).

10. Here I am drawing directly upon the arguments and research of Angela McRobbie's study of British teenage girls' magazines (McRobbie, 1978a).

11. There is an important series of stylistic connections, both at the musical and wider cultural levels, at this point to the later lacerated romanticism of Patti Smith and the street poetics of Bruce Springsteen.

12. Such self-referring constructs were the shifting personae of David Bowie and Lou Reed, the ironic, glossy packaging of Roxy Music, and, more indirectly, the subsequent facial masks and sartorial kaleidoscope of punk and such post-punk manifestations as the 'new romantics': 'three times removed from fiction' (Steve Strange).

13. Directed by Nicolas Roeg, the film *The Man Who Fell To Earth* appropriately featured David Bowie as an extra-terrestrial humanoid moving blankly through a science fiction script.

14. Amongst the liberal reforms put on the statute book by the Labour government of the day was the Abortion Act of 1967, the Sexual Offences Act in the same year decriminalising private adult male sexual activities, the abolition of the Lord Chamberlain's censorship of the theatre in 1968, and divorce reform in 1969.

15. It is no accident that much of the most illuminating research into how consumer goods are *actively* transformed into meaningful cultural signs and expression has been that examining the particular situations and experiences of those generally assumed to be the most 'passive' in their consumption: women. See notes 28 and 29 of Chapter 3, and Winship (1981). Arguments about the contradictory potentialities of consumption and its active appropriation/transformation, runs completely counter to Taylor and Wall's wholly negative view of 'glamrock' (Taylor and Wall, 1976). For them, Bowie was a 'plastic' disguise, an offensive commercial and cultural 'emasculation' of the once 'authentic' values of the 'underground'. (How the latter's music escaped 'marketing' they are reluctant to explain.) So while they acknowledge glam rock's importance in permitting working-class girls to enter directly into new leisure institutions, they conclude: 'this process has been accelerated, if not actually precipitated, by the new marketing of leisure' (p. 110). All the *contradictory* evidence of glam rock's and Bowie's success is reduced to being merely the latest move by capitalism to organise proletarian leisure. But the real question, given that the commercialisation of popular culture has been in act for at least a century or more in

Britain, is not whether this tendency exists, but how it *exists*. To adopt an epochal explanation of the details of British popular culture – the contradiction between capital and working-class culture – does not carry us very far towards understanding the active and imaginative changes made in the cultural textures and social experiences of popular culture by subordinate groups as they transform cultural commodities into their own (determined) culture.

16. For a revealing account of the construction of 'masculinity' in the male working-class experience of school, see Willis (1977). It should be read alongside Angela McRobbie's important criticisms of male oriented subcultural studies (McRobbie, 1980).

6 The Release From Obscurity: Black Musics, 1966–76

1. A listen to the contemporaneous recordings of fellow Chicagoans Muddy Waters and Gene Chandler (noted in Britain for his hit 'Duke of Earl'), clearly reveals the distance between urban blues and its subsequent reworking in the emerging context of soul music in the early 1960s (see the Discography).

2. It is in the mid-1960s that a *direct* bridge between black US music and white British pop is established. The early examples of isolated black performers – Fats Domino, Little Richard, Chuck Berry – were replaced by identifiable black sounds and labels: soul music, 'Stax', 'Tamla'.

3. The requisite male dress at one time involved baggy trousers with 40-inch bottoms and waistbands 6 inches thick, short-sleeved, collared bowling shirts or singlets, and generally short hair. A change of clothing to replace those saturated in sweat after a steamy 'all-niter' would be carried in a sports bag emblazoned with Northern Soul venue badges and slogans.

4. Such changes in location were regularly induced by police raids for drugs. As with the mods a decade earlier, amphetamines, known in northern argot as 'gear', frequently go hand in hand with the all-night allegiance to dance and soul. The Wigan Casino – the principal monument of 'Northern Soul' – finally closed its doors in the autumn of 1981. But the soul enthusiasm and the 'all-niters' still continue.

5. The change in terminology from 'coloured' (or 'Negro') to 'black' was only the most blatant illustration of the widespread practice in black culture of reversing the semantic tokens of the English language. Apart from the particular morphology of speech rhythms and syntax, a black idiolect can also be traced in the semantic transformation of the linguistic labels of a daily repression. The negative and feared connotations of 'black' is proudly adopted, and words like 'bad', 'dirty' and 'mean' come to be employed as adjectives of approval. Language, as the prime medium of daily consciousness, is refined in US black popular culture into a communicative practice (subsequently displayed in the

'rap' format) that simultaneously includes all its potential users while eliding the participation of the white outsiders.

6. One of the later consequences of the development of lengthy soul pieces was the baroque 'symphonic funk' associated with Barry White and his protégé Love Unlimited. Another was the role this development played in the shift from soul to disco music. For further details of this second aspect see the next chapter.

7. Apart from 'soul', the expression 'funk' conjures up almost as much semantic power in US black popular culture.

8. Doubly emarginated by sex and race, the more 'extreme' accounts of sexual and social margins were widely deemed – by both white and black audiences – to be the 'natural' property of black women singers. The few white female singers – Janis Joplin in the USA, Maggie Bell and Carol Grimes in Britain – who have sought their musical inspiration in Afro-American music have either rarely been permitted to sustain such an alliance for long or else have received only guarded acknowledgement.

9. The corporeal sense of disco music is further emphasised in many discothèques with the use of the 'Boom Box'. This instrument reproduces the bass notes a full octave below their recorded level. The music literally hits the bodies of the dancers as a series of physical/sound waves.

10. Significantly enough, the real breakthrough for Bob Marley in Britain occurred after the original Wailers had broken up and was engineered by Chris Blackwell of Island Records. It was not the distinctive 'roots' sound on *Burning* (1973), but the 'cross-over' LP, *Catch A Fire*, released in the same year, that proved most successful. Marley's distinctive voice and lyrics were mixed in with additional studio textures in London. The result was a rock 'mix' or 'progressive' reggae LP.

11. See Chapter 3.

12. According to Nettleford (1972), who refers to the 1960 Jamaican census, 76.8 per cent of Jamaica's population are of pure African descent. Less than 1 per cent are European or white. The rest are Chinese, East Indian and various mixtures (Afro-European, Afro-Chinese, etc).

13. For an account of an attempt to translate Rastafarian prophecies into present day Ethiopian realities, see Derek Bishton 'The Promised Land', in *The Face*, n. 31, November 1982.

14. For further details of these Jamaican aspects, see Rex Nettleford's excellent discussion of Jamaica's 'national identity' in Nettleford (1972). On reggae and black Jamaican popular culture, see S. Davis and P. Simon (1979), H. Johnson and J. Pines (1982), and Michael Thelwell's novel *The Harder They Come* (1980).

15. This procedure is well documented in a memorable scene in Perry Henzell's Jamaican film *The Harder They Come* (1972). The above mentioned novel by Michael Thelwell is an extended literary homage to the power of the original film.

16. For a clear discussion of the Afro-Caribbean context of African influences and traces in Jamaican popular music, see Johnson and Pines (1982), pp. 12–35.

17. As Garth White describes it: 'the piano or rhythm guitar emphasised the "and" of one-*and*-two-*and*-three-*and*-four-*and*-etc. The drummer meanwhile played the conventional four beats to the bar on the bass drum and the back beat on the snare' (in Johnson and Pines, 1982, p. 49).

18. Garth White once again offers a useful description of reggae's basic structure: 'A half-note is added to the classic "after-beat" of the Ska/Rock Steady, which gives one-*anda*-two-*anda*-three-*anda*-four-*anda* etc'. He goes on to observe that the drummer continues to drop in between the beats, but in a manner that results in 'a more "sinuous" and less "jumpy" rhythm' (Johnson and Pines, 1982, p. 61).

19. A nightmare vision of skinhead was graphically recreated for the peaceful citizen browsing through W.H. Smith in a series of vicarious reports from the youth front represented by the novels of Richard Allen: *Skinhead, Skinhead Farewell, Boot Boys, Skinhead Girls*. The connection of skinhead to popular currents of cultural parochialism perhaps also explains why it is the only subculture whose inner conservatism has permitted it to stage a successful revival. For the 'return' of the skinheads in the late 1970s, this time ostentatiously organised around the white rage of 'Oi' music, see the next chapter.

20. Already by the end of the 1960s, various official reports were revealing that black youth was heavily discriminated against in the British job market.

21. The authors of *Policing the Crisis* note: 'Policing the *blacks* threatened to mesh with the problem of policing *the poor* and policing the *unemployed*: all three were concentrated in precisely the same areas – a fact which of course provided that element of geographical homogeneity which facilitates the germination of a militant consciousness. The ongoing problem of policing the blacks had become, for all practical purposes, synonymous with the wider problem of *policing the crisis*' (Hall *et al.* 1978, p. 332; authors' italics).

22. The limited tolerance and respectability that the Rastas have won for themselves in Jamaica, a fitting recognition of their almost direct descent from Marcus Garvey, Jamaica's national hero, has found no echo in British public life.

23. It has to be said that not everywhere was common sense punctured so effectively. The predominant maleness of black urban street culture and much reggae music imagery has often been focused on the reggae equivalent of the mythical blues figure of 'Staggerlee'. 'Natty Dread' is a Caribbean hero who can out-smart and out-fuck all male competitors. Until very recently, the 'sisters' or 'queens' in the Ras Tafari movement have also regarded Women's Liberation and feminism as 'foolish'; they considered the Rastaman's preservation of his 'maleness' to be intrinsic to insulating himself against the forces of Babylon. In the Rasta's programme to recover his lost dignity and his enslaved 'manhood', homosexuality is also regarded as 'unnatural' and 'ungodly'. As for birth control, the reply has often been abrupt: 'They want to turn our queens into graveyards' (Nettleford, 1972, p. 93). Ontological 'reasoning' has predictably meant that the 'natural' role and place of women

becomes a point where such logic refuses to digest historical forces and contemporary realities. However, there are signs, both in Jamaica and in Britain's black communities, that this may be changing (see Gilroy, 1982).

24. It should not be forgotten that reggae is not the unique Caribbean music to be 'hidden' like this. There are also substantial audiences in Britain, particularly among older generation West Indians, for other Jamaican and Caribbean popular musics. The calypso of the Mighty Sparrow and Lord Kitchener are probably the most well known of this genre. But apart from calypso there is also 'soca' and 'spooge' (a cross between soul and reggae). For some fascinating details on the presence and popularity of these musics in Britain, see the interviews in 'Invisible Hits: The Caribbean Connection' (*Collusion*, n. 4, 1983).

7 Urban Soundscapes, 1976–

1. The American film director Jon Jost offers a suggestive vision of such a possibility in his film *Chameleon* (1978). Terry is a Los Angeles dealer whose main line is cocaine, but also includes art forgeries. We follow him as he wheels and deals and cruises around the endless intersections of the American metropolis talking to the night. He floats in the world of the artistic radical-chic; the one so mercilessly lampooned by Tom Wolfe in *The Painted Word* (1976). But he survives on 'street' logic, by hustling. Terry is a lizard, constantly changing skins. He lives on the urban margins and, sliding through the slick habits of the city, moves between the vague boundaries of an artistic 'hyperrealism' and a cocaine-induced freeze shot of the world: between the postures of the art world and the art of posing life. A more obvious cinematic metaphor is John Carpenter's *Escape From New York* (1981). It is 1997, Manhatten has been transformed into a quarantined penal colony, populated by criminals, punks and other urban mutants.

2 .While British punk represented a brutal musical overthrow of its present and immediate past, New York's punk scene involved an altogether more sophisticated, albeit neurotic, distillation of the dark 'highs' in US rock music, from Chuck Berry to the Doors, Jimi Hendrix to the Velvet Underground. A trash aesthetics, liberally strewn with literary referents – Wilson Pickett rubbing shoulders with Rimbaud, Genet with Van Morrison, as it were – set it in a cultural context quite distinct from the provocative cultural nudity and musical basics of British punk. The projected street corner dumbness of the Ramones was the only major exception.

3. Patti Smith's records (*Horses*, 1975, *Radio Ethiopia*, 1976), although deeply influenced by a pantheon of male rock romantics (Keith Richards, Brian Jones, Jim Morrison, Jimi Hendrix, Van Morrison), was an important step for woman's voice. She established an assertive, yet distinct, female vocal style within white pop.

4. *Melody Maker*, 7 August 1976. This rather predictable defence of 'artistic' qualities – 'eloquence', 'sensibility' – was unconsciously an ironic reincarnation of a similar attack by Steve Race against rock 'n' roll published in *Melody Maker* twenty years previously; see Chapter 2.

5. Tony Parsons, soon to be co-author with Julie Burchill of *'The Boy Looked At Johnny'. The Obituary Of Rock And Roll* (1978), *New Musical Express*, 11 December 1976.

6. The International Situationist Group emerged in the mid-1950s. Perhaps their most famous public statement was Guy Debord's global critique of the fetishised spectacle of advanced capitalism, *The Society of the Spectacle* (1970). In England, the Angry Brigade launched a bombing campaign in the early 1970s in a Situationist inspired attempt to spark off revolution. But it is hardly to this isolated, political activist strain that punk can be compared. It was rather with the immediate forebearers of L'Internationale Situationniste, L'Internationale Lettriste, a small offshoot of the Parisian Dada movement, that we find a certain affinity. The Lettrists specialised in painting slogans down their trousers, their ties, and across their shoes. They encouraged the practice of urban 'drifting' and 'psychogeography': 'the study and correlation of the material obtained from drifting. It was used on the one hand to try to work out *new emotional maps* of existing areas and, on the other, to draw up plans for bodies of "situations"' (Grey, 1974, p.5). Malcolm McLaren has been connected with the Notting Hill 'situationists' group known as 'King Mob'. The latter's claim to fame largely rested on an invasion of Harrods one Christmas and their distribution of 'free' goods to surprised shoppers until the police arrived.

7. Sometimes, of course, the perpetuators of startling mythologies become its most clamorous victims as a blinding circle of shock blocks everything else from view. The demise of the Sex Pistols, after a chaotic US tour in January 1978, tottered over into such an end. While Johnny Rotten quit the group, guitarist Steve Jones and drummer Paul Cook flew off to Rio De Janeiro to record with the Great Train robber Ronnie Biggs. Sid Vicious and girlfriend Nancy Spugen meanwhile entered their own horror comic script in New York City. Nancy was knifed to death and Sid, charged with her murder, finally escaped out of the picture on a heroin overdose.

8. Two broken contracts, the partial release of 'Anarchy In The UK' (immediately withdrawn after EMI terminated their contract), and £125,000 paid out to the group in compensation lay behind the Pistols before they signed for the third time in less than a year to Virgin Records in May 1976 and 'God Save The Queen' was released.

9. For a stimulating guide around some of the historical and institutional reasons for which this crisis may turn out to be irreversible in its effects, see Tom Nairn (1979) and Gamble (1981).

10. On 'English ideology', 'Thatcherism' and common sense conservatism, see Hall (1979) and Nairn (1981).

11. *Black Music & Jazz Review* (formerly *Black Music*), November 1978.

12. Hendrix had also been a direct influence on Davis's electro-jazz music. An interesting article on the Cuban roots of 'salsa' is Nestor Figueras's 'A Gozá', in *Collusion*, n. 1, 1981.

13. With a white John Travolta, the Australian Bee Gees and the Robert Stigwood organisation, disco's commercial 'conspiracy' seems complete. But appearances can be extremely deceptive! And even if they turn out to be real, no one can foresee the diverse pleasures they might meet.

14. I have largely relied on Tony Cummings's article 'Gloria Gaynor and the Disco Boom', *Black Music*, June 1975, for these details.

15. Disco is firmly wedded to soul, a tradition which itself has had a share of fussy styles that have undercut prevailing concepts of masculinity: falsetto voices, the high camp of Little Richard, the burlesque extravagancy of the James Brown Revue, etc.

16. This is the 'Northern Soul' DJ Ian Levine speaking, *Black Music & Jazz Review*, May 1977. For the clubs the DJs were continually searching out new sounds to establish and extend their reputations. In some cases, this reached such a pitch that Manchester's Ian Levine began flying out to the USA to produce 'Northern Soul' style records in American studios. By the late 1970s, Independent Local Radio did give a greater outlet to soul and disco music with programmes like Greg Edwards' *Soul Spectrum* (Capital Radio) and Andy Peeble's *Soul Train* (Piccadilly Radio, Manchester).

17. The success of disco music exercised an influence also on parts of reggae. Some groups and performers – Bob Marley, Third World, Inner Circle, Peter Tosh, Big Youth – slackened reggae's characteristic off-beat and moved nearer to the regularity of disco rhythms, sometimes passing directly into 'disco-mixes'. The famous bass/percussion partnership of Robbie Shakespeare and Sly Dunbar became a regular component of Grace Jone's disco success: listen to *Nightclubbing*.

18. Apart from the regular musical press, the London magazine *Collusion* has carried some interesting details on the New York rap situation. See Sue Steward's 'Rapping NYC' in *Collusion*, n. 1, 1981, and S. Cosgrove, S. Harvey and J. Nichols, 'Three Way Rapping' in *Collusion*, n. 3, 1982. The rap group that employs classical records on the turntable is The Symphonik B-Boys Mixx.

19. From an interview conducted with members of the *Temporary Hoarding* collective in London in September 1978.

20. The number of publications devoted to black music in Britain is notable; especially if compared to the situation in the United States where there exists no magazine specialising solely in black music. In Britain, *Blues and Soul*, *Black Music* (later *Black Music & Jazz Review*), *Black Echoes*, and a more occasional publication like the reggae specialist *Pressure Drop*, along with a host of fanzines (*Hot Buttered Soul*, *Black Wax*, *Soul To Inspect*), has revealed a major audience, which includes many white readers, for publications dealing only in black music.

21. Around the time of punk there was also a public re-emergence of teddy boys and a rockabilly revival. On the fundamental cultural (and political) conservatism of these born again teds, on their now seemingly 'quaint' combinations of clothing and music, their Little Englander patriotism, and their antipathy towards the punks for being 'too clever', see Hebdige (1979), pp. 80–4.

22. Beginning with Junior Murvin's 'Police And Thieves' on their first LP (1977), reggae had become an integral part of the Clash's sound by the time of their fourth album, *Sandinista* (1980). By this time the Jamaican Mickey Dread had materialised at the studio console and Don Letts was making their promotional videos.

23. In the provinces bondage trousers and spiky coloured crops continued to be seen long after their London inspiration had dried up or else been transformed into something else. In 1982 one commentator observed: 'punk has gone from capital fashion to provincial obsession' (*New Musical Express*, 1 May 1982).

24. For a description of certain aspects of New York's 'noise' music and interviews with Glenn Branca, Rhys Chatham and James Chance, see *ZG*'s special issue on New York, *ZG*, n. 3, 1981.

25. By the late 1970s, the music of the 'free' improvisation, avant-gardist groupings involved in the London Musicians's Collective at 42 Gloucester Road, NW. 1, and around their magazine *Musics*, was showing considerable signs of being affected by punk. Elsewhere, taking the Flying Lizards's first LP (1979), we find a now seemingly obvious marriage between the disruptive syntax and rumour scores of the historical avant-garde and the inheritance of subcultural 'noise'. This type of suggestive connection eventually crops up all over the place. We need only think of the precise theories and applications of the American composer John Cage and then listen to Brian Eno, PIL, Rhys Chatham, or, more unexpectedly, the 'cut-up' of reggae dub and interruptive 'street' sounds of rap.

26. The term 'post-modernism' came into circulation with the crisis of modernism in American architecture and the visual arts, and as an initiative in US literary criticism. In Europe, Jean François Lyotard's *La condition postmoderne* (1979) is probably most noted for this discourse. But the absence of 'respect' for official chronologies and historical 'authority' represented by European post-modernism is not exactly the same as its American cousin, although it often shares a French post-structuralist platform – Barthes, Derrida, Kristeva, Baudrillard, Foucault – in common. In particular, the European version is informed by a wider sense of 'crisis': one that is extensively political and ideological. It involves a profound sense of loss, of losing the coherence and explanatory authority, including marxism's, once assumed to emanate from the conscious, rational subject. The result is that existing rationalities, and the projects constructed upon them, have been forced into a deep reassessment.

Conclusion

1. Inside the elastic and continually reproduced contours of present day popular culture, the relative stasis of 'tradition' finds itself hard pressed to guarantee a beseiged 'authenticity'. For the traditionalists there lies only one exit: the 'idea of freedom recedes from social theory to aesthetics' (Fekete, 1977, p. 6). The presumed unity of an authoritative 'knowledge' or 'Culture' is undermined and dispersed by the heterogeneous pressures of diverse knowledges–cultures.

2. Leaving aside these broad sweeps for a moment, it would be possible to go even further and examine, for instance, the shifts within pop music journalism – from an insistence on a certain type of musical 'authenticity' in the late 1960s to the brandishing of 'street credibility' in the subsequent decade – as major signals in the changing rhetoric of a more generalised urban romanticism.

3. Pushed beyond previous limits by wider events and by the insistent demand for the 'new', male romanticism has in recent years begun to discover a conspicuous identification with its own sex: David Bowie, Michael Jackson, Boy George. But male beauty and narcissism, playing with 'self' and sexual ambiguities, often under the rubric of 'camp', still indicates a male privilege in public life. Existing gendered powers, even here, maintain the limits of the sexually permissible. Pop culture acknowledges the sign of 'gayness', but there is not yet a whisper of female sexual autonomy, of lesbianism.

Bibliography

Bibliography

ABRAMS, M. (1959), *The Teenage Consumer*, London Press Exchange, London.
ATTALI, J. (1977), *Bruits*, Presses Universitaires de France, Paris.
BARNES, R. (1976), *Coronation Cups and Jam Jars*, Centerprise Publications, London.
BARNES, R. (1979), *Mods!* Eel Pie, London.
BARTHES, R. (1970), *L'Empire des signes*, Skira, Ginevra.
BARTHES, R. (1973), *Mythologies*, Paladin, London.
BARTHES, R. (1977), 'The Grain of the Voice', in *Image–Music–Text*, Fontana, London.
BECKETT, A. (1968), 'Stones', *New Left Review*, 47, London.
BENJAMIN, W. (1973), 'The Work of Art in the Age of Mechanical Reproduction', in *Illuminations*, Fontana, London.
BIRD, B. (1958), *Skiffle*, Hale, London.
BIRMINGHAM FEMINIST HISTORY GROUP (1979), 'Feminism and Femininity in the Nineteen-Fifties', *Feminist Review*, n 3, London.
BLACK, M. and COWARD, R. (1981), 'Linguistic, Social and Sexual Relations: A Review of Dale Spender's Man-Made Language', *Screen Education*, 39, London.
BOOKER, C. (1970), *The Neophiliacs*, Fontana, London.
BROOKS, R. (1982), 'Everything you want... and a little bit more', *ZG*, 7, London.
BURCHILL, J. and PARSONS, T. (1978), *'The Boy Looked At Johnny'. The Obituary of Rock and Roll*, Pluto, London.
BURROUGHS, W.S. (1973), *The Wild Boys*, Corgi, London.
CARDIFF, D. and SCANNELL, P. (1981), 'Radio in World War II', Unit 8 of the Open University Popular Culture Course, U203, The Open University Press, Milton Keynes.
CASHMORE, E. (1979), *Rastaman*, Allen & Unwin, London.
CHAMBERS, I. (1982), 'Some Critical Tracks', *Popular Music*, 2, Cambridge University Press, Cambridge.
CHESTER, A. (1970), 'Second Thoughts on a Rock Aesthetic: The Band', *New Left Review*, 62, London.
CHRISTGAU, R. (1973), *Any Old Way You Choose It*, Penguin, Baltimore.
CLARKE, S. (1980), *Jah Music*, Heinemann, London.

COHEN, S. (1973), *Folk Devils and Moral Panics*, Paladin, London.

COHN, N. (1970), *AwopBopaLooBopAlopBamBoom*, Paladin, London.

COWIE, C. and LEES, S. (1981), 'Slags or Drags', *Feminist Review*, 9, London.

CUMMINGS, T. (1975a), 'The Northern Discos', in C. Gillett and S. Frith, (eds), *Rock File 3*, Panther, London.

CUMMINGS, T. (1975b), 'Northern Soul', *Black Music*, November, London.

CUNNINGHAM, H. (1980), *Leisure in the Industrial Revolution*, Croom Helm, London.

DAUFOUY, P. and SARTON, J-P. (1972), *Pop music/rock*, Editions Champ Libre, Paris.

DAVIS, S. and SIMON, P. (1979), *Reggae Bloodlines*, Anchor/Doubleday, New York.

DEBORD, G. (1970), *The Society of the Spectacle*, Red and Black, Chicago.

DYER, R. (1979a), *Stars*, British Film Institute, London.

DYER, R. (1979b), 'In Defence of Disco, *Gay Left*, 8, London.

EISEN, J. (1969), *The Age of Rock*, Vintage Books, New York.

EWEN, S. (1972), 'Charlie Manson and the Family', *Working Papers in Cultural Studies*, 3, Centre for Contemporary Cultural Studies, Birmingham.

FEKETE, J. (1977), *The Critical Twilight*, Routledge & Kegan Paul, London.

FIEDLER, L. (1972), *The Return of the Vanishing American*, Paladin, London.

FRITH, S. (1978), *The Sociology of Rock*, Constable, London.

FRITH, S. (1981), '"The magic that can set you free": The Ideology of Folk and the Myth of the Rock Community', *Popular Music*, 1, Cambridge University Press, Cambridge.

GAMBLE, A. (1974), *The Conservative Nation*, Routledge & Kegan Paul, London.

GAMBLE, A. (1981), *Britain in Decline*, Macmillan, London.

GAYLE, C. (1973), 'Reggae: Soul of Jamaica', in *The Story of Pop*, Phoebus Publications, Leeds.

GILROY, P. (1982), 'Steppin' out of Babylon – Race, Class and Autonomy', in P. Gilroy, E. Lawrence, H. Carby, *et al.*, *The Empire Strikes Back. Race and Racism in 70s Britain*, Hutchinson, London.

GOLDMANN, A. (1982), *Elvis*, Penguin, Harmondsworth.

GRAHAM, D. (1981), 'The End of Liberalism', *ZG*, 2, London.

GREEN, A. (1979), 'On the Political Economy of Black Labour and the Racial Structuring of the Working Class in England', *Stencilled Occasional Paper*, 62, Centre for Contemporary Cultural Studies, Birmingham.

GREY, C. (1974), *Leaving the 20th century*, Free Fall Publications, London.

GURALNICK, P. (1978), *Feel Like Going Home*, Omnibus Press, London.

GURALNICK, P. (1979), *Lost Highway*, Godine, Boston.

HALL, S.(1969), 'The Hippies: An American "Moment"', in J. Nagel, (ed.), *Student Power*, Merlin, London.

HALL, S. (1979), 'The Great Moving Right Show', *Marxism Today*, January, London.

HALL, S. AND WHANNELL, P. (1964), *The Popular Arts*, Hutchinson, London.

HALL, S. and JEFFERSON, T. (eds), (1976), *Resistance Through Rituals*, Hutchinson, London.

HALL, S. CRITCHER, C., JEFFERSON, T., CLARKE, J., ROBERTS, B. (1978), *Policing the Crisis*, Macmillan, London.

HAMBLETT, C. and DEVERSON, J. (1964), *Generation X*, Tandem, London.

HARALAMBOS, M. (1974), *Right On: From Blues to Soul in Black America*, Eddison, London.

HEBDIGE, D. (1976), 'The Meaning of Mod', in Hall and Jefferson (1976).

HEBDIGE, D. (1979), *Subculture: The Meaning of Style*, Methuen, London.

HEBDIGE, D. (1981), 'Towards a Cartography of Taste, 1935–62', *Block*, 4, Middlesex Polytechnic. Reprinted in an abridged version in B. Waites, T. Bennett and G. Martin (1982).

HEBDIGE, D. (1982), 'This is England! And they don't live here', in Knight (1982).

HOARE, I. (1975), 'Mighty, Mighty Spade and Whitey: Soul Lyrics and Black–White Crosscurrents', in I. Hoare, C. Anderson, T. Cummings, S. Frith, *The Soul Book*, Methuen, London.

HOGGART, R. (1958), *The Uses of Literacy*, Penguin, Harmondsworth.

HOSKYNS, B. (1982), 'As Years Go By', *New Musical Express*, 9 January, London.

HOWELL, D. (1976), *British Social Democracy. A Study in Development and Decay*, Croom Helm, London.

JACKSON, B. (1968), *Working Class Community*, Routledge & Kegan Paul, London.

JASPER, T. (1979), *British Record Charts 1955–1979*, Macdonald/Futura, London.

JENKINS, D. (1975), *Black Zion: The Return of Afro-Americans and West Indians to Africa*, Wildwood, London.

JOHNSON, H. and PINES, J. (1982), *Reggae. Deep Roots Music*, Proteus, New York & London.

JOHNSON, L.K. (1975), *Dread Beat and Blood*, Bogle-L'Ouverture, London.

KEROUAC, J. (1958), *On the Road*, Deutsch, London.

KNIGHT, N. (1982), *Skinhead*, Omnibus Press, London.

LAING, D. (1969), *The Sound of Our Time*, Sheed & Ward, London.

LEFEBVRE, H. (1961), *Critique de la vie quotidienne. 2. Fondements d'une sociologie de la quotidienneté*, l'Arche Editeur, Paris.

LEFEBVRE, H. (1969), *The Explosion*, Monthly Review Press, New York & London.

LYOTARD, J-F (1979), *La condition postmoderne*, Editions de Minuit, Paris.

MABEY, R. (1969), *The Pop Process*, Hutchinson, London.

MALONE, B.(1969), *Country Music USA*, University of Texas Press, Austin.

MARCUS, G. (1977), *Mystery Train*, Omnibus Press, London.

MARCUSE, H. (1972), *An Essay on Liberation*, Penguin, Harmondsworth.

McARTHUR, C. (1972), *Underworld USA*, Secker & Warburg, London.

McGLASHAN, C. (1973), 'The Sound System', *Sunday Times Colour Magazine*, 4 February, London.

McINNES, C. (1959), *Absolute Beginners*, MacGibbon & Kee, London.

McINNES, C. (1961), *England, Half English*, MacGibbon & Kee, London.

McINNES, C. (1969), *Sweet Saturday Night*, Panther, London.

McROBBIE, A. (1978a), '*Jackie*: An Ideology of Adolescent Femininity',

Stencilled Occasional Paper, 53, Centre for Contemporary Cultural Studies, Birmingham.

McRobbie, A. (1978b), 'Working Class Girls and the Culture of Femininity', in Women's Study Group, *Women Take Issue*, Hutchinson, London.

McRobbie, A. (1980), 'Settling Accounts with Subcultures', *Screen Education*, 34, London.

McRobbie, A. and Gerber, J. (1976), 'Girls and Subcultures', in Hall and Jefferson (1976).

McRobbie, A. and Frith, S. (1978), 'Rock and Sexuality', *Screen Education*, 29, London.

Meller, H.E. (1976), *Leisure and the Changing City*, Routledge & Kegan Paul, London.

Mellers, W. (1976), *Twilight of the Gods*, Faber & Faber, London.

Melly, G. (1970), *Owning-up*, Penguin, Harmondsworth.

Melly, G. (1972), *Revolt into Style*, Penguin, Harmondsworth.

Merton, R. (1968), 'Comment', *New Left Review*, 47, London.

Middleton, R. (1972), *Pop Music and the Blues*, Gollancz, London.

Middleton, R. (1980), 'All Shook Up', in J.L. Tharpe (ed.), *Elvis: Images and Fantasies*, University Press of Mississippi, Jackson.

Miles, J. (1981), 'Terrorism in Disneyland', *ZG*, 2, London.

Millar, B. (1971), *The Drifters*, Studio Vista, London.

Mitchell, J. (1971), *Woman's Estate*, Penguin, Harmondsworth.

Morin, E. (1962), *L'esprit du temps*, Grasset, Paris.

Morse, D. (1971), *Motown*, Studio Vista, London.

Mulvey, L. (1975), 'Visual Pleasure and Narrative Cinema', *Screen*, v. 16, 3, London.

Mungham, G. (1976), 'Youth in Pursuit of Itself', in G. Mungham and G. Pearson (1976).

Mungham, G. and Pearson, G. (eds), (1976), *Working Class Youth Culture*, Routledge & Kegan Paul, London.

Nairn, T. (1979), 'The Future of Britain's Crisis', *New Left Review*, 113–14, London.

Nairn, T. (1981), *The Break-up of Britain*, Verso/NLB, London.

Nettleford, R. (1972), *Identity, Race and Protest in Jamaica*, Morrow, New York.

Neville, R. (1971), *Playpower*, Paladin, London.

Nuttall, J. (1970), *Bomb Culture*, Paladin, London.

Orwell, G. (1970), *Collected Essays. Volume 2, 1940–43*, Penguin, Harmondsworth.

Paddison, M. (1982), 'The Critique Criticised: Adorno and Popular Music', *Popular Music*, 2, Cambridge University Press, Cambridge.

Palmer, T. (1977), *All You Need Is Love*, Futura, London.

Pryce, K. (1979), *Endless Pressure*, Penguin, Harmondsworth.

Quattrocchi, A. and Nairn, T. (1968), *The Beginning of the End*, Panther, London.

Robins, D. and Cohen, P. (1978), *Knuckle Sandwich*, Penguin, Harmondsworth.

Russell, J. and Gablik, S (1969), *Pop Art Redefined*, Thames & Hudson, London.

SAVAGE, J. (1982), 'Is This The End?', *ZG*, 8, London.

SCANNELL, P. and CARDIFF, D. (1982), 'Serving the Nation: Public Service Broadcasting Before the War', in B. Waites, T. Bennett and G. Martin (1982).

SHEPHERD, J. *et al.* (1977), *Whose Music?* Latimer, London.

STEDMAN-JONES, G. (1974), 'Working-Class Culture and Working-Class Politics in London, 1870–1900: Notes on the Remaking of a Working Class', *Journal of Social History*, vol. vii, 4. Republished in an edited version in B. Waites, T. Bennett and G. Martin (1982).

TAYLOR, I. and WALL, D. (1976), 'Beyond the Skinheads', in G. Mungham and G. Pearson (1976).

TAYLOR, J. and LAING, D. (1979), 'Disco–Pleasure–Discourse', *Screen Education*, 31, London.

THELWELL, M. (1980), *The Harder They Come*, Pluto, London.

THOMPSON, H.S. (1980), *The Great Shark Hunt*, Picador, London.

VULLIAMY, G. and LEE, E. (1982), *Popular Music. A Teacher's Guide*, Routledge & Kegan Paul, London.

WAITES, B. (1981), 'The Music Hall', Unit 5 of the Open University Popular Culture Course, U203, The Open University Press, Milton Keynes.

WAITES, B., BENNETT, T., MARTIN, G. (eds), (1982), *Popular Culture: Past and Present*, Croom Helm, London.

WALE, M. (1972), *Vox Pop*, Harrap, London.

WEEKS, J. (1981), *Sex, Politics and Society*, Longman, London.

WHEEN, F. (1982), *The Sixties*, Century, London.

WILD, P. (1979), 'Recreation in Rochdale, 1900–40', in J. Clarke, C. Critcher and R. Johnson (eds), *Working Class Culture*, Hutchinson, London.

WILLIAMS, R. (1963), *Culture and Society 1780–1950*, Penguin, Harmondsworth.

WILLIS, P. (1977), *Learning To Labour*, Saxon House, Farnborough.

WILLIS, P. (1978), *Profane Culture*, Routledge & Kegan Paul, London.

WINSHIP, J. (1980), 'Sexuality For Sale', in S. Hall, D. Hobson, A. Lowe and P. Willis (eds), *Culture, Media, Language*, Hutchinson, London.

WINSHIP, J. (1981), Woman Becomes an "Individual" – Femininity and Consumption in Women's Magazines, 1954–69', *Stencilled Occasional Paper*, 65, Centre for Contemporary Cultural Studies, Birmingham.

WOLFE, C. (1981), '"Gospel boogie": White Southern Gospel Music in Transition, 1945–55, *Popular Music*, 1, Cambridge University Press, Cambridge.

WOLFE, T. (1969), *The Electric Kool-Aid Test*, Bantam, New York.

WOLFE, T. (1972), *The Pump House Gang*, Bantam, New York.

WOLFE, T. (1976), *The Painted Word*, Bantam, New York.

WOLFE, T. (1982), 'Wolfe in Chic Clothing', *New Musical Express*, 6 February, London.

WOLLEN, P. (1982), *Readings and Writings*, Verso/NLB, London.

YORK, P. (1980), *Style Wars*, Sidgwick & Jackson, London.

Index

258